DATE DUE

FEB 0 1 1993	
FEB 0 8 1993	
MAR 26 1993	
APR 1 0 1993	
FEB 1 1 1994	
MAR 0 2 1994	
APR 0 5 1994	
APR 2 1 1994	
APR 2 8 1994	
NOV 1 4 1994	
FEB 0 8 1996	
FEB 2 0 1996	
MAR 1 1 1996	
APR 1 0 1996	
FEB 0 4 1997	
BRODART	Cat. No. 23-221

LAWRENCE
among the Women

*Wavering Boundaries in
Women's Literary Traditions*

FEMINIST ISSUES

Practice, Politics, and Theory

Kathleen M. Balutansky and Alison Booth, editors

———————————————————

Carol Siegel, *Lawrence among the Women: Wavering Boundaries in Women's Literary Traditions*

Harriet Blodgett, *"Capacious Hold-All": An Anthology of English-women's Diary Writings*

LAWRENCE
among the Women

*Wavering Boundaries in
Women's Literary Traditions*

Carol Siegel

University Press of Virginia
Charlottesville and London

THE UNIVERSITY PRESS OF VIRGINIA
Copyright © 1991 by the Rector and Visitors
of the University of Virginia

First published in 1991

ISBN 0-8139-1330-6

Library of Congress Cataloging-in-Publication Data

Siegel, Carol, 1952–
    Lawrence among the women : wavering boundaries in women's
literary traditions / Carol Siegel.
        p.   cm. — (Feminist issues)
    Includes bibliographical references (p.   ) and index.
    ISBN 0-8139-1330-6
    1. Lawrence, D. H. (David Herbert), 1885–1930—Political and
social views.   2. Feminism and literature—Great Britain—
History—20th century.   3. Women and literature—Great
Britain—History—20th century.   4. Sex role in literature.
I. Title.   II. Series: Feminist issues (Charlottesville, Va.)
PR6023.A93Z9134   1991
823'.912—dc20   91-6786
                                                                      CIP

Printed in the United States of America

To Gerhard

Contents

Acknowledgments

DURING THE YEARS I have spent working on this book, many people have discussed it with me and made wonderfully helpful suggestions. I received invaluable criticism of various sections of the manuscript from Julia Bader, Sara Blair, Keith Cushman, Carol Christ, Paula Fass, Eva Fuchs, Dennis Jackson, Elizabeth Langland, Elisabeth Magnus, Peggy McCormack, Thaïs Morgan, Gail Kern Paster, Lillian Taiz, and Louise Yelin. I especially want to thank Elizabeth Abel and Bruce Henricksen for reading the entire manuscript and responding with good ideas for its improvement. And most of all, I want to thank Alex Zwerdling, whose active interest in every stage of this project has been an unparalleled source of inspiration for me. In addition, I am very grateful to Nancy Essig, my editor at the University Press of Virginia, who has helped me shape this into the book I wanted it to be, and to Alison Booth, whose extraordinarily sensitive and perceptive reader's comments were a pleasure to work with. I would also like to thank my students at U.C. Berkeley and Loyola, New Orleans, for their contributions to my understanding of reader response. Without the generous support I have received from all of these people, writing this book would have been a nightmare.

I am grateful, as well, to the editors of *The D. H. Lawrence Review* and the collections *Men Writing the Feminine* and *D. H. Lawrence's Literary Inheritors* for their willingness to allow me to reprint here versions of the essays of mine that they originally published.

LAWRENCE
among the Women

Wavering Boundaries in
Women's Literary Traditions

D. H. Lawrence and the Idea
of Sexual Difference

A Convenient Other

TO APPROACH THE TOPIC of women's literary tradi-
tions through a study of D. H. Lawrence's work may seem deliberately
bizarre, even perverse. In recent years, some feminist critics have devoted considerable attention to Lawrence, but generally only to emphasize the distance between his writings and those of women. Lawrence's
position is usually understood as antithetical to women's literary traditions. One might think that critics interested in these traditions could
now begin to ignore Lawrence and, if we wish to discuss male authors at
all, turn our attention to men like Richardson and James, whose gender
allegiance appears less certain. Yet there seems to be something about the
feminist study of women's literature that brings us back again and again
to Lawrence.

The most obvious reason for the persistence of feminist critical interest in Lawrence is the extensiveness of his participation in the formative
processes of women's literature. As I will show, Lawrence often wrote in
response to directions from his women friends, represented himself as
the inheritor of Victorian women novelists, and influenced his literary
female contemporaries' thinking about women's creativity. He also affected the development of the next generation of women writers, as both
a precursor and a figure for the male artist. He still contributes to our
concept of a gendered literary heritage, through the role he plays as a
subject of feminist criticism. Although I hope to call into question the

value of reading Lawrence's works against women's literature, my main purpose is not to present a friendly feminist reading of Lawrence. Instead, I intend to suggest how recognition of Lawrence's connections to women's literary traditions can increase our understanding of the development and continuance of these traditions.

By beginning with two controversial assumptions, that "women's literature" is a useful descriptive term and that a diachronic approach to this literature can be of value, I reveal my belief in a concept of gender that some poststructuralist critics would condemn as essentialism. I am aware that this position brings me dangerously close to the ideology in which supposed inherent differences between men and women are used to justify differences in their cultural positions. Proximity is not accord, however. A certain type of essentialism, which I will discuss in the pages that follow, seems inseparable from feminist criticism, and thus highly relevant to the use feminist criticism has made of Lawrence. Consequently, I will defer discussion of Lawrence's relationship to women's literature until I have clarified my own relationship to conflicts in feminist theory over the concept of gender difference.

From its beginnings, feminism has needed its own type of literary criticism because representations of women have traditionally both naturalized their subordinate position, as appropriate to essential femininity, and treated feminine difference as a sinister power source. Feminist psychologists, like Nancy Chodorow and Dorothy Dinnerstein, have persuasively argued that early perceptions of the mother as omnipotent are never completely eradicated by adult experience, but instead inform the myths upon which we base our understanding of reality. Almost as long as there has been literature, men have used it to complain about the dangerous power of woman and to argue that she must be controlled. And women writers have responded, attempting in hundreds of different ways to show that male depictions of woman are fantasies and self-justifications. One might say, feminism begins with the struggle of women to define themselves and their own situation in the world. And in the word because, in literate societies, this struggle must include women's writing against a literary canon formed in accordance with masculine values. Thus, the first feminist criticism appeared as an aspect of literature written by women.

As common sense quickly shows us, however, "literature written by women" and "feminist literature" are not synonymous. An adequate self-definition for women cannot come directly from women's literary works because women are products of the same culture as men. Women writers need to question their own culturally determined concepts of woman. The aim of a great deal of feminist criticism is to reveal the ways women writers attempt to do this. Critics from Ellen Moers to Nancy Miller, who place women writers in a female literary tradition, have scrutinized what Sandra Gilbert and Susan Gubar call the palimpsest of texts written by women, in order to find individual women's subversive voices beneath the authors' ostensible affirmations of patriarchal values.[1] The problem with this method is that its aim of uncovering the female beneath the socially constructed feminine sometimes seems to valorize gender difference as existing in some space outside culture, allowing us to contrast "real" women with women-in-fiction. Critics like Shoshana Felman and Mary Jacobus who focus on the feminine voice rather than the historical figure of the female author object to this vision of layered femininity and femaleness because they see "the production of sexual difference . . . as textual, like the production of meaning."[2] These critics look at works by both men and women to find the feminine manifesting itself as a disruptive force within the masculine.

Still both of these feminist approaches to literature depend on some agreement about what the masculine and feminine are. If, for the latter group, the feminine is "unfixed," it does retain recognizable attributes coded as not-masculine. This emphasis on gender difference is unacceptable to some critics, like Nina Baym who rejects "all current [feminist] theory [because it] requires sexual difference as its ground."[3] Theorists as well as antitheoretical critics have tended to reject Lawrence's work for similar reasons. Beginning with *A Room of One's Own* (as I will discuss in chapter three), feminist criticism has treated Lawrence as an adversary to women's writing because of his insistence on irreducible gender difference. This attitude about Lawrence points up a profound disjunction between some feminist practices and goals.

Most feminist theorists see their endeavor as paradoxical in its treatment of the concept of gender difference. One strategy that centuries of feminists have found useful is to assert woman's difference from man while rejecting the negative valuation this difference has been given in patriarchal discourse. While this strategy remains popular with many cultural feminists, most literary theorists find it objectionable because of its reinscription of a restrictive definition of femaleness. Linda Alcoff, however, seems right to urge a skeptical attitude toward a poststructuralist, "posthumanist" feminism that rejects the concept of woman's difference. She argues that this position "unintentionally but nevertheless, colludes with [the] 'generic human' thesis of classical liberal thought, that particularities of individuals are irrelevant or improper influences on knowledge."[4] The denial of any natural female subjectivity seems antithetical to the idea of a gendered speaking position and thus the possibility that women can speak as or for women. As Toril Moi puts it, "the feminist struggle must both try to undo the patriarchal strategy that makes 'femininity' intrinsic to biological femaleness, and at the same time insist on defending women precisely *as* women."[5]

In recent years, "defending women" has become increasingly problematic. Alcoff asks, "How can we ground a feminist politics that deconstructs the female subject?"[6] Alice Jardine sees feminist theorists as uneasily poised between reducing "woman" to metaphor and returning "to metaphysical—anatomical—definitions of sexual identity."[7] To treat the feminine as metaphor certainly undermines the concept of difference, but only at the expense of erasing woman. Like Alcoff, Jardine, and Naomi Schor, and in some ways also like Lawrence, I find this cost unpayable. Schor opposes critics who take a utopian view of gender indeterminacy and protests the dominance, in gender studies, of what she calls "the discourse of indifference," which she believes reasserts the alterity of woman while denying her specificity.[8]

That privileging indeterminacy is of little immediate political use to feminist critics seems to me self-evident. True gender indeterminacy is extremely rare. Even in times and places that promote androgyny, we see men and women whose very mode of behaviorally deconstructing gender roles is meant to reveal their own gender.[9] As Eve Sedgwick shows, in "Epistemology of the Closet," what we commonly call androgyny is just what an earlier, less approving, age called inversion, the recognizable presence of one sex within another.[10] This inversion trope would be impossible without a belief in two separate and definable genders.

We can only imagine an indeterminacy that underlies and negates the cultural inscription of gender difference on our bodies if we believe in an unseen essence of human nature. Because such an essence is unknown and seemingly undiscoverable in the present world, it is hard to see what sort of literature could take it as a subject. The problem of focusing on gender indeterminacy in literary criticism is even more acute. Although we may "dream beyond the number two," as Susan Suleiman regretfully admits, the few feminist texts in theory or fiction that seem intended to do so actually do not go beyond privileging attributes traditionally associated with woman; and even more troubling, as Frances Restuccia has shown, the common modernist elision of woman and indeterminacy often serves misogyny by covering crimes against women and their agents with a feminized cloud of mystery.[11] Thus it is not surprising that despite profound disagreements about what sorts of texts to study, about appropriate methodology, and even about the immediate purpose of their endeavor, most feminist critics begin with the idea that gender difference exists—and matters. Nor is it hard to understand why increasing numbers of feminist critics insist on treating both authors and literary characters as beings with a specific gender.[12]

What is surprising is that when they reach a place in their arguments where it is useful to identify a particular writer as representative of the masculine, feminist critics so frequently turn to (or on) D. H. Lawrence. As we journey through early feminist criticism, it seems Lawrence is always with us. In *The Second Sex,* Simone de Beauvoir gives him a prominent place in her discussion of writers who have created the myth that the ideal and only real woman is she "who unreservedly accepts being defined as Other."[13] But if Lawrence does make woman Other, she returns the favor in text after text, defining her vision in contrast to his. This attitude is understandable because of Lawrence's railings against women and feminism in his own texts. Furthermore, as Kate Millett shows in *Sexual Politics,* some of the most virulently antifeminist writers of our time claim Lawrence as an authority for their male supremacist position. Just as for Henry Miller and Norman Mailer, Lawrence is the masculine fighting back against the devouring feminine, for critics as diverse as Annis Pratt and Eve Sedgwick, Lawrence is the convenient masculine Other against whom the feminine can be defined. It often seems that before women writers can be placed, Lawrence must be.

Whether their approach is thematic, deconstructive, historicist, or psychoanalytic, feminist critics seem to find Lawrence useful. Almost as predictably as their works tell us that gender differences exist, they also tell us that Lawrence represents all that does not belong to woman. Pratt believes that we can better understand woman's relationship to nature by comparing Lawrence's depiction of it to that of women writers.[14] Gilbert and Gubar quote Lawrence to explain the foundation of "patriarchal poetics"; they find his remarks on Jane Austen representative of conventional masculine hostility toward "the lady writer."[15] Jacobus depicts the feminine sense of fluid identity, free expression, and openness by contrasting it with what she believes is Lawrence's dichotomized world view and consequent desire to silence woman, "to consider her not as an image but as a sign."[16] Sedgwick describes our present, "schizoid" homosocial culture as determined by "the triumph of Lawrence and 'Wilde'": the polarization of male attitudes into Lawrencian masculinist homophobia or the feminine but misogynous homosexuality represented by the public concept of Oscar Wilde.[17] Like other feminist critics, Sedgwick seems to see no reason to consider the standard opinion of Lawrence as other than fact. Wilde goes into quotes; Lawrence does not.

A recognition of what "Lawrence" stands for in feminist criticism seems basic to a practical concept of the underlying agreements about gender difference that support feminist theory in all its variations. But whether feminist critics' almost reflexive tendency to refer to Lawrence as the opposite to the feminine in literature is as helpful as it is easy remains to be decided. It seems to me necessary for feminist criticism to concentrate on gender differences, but it is unnecessary for us to simplify them by creating allegorical figures to embody them. We should look as skeptically at feminist descriptions of Lawrence that reduce him to a symbolic Other as we do at patriarchal reductions of women writers. Since it does an injustice to the seriousness of feminist criticism to suggest that so many critics write about Lawrence as they do simply because it is a convenient and satisfying way to respond to his misogyny, we might begin by asking why he so often comes to mind when women's literature is being discussed. I believe the answer to this question must ultimately be found through an examination of the long and close relationship between Lawrence's work and women's literature. However, the most sensible way to begin to determine where Lawrence's writings stand in relation to women's is with a working knowledge of his stated literary intentions. In this way we can evaluate the common feminist assumption that Lawrence conceived his literary persona in opposition to the female voice.

"The Battle of Tongues"

Lawrence's work is particularly resistant to any reading that dismisses the importance of authorial intention because, since the banning of *The Rainbow* in 1915, his intentions have been a recurrent topic of legal discourse. It is also hard to think of a writer about whom more biographical material has been written than D. H. Lawrence, but easy to see why this is so. The greatest difficulty presented by Lawrence's work—that he continually contradicts himself—is exactly paralleled in what we know of Lawrence's life. Moreover, the contradictions in Lawrence's work and in his life cluster around the same issue: the relations between men and women. Perhaps the greatest mistake that a reader of Lawrence can make is to treat the contradictoriness of his writings as an unconscious intrusion of personal conflicts. Such readings seem based on the assumption that Lawrence wished to produce texts that would communicate coherent, unified statements, that he tried but failed to make his works speak with one voice. On the contrary, some of Lawrence's nonfictional writings reveal his dedication to allowing what he perceived as an external, female voice intrude into his work to challenge the voice he identified with himself.

It is true that in 1914, when Lawrence wrote his "Study of Thomas Hardy," he said the most difficult problem faced by fiction writers was "reconciling their metaphysic, their theory of being and knowing, with their living sense of being."[18] In his specific comments on the novels, Lawrence makes it clear that he is most disturbed by the gap he sees between Hardy's implicit theorizing about gender relations and his depictions of female characters. Whether Lawrence ever believed that these two aspects of a text could be brought into harmony remains doubtful, however. He seems unable to think of an author who successfully aligns metaphysics and art. In the 1918 version of "The Spirit of Place," Lawrence sees as "one of the outstanding qualities of American literature: that the deliberate ideas of the man veil, conceal, obscure that which the artist has to reveal."[19] Again, Lawrence shows us compelling female characters veiled by their authors' socially prescribed statements of their meaning. By 1923 he had revised the passage to emphasize the universality of the writer's inability to communicate with one voice: "Truly art is a sort of subterfuge. . . . The artist usually sets out—or used to—to point a moral and adorn a tale. The tale, however, points the other way, as a rule."[20] To believe that Lawrence makes such statements in hopes that his critics will save the truth of his own art from the lie of his metaphysics is naïve. Nothing in Lawrence's work or life gives the impression that he was so humble about his talents or his role as an author.

In Frank Kermode's study of the conflict between doctrine and art speech (what Lawrence calls the metaphysic and the tale) in the novels, he demonstrates that Lawrence is aware of the contradictions in his works; indeed, that he emphasizes them with complex techniques of narration.[21] Kermode shows that Lawrence's best fiction is governed by the standard articulated in the "Study of Thomas Hardy": "The degree to which the system of morality, or the metaphysic of any work of art is submitted to criticism within the work of art makes the lasting value and satisfaction of that work" ("Study," 476). Lawrence's apparent skepticism about his own beliefs is not the unifying force that Kermode suggests it is, however. Like most artists, Lawrence often calls upon his readers to accept some apparent contradictions as part of the mystery of life, which is made up of many truths, but he also presents us with voices within his fictions that make assertions which cannot be simultaneously accepted as truths.

As Wayne Booth points out, "Again and again, Lawrence simply surrenders the telling of the story to another mind, a mind neither clearly approved nor clearly repudiated yet presented in a tone that seems to demand judgment."[22] However, Bakhtin's dialogics, which Booth draws on to explain Lawrence's "double voiced" texts, seem less useful than Dale Bauer's modification of the theory into feminist dialogics, because Lawrence's voices in opposition are almost always also oppositely gendered. As Bauer asserts, dialogic community, which inheres in the struggle of competing voices, "does not exist without the tension between the marginal and the central, the eccentric and the phallocentric," positions that are always gendered.[23] And in Lawrence's texts this tension is foregrounded as the battle for reader identification going on between male and female voices. For instance, Ursula and Birkin in *Women in Love* can be seen as having equally plausible views of their shared experiences, but only one of them can be right when they disagree, at the end of the novel, over whether or not it is possible to "have two kinds of love."[24] Ursula's criticism of the doctrine does not simply modify our understanding of the doctrine; if we accept the criticism as correct we must reject the doctrine.

E. M. Forster amusingly describes the sort of demands Lawrence's fiction makes on the reader by categorizing Lawrence as both visionary prophet of nature and annoying preacher.[25] This complaint is not an adequate assessment of the conflicting demands of Lawrence's fiction, because it implies that the reader is forced to put up with the preacher in order to enjoy the prophet, read through the metaphysic in order to see the art, when, in fact, we are presented not with a sermon, but a trial which the hectoring author insists we judge. Although Lawrence's lyrical evocations of nature are often gratingly disrupted by his outbursts of narrowly moralistic interpretation, this may annoy but should not confuse the reader. Many writers before Lawrence found "sermons in stones" and insisted on preaching them. There is no intrinsic conflict between an author's ability to describe the physical world delightfully and his propensity to philosophize tediously about it.

The characters in Lawrence's landscape, not the landscape itself or the sermonizing about it, jumble Lawrence's message. Forster's metaphor of a man divided into two (male) selves is inaccurate because he leaves out the fundamental conflict in Lawrence's fiction: the discrepancy between male and female world views. Still, in describing Lawrence's conflicting voices as conflicting personas and linking the more attractive and artistic persona to Lawrence's celebrations of nature, Forster does, although unknowingly, draw attention to one area in Lawrence's work where real female voices successfully compete with Lawrence's dictatorial male pronouncements. Lawrence frequently used material written by his female friends as sources for his famous descriptions of nature.[26] Nonetheless, Lawrence's fiction does not present us with a female representation of nature lying helpless in the grasp of a hermeneutics of male supremacy, but, instead, with female characters who, as Kermode points out, consistently undercut the doctrinal pronouncements of both the author and his fictional spokesmen.[27]

In accordance with sound rhetorical practice, Lawrence seems to present what he imagines to be his opponent's argument in order to destroy it. What is so unusual about Lawrence's use of this rhetorical technique is that he usually makes such a good case for the opposition that he is unable to refute it. F. R. Leavis sees the oppositional female voices in Lawrence's fiction as representative of his wife's criticisms ("the voice is unmistakably Frieda's") and takes it as a sign of Lawrence's brilliance that he represents that voice as "unanswerable" in novels like *Aaron's Rod* and *Kangaroo*.[28] Certainly Lawrence's honesty in these instances is admirable, but it also causes him to cut the doctrinal ground right out from under himself. This effect is not limited, as Leavis suggests, to Lawrence's weakest novels. *Women in Love, The Lost Girl, The Plumed Serpent,* and *The Fox* all have major female characters who assert their own wills against men who apparently speak for Lawrence in demanding that women submit to male authority.

In each of these novels, the view of life Lawrence gives us seems to support the women's final assertions. For example, in *Women in Love,* Lawrence never shows that it would be possible for Birkin to add a blood brother to his ménage, and he gives us every indication that Ursula's instincts are superior to Birkin's. Moreover, in the other three stories the woman is the protagonist, and in all four her commonsensical views further invite reader identification. While Lawrence associates the major male characters with death, he depicts the women as wholesome. Their unanswerable criticisms of male authority are presented as intrinsic to a healthy will to survive rather than the "deadly female will" Lawrence so often rails against in his essays. Thus, even if we want to belief that Lawrence wrote his fiction with misogynous intentions, the texts confound us because of their presentation of patriarchal discourse within not only what Booth calls "a chorus of voices, each speaking with its own authority,"[29] but also a feminized cosmos that most often seems to affirm a female character's point of view.

"Supreme Servant-in-Command"

Just because Lawrence did not write fiction that can persuade the unconverted to accept his patriarchal doctrines, we should not be tempted to see him as a feminist writer despite himself. Instead, in his relegation of the male voice to a subsidiary narrative role, we might see the importance Lawrence gave the representation of women's dissenting and contradicting voices. We cannot hope to understand why Lawrence considered this so important without examining his attitudes toward women. Most of Lawrence's critics see, in his life as well as his work, an underlying pattern of ever-increasing hostility to women (usually attributed to resentment of his mother's dominance, inability to accept his own homosexual desires, and misery over his unhappy marriage) and a consequent progressive advocacy of male supremacy. This movement is generally conceived of as being accompanied by a desire to force women into silence.

Julian Moynahan finds the male characters in Lawrence's early novels weak, passive, and "pathologically oversensitive to feminine rebuke and resistance," and discusses much of Lawrence's subsequent work in terms of his entrapment in the narrow and ugly view of male heroism embodied in such later protagonists as Richard Lovat Somers in *Kangaroo* and Don Ramón in *The Plumed Serpent*.[30] Graham Hough believes that the development of Lawrence's work is, to a large extent, determined by his struggle to shift its focus away from women and instead to depict men "in the world of men."[31] Hilary Simpson introduces a welcome break from the usual biographical explanations of misogyny in Lawrence's work with her theory that he was simply deeply influenced by social and historical trends of intensifying misogyny. But Cornelia Nixon, partly in response to this idea, uses her excellent textual research to support her belief that Lawrence's personal problems resulted in a sudden turn against "motherhood and female sexuality" during the first World War followed by increasing aversion toward women, too intense to be considered characteristic of the age.[32] We seem to be returning to Middleton Murry's view (in *Son of Woman*) of Lawrence's work as the record of a sick man's descent into pathological misogyny.

Such theories leave little room for recognition of what Philip Callow calls "Lawrence's habit of swerving from passionate attachment to the most violent hatred," or, in less extreme terms, Lawrence's radical inconsistency about all that moved him most.[33] Lawrence does change suddenly, but he also changes back again. In *The Virgin and the Gipsy,* which has been regarded as the prototype of *Lady Chatterley's Lover,* the female protagonist cannot survive without her admirer, while he desires but does not need her. As Lawrence takes the story through three revisions, the lover becomes more dependent. In the final version, the sexually damaged and despairing gamekeeper can only be saved by his lady's love. Yet, even here, there is no linear progression in Lawrence's attitudes. *John Thomas and Lady Jane,* the third version of the story, ends with the absolute submission of the gamekeeper to his mistress's will ("I'll do anything you like"), while in the last version Connie more or less submits to Mellors.[34] *John Thomas and Lady Jane* also presents a marked contrast to the views on marriage in *Kangaroo*. In *Kangaroo*, the earlier novel, Lawrence compares marriage to a ship in order to stress the importance of male leadership. In *John Thomas and Lady Jane*, he revises the analogy to compare husband and wife to separate ships, each of which must travel "according to its own skill and power" (*JTLJ*, 302). Lawrence's nonfictional preaching is sometimes even more blatantly contradictory. In one chapter of *Fantasia of the Unconscious*, he strongly advises woman to "stick to her own natural positivity" and love her man come what may; then, in a subsequent chapter, he commands, "Wives don't love your husbands anymore."[35]

Lawrence was inconsistent about most issues concerning women except the representation of women's views in fiction. On that issue his constancy suggests that far from wanting to still woman's voice, he was often so desperate for its continuance that he tried to make himself its medium. He does seem to have lacked confidence in women's ability to speak for themselves, as is implied by his famous promise to Sallie Hopkin, "I shall do my work for women, better than the suffrage."[36] Lawrence's goal could perhaps best be described as helping women articulate their deepest emotions. In *Sons and Lovers* Lawrence answers, in a very complex way, the call he felt to speak for woman. Paul translates Miriam's emotional reactions to the world into artistic speech, thus enacting within the novel the role that Lawrence played in creating it from Jessie Chambers's memories of their shared past. But Lawrence does not stop here. He also incorporates into his story female criticisms of his interpretations of female experience. For instance, Clara tells Paul that his belief that Miriam wants "soul communion" rather than physical love is his "own imagination," and Miriam confirms Clara's theory with her complaint, "It has always been you fighting me off."[37] This technique shows the extent to which Lawrence's desire to prescribe a course for woman is overcome by his conviction that her inevitable rejection of his prescription must be heard.

Some clarification of the source of this conflict can be found in the "Foreword" to *Sons and Lovers*, which Lawrence wrote in 1913 not for publication but, as Callow puts it, as "his first deliberate attempt at the formulation of a doctrine for himself."[38] One of the major ideas in this cryptic and Biblically phrased work is that the business of man is to express the truth of "the Father—which should be called Mother."[39]

Lawrence's deliberate replacement of the Father with the Mother as the primary source of life and art should be considered as a context for his representations of gender relations. If he makes a religion of sexual difference, it is not in service of God the Father.

Many critics have accused Lawrence of writing quasi-mystical texts in which submission to a male is depicted as the means of woman's salvation. Simone de Beauvoir sums up her commentary on male and female roles in Lawrence's works with the observation, "We can see why Lawrence's novels are above all 'guide books for women.' It is much more difficult for woman than for man to 'accept the universe,' for man submits to the cosmic order autonomously, whereas woman needs the mediation of the male."[40] Kingsley Widmer, likewise, asserts that "Lawrence is but restating Milton, and the Bible: 'He for God only, she for God in him'"; and Catherine Carswell, always seemingly willing to accept patriarchal authority, says approvingly that Lawrence imagined the true man as giving "his woman" "the full satisfaction of being the 'she for God in him.' "[41] However, not only the "Foreword" to *Sons and Lovers* but Lawrence's lifelong determination both to find divine truth in woman and to express it seem to contradict this view of him as a priest of the Father.

One might argue that Lawrence sees woman as the unconscious repository of truth, a passive fleshly object who is intermediary between man and the gods simply through her existence, not by any choice. But how far Lawrence departs from what Gayatri Spivak says "we are obliged 'historically' to call the discourse of man" becomes evident when we compare Lawrence's "Foreword" with Spivak's examples of the sort of male discourse that demands the *silent* participation of woman.[42] As Spivak shows, the displacement of woman is based on the valuation of woman's reproductive function over the rights of woman as an individual. Spivak connects the "official view of reproduction" (women are only the guardians of the father's children) with the "privileging of marriage, the Law that appropriates the woman's body over the claims of that body as Law."[43] Lawrence warns against such privileging in the "Foreword." The man who believes that he can claim a woman as "flesh of his flesh" has, in Lawrence's view, "blasphemed" against "the Father" (who is "more properly [called] the Mother") ("FSL," 100). Likewise the man who would deliberately use woman to produce a copy of himself has missed her significance. To Lawrence, procreation is always, as he says in the poem "Rose of All the World," "just left over" from the communion of man with woman. And, as he argues, against the traditional valuation of woman-as-mother evoked by the poem's title, for a man to love a woman is for him to understand her as "purposeless; a rose / For rosiness only, without an ulterior motive." Having designated the woman's body as Law, Lawrence sees no law beyond it.

Yet even woman as Truth and Law can be powerless if, as Spivak says, "she has never been considered a custodian of truth anyway (only its mysterious figure)."[44] As Diana Fuss explains, in a defense of Luce Irigaray's essentialism, Western philosophy has followed Aristotle's view that "[o]nly man properly *has* an essence" because of his unique claim to subjecthood, while "woman is the ground of essence, its precondition in man, without herself having any access to it."[45] Lawrence's writing generally opposes this Aristotelian position, and his essentialism sometimes resembles Irigaray's in its affirmation of a female essence accessible to women as individuals. Such essentialism informs his female characters' parodies of the male characters' ideological statements. For example, in *Kangaroo* Harriet restates her husband's proposal that she act as nest to his dominant male phoenix-self thus: "So that he could imagine himself absolutely and arrogantly It, he would turn her into a nest, and sit on her and overlook her, like the one and only phoenix in the desert of the world, gurgling hymns of salvation."[46]

In the "Foreword," Lawrence writes, "For in the flesh of the woman does God exact Himself. And out of the flesh of the woman does he demand: 'Carry this of me forth to utterance,'" and then adds, "And if the man deny, or be too weak, then shall the woman find another man, of greater strength" ("FSL," 104). For Lawrence, woman is not only the bearer of truth but the judge of it. Although allowed no creative role in this system, woman is active as the judge of truth. This function implies her situation as an intellectual, as well as a physical, intermediary between man and the sacred. The truth written into woman's flesh by God the Father/MOTHER seems always preinterpreted by its bearer. If she cannot always speak the truth she carries, still, she apparently knows it and passes judgment accordingly. She withdraws herself, and so the means of understanding, from men whose words fall short of what she knows her truth to be.

This belief accounts for much of Lawrence's ambivalence about his literary "work for women." Although he granted himself the elevated position of the author who gives form to discourse, he imposed on himself a program of speaking primarily for women, a program that denied him a sense of true creative power. He could never be more than the "supreme servant-in-command" of the Mother Goddess because, according to his own philosophy, the truth he dedicated himself to expressing could not originate with him and could only be validated by female approval.[47] In arguing in favor of an "essentialism with a [feminist] difference," Rosi Braidotti observes that "the male subject has historically chosen to conjugate his being in the universalistic logocentric mode," and implies that it would represent a change for the better if men were to conceive of their own subjectivity in relation to gender.[48] Lawrence's vision of himself as the speaker for woman might be seen as representative of just such a relationally gendered subjectivity. He can construct himself as a speaker only in reference to female presence and desire.

Perhaps because he thought the consequences of failure to speak for woman would be devastating, Lawrence did not trust to his experiences with woman's inarticulate flesh for material for his utterance of her truth, but instead incorporated the spoken and written words of the women he knew into his works, where they bore the force of truth. That Lawrence worked closely with Chambers on *The White Peacock* and *Sons and Lovers,* his wife Frieda on the final version of *Sons and Lovers,* and Helen Corke on the *The Trespasser* has been established beyond dispute. Both Chambers and Frieda seem to have contributed to *The Rainbow.*[49] Lawrence himself described *The Boy in the Bush* as a collaboration (with Mollie Skinner), and he tried to work with other women, like Catherine Carswell and Mabel Luhan, in the same way. While the philosophy that prompted this practice seems extreme and unique, there is nothing exclusively Lawrencian about this writing technique. As Simpson points out, the "male *editing* of women's experience" and the incorporation of women's private writings into published works have always been among male novelists' techniques.[50]

Although Lawrence's use of women's experience was in some ways similar to the techniques of his male predecessors, in other ways it had to be different because Lawrence's goals were different. In his high valuation of female sexual fulfillment, his sympathy with women's direct expressions of rage against men, his insistence on the unimportance of procreation, and his scorn for Christian meekness and self-sacrifice,

Lawrence is obviously unlike novelistic forefathers whose use of female protagonists involves emphasis on the importance of virtues tradition-ally demanded of women in patriarchal societies: religious humility, gentleness, selfless love of children, and deference to worthy men. In depicting women as innately active, angry, and resistant to masculine control, Lawrence also sets himself apart from cultural feminists who, as Alcoff points out, have traditionally based their defense of women on our "innate peacefulness and ability to nurture."[51]

Rather than dramatizing the world's deplorable treatment of attrac-tively feminine heroines, as do Defoe, Richardson, and Dickens, or celebrating the destructive energy of female villains produced by an unnatural society, as do Thackeray, Trollope, and Flaubert; Lawrence consistently depicts the natural female state as furious rebellion. For Lawrence the female voice must always undercut rather than affirm the male author's message. Because of this concept of female nature as essentially oppositional, his female characters deconstruct from within the fictions that (attempt to) contain them. As Jonathan Dollimore has shown, in discussing Gide, an essentialism that is used to legitimize desires that society seeks to repress is "incompatible with conventional and dominant sexual ideologies, bourgeois and otherwise."[52] At his most essentialist moments Lawrence seems most subversive of the ide-ologies that generally inform the representation of women in nonfemi-nist texts.

Lawrence's treatment of women differs markedly from that of mod-erns like Hardy, James, and Shaw, who used the problems of female heroes to represent those of the modern individual (or generic man). Daniel Schneider argues that Lawrence's early novels belong to a tradi-tion dominating "postromantic writing" that is characterized by atten-tion to the individual's struggles with limitations imposed by fate and society and by use of "the plight of woman" to represent "the general problem."[53] If this were strictly true, one would expect Lawrence to emphasize the relations of his female heroes to their society. Instead, as Emile Delavenay points out in his discussion of *The Rainbow,* Lawrence tends to concentrate "exclusively on the emotional and sexual, as op-posed to the economic and social" aspects of his protagonists' lives.[54] This emphasis on inner, and to Lawrence gender-determined, experi-ence makes it difficult to believe that Ursula Brangwen in *The Rainbow,* for example, was meant to symbolize modern man. Even when her circumstances and behavior resemble those of her fellow schoolteacher, Mr. Brunt, Ursula suffers differently because of the femaleness of her perceptions. The headmaster, Mr. Harby, is annoying to her because he appears "very manly and incontrovertible," and she "detest[s] him for his male triumph."[55] Her unhappiness comes not from an essential similarity to man, which would make her resent her oppression as he would, but from her deep difference.

From the beginning of the novel Lawrence insists on the differences between men's and women's perceptions and emotional needs. When Ursula feels alienated by the unnaturalness of modern society and fights against it, she is depicted neither as a potentially good woman driven to become evil nor as the modern representative of the entire Brangwen family; rather she is the natural heir of a long line of Brangwen women, all of whom "were different" from the men (*RB,* 2). In this respect Ursula is typical of Lawrence's fictional women, who almost uniformly stand (and speak in the self-assertive manner he trusted most) not for mankind as a whole, but exclusively for themselves as women. Through these characters, Lawrence tries to articulate female resistance to the male definition of their world, including his own creation of it. Their questioning of the world of seeming, which man has made, moves beyond the confines of their fictionality, and they challenge the authority of Lawrence, their author, as well.

Ursula is often brought up by critics like Bonnie Kime Scott who believe that Lawrence's early work "presents images of women who are strong, generative, and autonomous. [But] It was a vision Lawrence did not sustain; instead he brought his women to kneel in homage to the phallus as part of his anti-modern, vitalist position."[56] However, Lawrence's later female characters reject such interpretations of their ritualistic sexual posturing. They themselves describe it as a means to escape the traditional confines of intimacy with a man and to discover their own selfhood. For instance, Kate, in *The Plumed Serpent,* after undergoing rites in which she kisses her husband's feet and allows herself to be celebrated as a female principle, learns that "she loved to be alone," that she is "not going to submit" even to being ruled by sexual desire (let alone by the man who arouses it), and that "I want myself to myself."[57] Within stories about women's enactment of exaggerated male worship, the inclusion of such articulations by female characters of their awakening to a passionate sense of autonomy works against Lawrence's occasional suggestions that female consciousness can or should be subsumed into male purpose. Lawrence's insistence on mixing, in the same texts, incompatible narratives of female self-discovery is modern in that it foregrounds the fictionality of stable identity. The experiences of Lawrence's female characters cannot be understood in reference to traditional visions of woman as man's subordinate or victim.

The distinction between Lawrence's approach to female experience and those of the moderns with whom he is often grouped can easily be seen if we compare Hardy's Tess to any one of Lawrence's heroines. As Laurence Lerner shows, Tess's motivations for the most important choices in her life are unclear.[58] We usually see Tess from such a distance that we might conclude that Hardy's subject is not a "pure" woman's emotional and intellectual responses to her society, but rather her victimization by that society. Because Tess is a vulnerable, feminine woman, the tragedy of her fate is fully achieved. But we are left wondering how much her (frequently opaque) character and the decisions it compelled helped shape her fate.

When Lawrence creates a female protagonist, he is uninterested in her weakness and victimization. Every Lawrence heroine, even those who fail miserably, forcefully determines the course of her life through her own choices. Moynahan points out the importance Lawrence places, in *Lady Chatterley's Lover,* on a woman's freedom to evaluate and choose.[59] The same could be said for *The Plumed Serpent,* which is generally considered Lawrence's most misogynous novel. Connie Chatterley does choose just as Lawrence at his most domineering might wish her to, but in this she differs from the majority of Lawrence's female characters. More typically, the choices made by Lawrence's heroines go against the male supremacist doctrines of his fictions.

Although Lawrence, who condemned liberalism as effete, would no doubt be aghast at the idea, his attitude toward his female characters certainly has affinities with liberal humanism in its emphasis on free choice and its fundamental assumption of an identity that transcends social and cultural forces. More importantly, his philosophy breaks away from humanism at precisely the same point that feminism does. He treats the problems that arise from gender identity as the ones most deserving of serious attention. Moreover, he takes as his first priority the articulation of female experience. No wonder Lawrence's work continues to fascinate women. And no wonder it continues to enrage so many of us, since, no matter how accommodatingly he may use the female voice, he is, as Simpson calls him, a literary trespasser invading the territory that rightly belongs to his female contemporaries in his insistence on speaking for them.

The paradoxical relationship between Lawrence's essentialism and feminist writings in some ways resembles the relationship between feminist theory and psychoanalytic theory, as it has traditionally been understood. On the one hand, many feminists resent, as limiting if not necessarily patriarchal, male theorists' attempts to describe or define woman or the feminine. On the other hand, many others find a biologically based theory of gender difference enabling because, as Fuss observes, "An essentialist definition of 'woman' implies that there will always remain some part of 'woman' which resists masculine imprinting and socialization."[60] And just as Freud's most apparently entrapping definitions of the feminine as what is outside normality and order have served to open gaps in patriarchal discourse wherein we women can describe ourselves Otherwise, Lawrence's writing *for* women as the embodiments of resistance to the masculine has opened spaces in the body of his writing *about* women for revisionary feminist responses. Thus, in the very exercise of his own (male) hermeneutic privilege over woman, he concedes the legitimacy of her response.

In the chapters that follow, I will compare various aspects of Lawrence's and several women's texts which place them in a common tradition: the biographical and cultural grounds of the texts' productions, the authors' stated intentions, their similar and recurrent use of certain images, their identical linguistic choices, and, above all, the commentaries the texts make on each other's concepts of gender, because long before feminist literary criticism took form as a separate discipline it was embedded within women's literature. The reappropriation "by means of ironic rereadings—and rewritings—[of] the dominant cultural productions of the past" that Suleiman identifies as a fundamental part of "the new 'feminine' poetics" seems to me at least as old as women's writing.[61] For this reason, I will look as closely at what women wrote about Lawrence as I will at what he wrote for women. My aim, always, is to uncover clues as to why and how Lawrence has become entangled in the way feminists think about women's literary traditions, because our approach to these traditions shapes them constantly anew.

CHAPTER ONE

"Those Who Washed Dishes with Lawrence": Voices Heard from the Periphery

I HAVE BEEN DISCUSSING the narrative strategies Lawrence uses in his attempts to define and delimit himself as an author. It should be apparent that these strategies are inextricable from his theories of the relationship between woman and literature. Now, it remains to consider how women participated in the creation of Lawrence-the-author. If what is in question is a relationship between texts, it might seem beside the point to talk about Lawrence as he existed outside his own narratives. Yet now, when no extratextual Lawrence exists at all, a certain "Lawrence" continues to affect the formation of feminist theory. This Lawrence cannot be described simply as the author implied in texts with that signature. Nor is he entirely what Wayne Booth calls a public myth, created by the shared speculations of "a fair number of real readers."[1] Rather, the figure called Lawrence first appears in the intertext of literature produced under that name and literature produced by women.

Like many writers before him, Lawrence went to the body of woman to give what he saw as her truth voice. But where was that body? To a certain extent, Lawrence conceived of woman's body as textual, as we can see in his conflation of femaleness and the literary when he assigns the oppositional voice of the tale to female characters. Female presence in his fiction deconstructs the discourse of the teller. Everywhere the text resists the interpretation the narrator would code into it, it belongs to woman. In his insistence that actual women must judge man's utterance, however, Lawrence also moves toward an affirmation of the importance of female authorship. He invited women to write about him, and they accepted the invitation. As he spoke, from the center of his own texts, what he believed was woman's truth, he was enfolded by the marginalized voices of actual women, describing him. Consequently, Lawrence was (and still is) constructed as an author not through his penetration of a female object/text but through an intertextual exchange between gendered subjects.

If we can believe that Lawrence's very creation as an author was so promising, we must ask why the promise was never fulfilled, why "his" women remained marginal while he grew into the phallocentric monster that feminist criticism now puts on display. In examining the first interchanges between Lawrence and women writers we can glimpse possible answers.

That Lawrence believed he must write as a spokesman for women should by now be clear, but why he had such a belief is difficult to say. An equally difficult and seemingly related question is why women allowed and even encouraged Lawrence to write for them despite his frequent misogynous pronouncements. Perhaps a woman who lacked the confidence to write for herself would find gratification in achieving a literary voice through Lawrence's mediation, but few of "Lawrence's women" fit this description. Even his first close friend and lover, Jessie Chambers, the most retiring of them, was able to bring herself both to write a novel of her own (about her early days with Lawrence) and to show it to prominent literary figures like Violet Hunt, Ford Madox Ford, and Edward Garnett.[2] Yet, beginning with Chambers, many women submitted their ideas, memories, and writing to Lawrence for him to rework into fiction.

Perhaps the strangest of these cases is the one in which a powerful, audacious woman relentlessly sought Lawrence's friendship in order to persuade him to write about her life. Mabel Dodge Luhan said, "I wanted Lawrence to understand things for me. To take *my* experience, *my* material, *my* Taos, and to formulate it all into a magnificent creation."[3] Later, disappointed with his efforts, she wrote about him, instead. Luhan seems to have been, self-consciously and deliberately, a particular type of 1920s New Woman, aggressively defining herself against the femininity of the previous generation. Her *Lorenzo in Taos* is a rich source of information about the ways it was possible for such a woman to read Lawrence's work and to encourage his participation in women's literature.

Lorenzo in Taos has been almost universally despised by Lawrence's critics and literary biographers, apparently because of Luhan's unusual beliefs and tendency toward self-aggrandizement.[4] Luhan happily defied conventions that still govern sexual behavior, and she triumphantly promoted herself as an authority on sex. Assisted by wealth, luck, intellect, and physical robustness, she became the center of a spiritual/artistic community and the dominant partner of a fulfilling marriage. In short, she achieved goals Lawrence pursued without success all his life. Yet Luhan was determined to make him her voice.

The poems Luhan includes in *Lorenzo in Taos* are interesting in that they were written for and about Lawrence. They simultaneously flatter and criticize him. Two of the most emotionally complex of these poems are "The Ballad of a Bad Girl" and "Plum." The former apparently succeeded in pleasing Lawrence since he drew an illustration for its publication in *Laughing Horse Magazine*. One can see why Lawrence might have approved of this narrative poem that portrays him as "a very, very angry man" who lives in God's heart and kicks down to earth the heroine who rises up to claim God's secrets. The Lawrence figure, in so doing, teaches her "a secret, the best one of any, / That a *woman* can be saved by a fall, fall, fall!"[5] But the poem is far more than a simple dramatization of Lawrence's doctrine of female subordination. The overt moral is as Freudian as it is Lawrencian. The bad girl's first crime is the theft of her "Father's silver-headed walking-stick" which she improperly places between her legs to ride "a-straddle" after "things no other woman knows." Moreover, like Freud's Dora, she is the victim of a negligent mother, who "pushed [her] from [her] cradle" and does not know of her absence "till Father told her so. / But she didn't care!" On the most immediately accessible level of the poem, Luhan seems to be endorsing the standard psychoanalytic description of female experience as determined by penis envy and the need to sublimate it in maternity. But she strikes many jarring notes that, considered together, make up a discordant subtext which both reverses the values implicit in Freudian theory, as it was popularized in Luhan's time, and reconstructs Lawrence as a dialogic voice necessary to her establishment of her own speaking position.

This subtext stands in direct contradiction to the poem's title, calling its value judgment into question. On this level the poem is self-congratulatory. The "bad girl" is extraordinary rather than eccentric, ultramature rather than immature. Rejection, by her mother, facilitates success. She rises above other females—"Little girls and women were gaping down below"—and the ancient wise men among whom, she says, "every day I higher went." In fact, *only* the Lawrence figure is posited as her equal. She encounters him upon reaching the plane on which she is most individual and most clearly distinguished from all others. The anger with which he greets her seems displaced from her own situation. Luhan emphasizes the gross injustice to women of the cosmos in which her ballad is set. The old, wise men are "gathered *safe* in rows, / *Safely* making magic" (emphasis mine), but the brave girl moves among them unprotected. She knows, and never in the poem recants the knowledge, that God "had the secret that it wasn't His to keep!" In driving her out of the divine presence because "This is no place for *women* here!" (Luhan's emphasis), the Lawrence figure explicitly acknowledges the gender bias in the cultural hierarchy, and thus, even while he upholds it, he defines her actions as feminist.

Although Luhan expresses gratitude for being forced "Back, back to earth where [she] belong[s]," as narrator she also implies that she is being thrown down into a hopeless situation. As heroine she ends by exclaiming, "Mother! Mother me / And teach me how to mother and that's all, all, all." But what hope is there that the mother will respond to this plea or command? It is "whispered," but even if it were shouted, the mother, who has shown nothing but indifference throughout the poem, can hardly be expected to pay any attention, and so we must assume that the heroine will neither learn maternity nor be loved. Which seems appropriate enough when we remember that the red-haired man, in ordering the bad girl to her place, called it interchangeably earth and "hell, hell, hell."

"The Ballad of a Bad Girl" is an astute (self-)portrait of a strong woman who is both proud of and frightened by her strength, who can remember the exhilaration of feeling lost and defiantly "glad [she] was lost," but who also wants to be connected to the earth she knows so that her experience can be represented in terms familiar to her and her audience. Her celebration of herself as a New Woman depends on a reconstruction of the traditional woman as a victim in Hell. To put this vision into language, she must be magically transported back to the familiar concept of gender against which she rebelled but which can, alone, contextualize and so give heroic meaning to her rebellion. And, obviously only a male writer would be acceptable as the magician to such a woman as Luhan, because it is the male voice that continually pronounces the cultural precepts that her actions violate. It is not so obvious why Luhan refused to accept any man but Lawrence in this role. Since Luhan was not alone in this insistence that she be saved from cultural irrelevance and meaninglessness by Lawrence, the question cannot be considered answered by reference to her personal eccentricity. Her own answer can, however, be used as a basis for understanding why other women felt the same way.

She gives her answer in "Plum."[6] "Plum" goes far toward explaining what drew women to Lawrence and often kept them unable to sever their conflicted relations with him. The theme of the poem is that Lawrence is a "never-never man," his chameleon-like nature feminizing him.[7] She suggests that there is something intrinsically feminine about many of his qualities as a writer. Those she names have been associated, at least since the Romantic period, with literary creativity: a fluid sense of self and consequently an empathic identification with other living things. There is nothing particularly insightful in her suggestion. The male artist's portrayal of himself as a double-sexed being is a constant of modern literature: Shelley's vision in "Alastor" of the Poet embracing a maiden who is both "Herself a poet" and a living poem, whose "voice was like the voice of his own soul," becomes the female alter ego of "The Lady of Shalott" and "The Palace of Art"; and in "The Waste Land" T. S. Eliot speaks as Tiresias "throbbing between two lives" and genders.[8] What is impressive about Luhan's poem is that she does not portray Lawrence as a man writing from his female side, but as one with an essential being that is antithetical to maleness.

The assumption underlying her text seems to be that marginal people do not simply have similar experiences, they are the same. Women are non-men, Lawrence is not a true man, so Lawrence and women must be in some way the same. The way is, in her words, "mystic." Because as a man he is at the heart of God, at the center of patriarchal power, he can speak with authority (which is always coded as masculine) to give recognizable form to experience. Because he is also, as a non-man, at the heart of woman, he can see through patriarchal culture's constructs to what Luhan believes is a female essence.

She asks "why do men hate him?" "why do women love him?" Her answer is given in her description of the plum, which represents the "available, invisible Being" Lawrence shares with women. In "Peach," the poem that probably provided Luhan's model, Lawrence emphasizes the fruit's stone. Like Lawrence, Luhan treats the fruit's inner hardness as symbolic. If her plum is the wonderfully seductive fruit at the heart of woman, its stone is the part of woman's being that remains unconsumable, the irreducible core femaleness. To Luhan, this "bitter, sacred fruit of women" and its stone are inseparable, even conflated, the fruit "heavy like a stone," "[h]ard like a stone." Like the sensual experience that she claims is locked in her own memory, it is indestructible but troubling. Lawrence is necessary to women (and anathema to men) because of his likeness to the hard, bitter female essence concealed within women, which only he knows how to "pull out." In fact, he is paradoxically both the plum that she envisions "weighing so heavily in female bosoms" and also the only one who "[p]lucks it, but devours it never." Both Lawrence and the plum are modified by the single-word-stanza "Unassimilable!" And in the last lines the "mystic Plum" is apostrophized as "self-harvested only."

Luhan succeeds in giving a plausible explanation of the desire to have Lawrence speak for them that a group of women shared. They see him as the physical/textual manifestation of an inner self, the essential being that they can neither sacrifice nor complacently conceal. Lawrence not only draws out this "bitter, sacred fruit," he lends it his own form. He does not, in Luhan's view, take on the feminine as a persona from behind which he can speak for mankind, as a more typical male artist might; rather, he speaks for women and so becomes (or comes to represent) the nonnourishing, literally self-centered femaleness that opposes traditional masculinity and the system that empowers it.

As "The Ballad of a Bad Girl" indicates, however, Luhan's own feelings are ambivalent about both essential femaleness and the femininity in which society conceals it. In *Lorenzo in Taos,* the femaleness and femininity Luhan sees in Lawrence are most often depicted in terms of flaws and weaknesses, yet it is when she joins Lawrence in some enactment of the female role—for example, when their "fingers touch in the soap suds"—that she feels closest to him.[9] In this she is typical of Lawrence's female, contemporary biographers.

Carroll Smith-Rosenberg's discussion of another man's transformation into a mythic figure may further illuminate the process through which Lawrence was first mythologized in women's writings. To introduce her study of the re-creation of Davy Crockett in fable, Smith-Rosenberg says, "Individuals, experiencing themselves as powerless in the face of massive and unremitting social transformation, respond by attempting to capture and encapsulate such change within a new and ordered symbolic universe. They seek through imagery and myth to mitigate their feelings of helplessness by deflecting and partially distorting change and thus bringing it within the control of the imagination."[10] At the nexus of such imagery and myth, liminal figures take form. Liminality may be culturally contained—like the sex change operation, which subverts the idea of biologically fixed gender only to reinscribe gender difference—or disruptive of culture through its representation of the repressed or marginalized as worthy of attention or even as heroic. The liminal figure may stand for a change in the society's concept of selfhood.

Smith-Rosenberg argues that the fictional Crockett fulfilled all these functions for the men of a patriarchal society in violent flux. He valorized the culturally contained but rebellious energies of the new adolescent while also symbolically acting out the anxieties and aggressions surrounding the social mobility of the bourgeois, lower, and immigrant classes. In Crockett, Jacksonian-era men could see themselves reflected not as lost, fragmented, disintegrating prodigal sons, but as heroes striking out for new territory on which to put their marks. And, in comparison to Crockett's comically exaggerated difference from the norm, their own deviations were minimized, allowing them to reaffirm their own connectedness to the dominant culture.[11] Similarly, a group of women in the midst of the confusion created by rapid changes in gender roles and gender-bound power structures in England and America in the early part of the twentieth century seem to have mythologized Lawrence in response to their need for a sense of stable identity from which to write.

It may seem that these women were moving against the stream of modernism. At the very moment that, according to most postmodern theories, many prominent writers of fiction were beginning to decenter the subject, a group of women writers in desperate pursuit of old-fashioned subjecthood were assembling around Lawrence. Rather than condemning their project as a reactionary retreat from change, we might consider it as a step toward achieving a change in class status. As Lillian Robinson succinctly points out, "Women are not the in-laws of class society."[12] Instead, women's class status has generally been seen as lower than that of their fathers, brothers, and husbands. In a culture in which men are paid for their work and women are not, women tend to be considered dependents and subordinates. As a provider of domestic service, or even as a lady who is responsible for overseeing the running of the home, woman in capitalist society cannot renounce subjectivity because she has not been granted it within any of the structural systems that determine her cultural meaning. Thus, as Rita Felski says, "For women, questions of subjectivity, truth, and identity may not be out-moded fictions but concepts which still possess an important strategic relevance."[13] And if these questions remain relevant to feminist writers now, they were even more pressing for the women in Lawrence's circle.

Although most of them were from affluent families, these women show a high degree of the "impulse toward wholeness" or unified self-definition that Robinson convincingly demonstrates is a prominent feature of lower-class women's writings.[14] This may have been a result of their attempts to define themselves outside the ideologies they inherited. Their defiant countercultural stance against consumerist values and the Victorian class hierarchy meant that they were aligned by default with the lower classes. And even though this alignment appeared mostly in their rhetoric and was only translated into action as occasional, playful housework, it reinscribed their position as silent objects in the metonymic chain woman-houseworker-slave. To gain the authority to write, they first needed to break the connections among role, gender, and status. The creation of the fictional Lawrence was one of their strategies.

In their memoirs, women as different as Mabel Dodge Luhan, Jessie Chambers, Cynthia Asquith, Frieda Lawrence, Catherine Carswell, and Dorothy Brett all stress Lawrence's traditionally feminine traits and behavior patterns; while insisting, often rather contemptuously, that he was excluded by men from normal society because of these indications of nonmaleness, they reveal how much the supposed inner femaleness that determined Lawrence's inability to play the male role delighted them. Definitions of Lawrence in terms of escape from and adherence to feminine norms thread through all of these women's self-definitions. In fighting to understand and contain him, to represent him as both non-male and valuable, they often seem to be struggling to come to terms with their own femaleness. If ultimately they bow, as the world demands they must, to his male authorization to name them, still, they call him a man so that he can call them women—even in the full flowering of their rebellion. Always constrained by their language's construction of gender difference, they write Lawrence as both male and female, while demanding that he write them as women beyond cultural definitions of gender.

Lawrence's female biographers consistently discuss his housekeeping as a sign of his inner nature. They demonstrate, in the process, their own (often mixed) feelings about the metonymy that links woman and her duties. Chambers introduces her memories of Lawrence's friendship with her parents by commenting on his unusual willingness to help both his own mother and hers. Whatever task she shows him performing, Chambers always praises Lawrence's efforts as delicately executed and expressive of conventionally feminine aesthetics. She never criticizes Lawrence for this effeminacy. She defines herself, however, as an awkward housekeeper "in a state of furious discontent and rebellion" against her enforced role as "the family drudge."[15]

A juxtaposition in her memoir suggests the identification she feels with Lawrence. She first reports that her father praised Lawrence for helping his mother and then explains that "Lawrence told me himself that he never minded father seeing him with a coarse apron tied round his waist, but if he heard my brother's step in the entry he whipped it off on the instant, fearing he would despise him for doing housework." Superficially Lawrence's situation seems to have little in common with Chambers's. While she is fighting to escape domestic work, he is helpful and cheerful under the direction of his own mother and hers. One suspects Mr. Chambers of praising "Bert" in order to shame a daughter who is not equally good to her mother. Two similarities exist, however: Lawrence is ashamed of having Chambers's brother see him doing housework, and Chambers "quarrel[s] continually with [her] brothers" because they treat her like a domestic servant. Neither Chambers nor Lawrence can bear to be subjected to the contempt of male peers for working like women, although neither refuses to do women's work. This first small bond between them leads to Chambers's view of Lawrence as differing from ordinary men and occupying a (superior) position between them and women. Acting in a way that defines femininity as a problematic choice, Lawrence stands at the border Chambers longs to cross.[16]

Both Chambers and Cynthia Asquith often represent Lawrence as more like an uncontainable creative force than a gendered being. Asquith ends her reminiscences of his homely skills with quotes from Chambers that support her own view of Lawrence as " 'like the naked flame of light.' "[17] To both women, Lawrence seems "preternaturally alive" because he dignifies women's traditional tasks by performing them as if they were religious rites. His domestic activity is not a parody of the feminine role but a glorification of it. He acts as their culturally ideal selves might, while at the same time he recognizes, with sympathy rather than condemnation, that their real selves scorn housework.

Thus, as he was by Luhan, Lawrence is imagined as mediating between the inner and outer woman, joyfully taking upon himself the signs by which the world knows her while paradoxically acknowledging that the female, in her essence, hates such signification. These women seem to have looked to Lawrence to articulate their sense of themselves as moderns, self-defined as the opposites of the domestic woman whose services to the patriarchal family define her, even while he reaffirmed the worth of their domestic compromises with the world's demands. As they straddled the threshold between what they felt they were and what they were said to be, what they thought and what perforce they did, he was to celebrate their presence in the territories on both sides. And in return they would make him a god of their new mythology.

Lawrence's marriage to Frieda, a self-proclaimed female force who had never learned how to boil water, created the perfect situation for his performance of this liminal role. From the beginning of their shared life, Lawrence frequently played the model matron with Frieda. By her account, she "suddenly . . . knew [she] loved him" after he showed that he knew his way around a kitchen far better than she did and took more interest in her children than she could. After their elopement, Lawrence daily put aside his manuscripts in order to do all their housework, even carrying "the breakfast to [her] with a bunch of flowers." Four months later, Frieda started her "first attempt at housekeeping," with Lawrence cheerfully leaving his work whenever she called for his help and still bringing her "breakfast in bed."[18] As Frieda stresses throughout *Not I, But the Wind . . .* , Lawrence never seemed to her to value his writing above the housework or even to think of the latter as her work. Frieda's daughter, Barbara Weekley Barr, writes, "He did not have the ordinary man's domineering dependence on his womenfolk, but could mend, cook and find his possessions."[19] Frieda, like Chambers, must have seen in Lawrence a man who recognized the world's low valuation of women's work but considered it important enough to merit his own participation, a man who not only insisted that the bread "had to be perfect," but also was not above baking it.[20] In a world that often equated women and their work, Lawrence's behavior as housekeeper and writer challenged not only the separate gendering of each role but also the prevalent idea that the two roles were mutually exclusive.

Lawrence's sharing of the work that culture assigns to women seems to have led to his sharing with them the work that culture forbade them, the articulation of that in female experience which defies patriarchal definition. This was the pattern even when the friendship was almost entirely literary, as it was with Catherine Carswell. Although most of the contact between them took the form of exchanges of manuscripts and ideas, Carswell seems to have felt closest to Lawrence not when they worked at writing but when they worked around the house. After a discussion of how she helped Lawrence with the household chores during one of her many extended visits to the Lawrences, Carswell writes, "Certain literary critics have found that in estimating Lawrence as a writer it is beside the point to note that even while washing up dishes he radiated life. But those who washed dishes with Lawrence know that it is not beside the point."[21] The point, according to Carswell, seems to be that Lawrence was capable of a unique kind of understanding of women. She valued the advice and encouragement Lawrence gave her about her writing because she saw it as arising from his capacity to draw close to women and share their experiences.

Carswell often distanced herself from traits she saw as female; she dismissively categorized the cantankerous and "illogical" Frieda as "mindless Womanhood." Yet, like Luhan, she yearned for this un-socialized and so unassimilable power. She confided to Lawrence her plans to write a novel based on an account of a baby girl raised by savages who "never [let] her mix with her kind" but teach her "to believe that she is no mortal but a goddess." Like many women writers, the Brontës and George Eliot for instance, Carswell sees the story of female rebellion as developmental, with childhood marking the female's wildest state. She is interested in explaining how the baby girl could avoid seeing herself as a mortal woman, her destiny determined by biology. But the plot structure she chooses (bildungsroman) predetermines the movement of the protagonist into the social world that will reduce her to impotence. She attempted to collaborate with Lawrence on the project. He revised the story to focus on "a woman of thirty-five." That Lawrence could envision an adult woman from whom culture's inscription of tameness would be easily wiped away must have convinced Carswell that he had a confidence she lacked in the resurgent power of the hidden, fierce greatness of woman. Since he acted the female role but remained strong and self-defined beneath, why should he not have faith in an underlying pure female essence that defies definition by function? She gave the project over to him.[22]

Ironically, the final form of the story is "The Woman Who Rode Away," a sort of dramatization of the essay "Give Her a Pattern" in which Lawrence complains about woman's failure to know herself outside of the texts man creates. The woman in the short story runs away from a male adventure story that negates her (her life with her husband recalls Conrad's *Nostromo*) to enter an Indian myth that literally kills her. Socialization is represented as inescapable, female essence as meaningful only at the moment of its destruction, as the woman passes into utility within a primitive patriarchal culture. Sharing women's work with Lawrence seems to have led to turning over to him the work for women's freedom. The results were bound to disappoint his female followers since one cannot be led into freedom by a member of the group one is struggling against.

For women like Carswell and Dorothy Brett, the most devoted and submissive of Lawrence's female friends, doing housework with Lawrence fostered a sense of modern escape from feminine servitude to men, without introducing any of the frightening demands of a more feminist posture of open resistance to masculine power. Like his own god(dess), the Father more properly called the Mother, Lawrence was textually constructed by his female followers as truth bearer, higher self, nurturer, and judge. Brett, who spiritualized housework, wrote more about his cooking, sewing, and cleaning than any of his other biographers. Her vision of Lawrence as a Christ figure, implicit throughout her memoir, is closely connected to her understanding of him as an unusually domestic man. She shows us Lawrence, shortly before his trip to Mexico, retreating from angry thoughts about the "Judases" that have betrayed him in the past by getting "a shirt out of the cupboard and with incredible neatness [turning] the frayed cuffs." Brett also implies that Lawrence's domestic activities serve as a sort of religious purification. She shows him, sick because of problems with Luhan, scrubbing the "rotten old planks" of his kitchen floor "on [his] knees." But if these activities make Brett see Lawrence as godlike, they also make her see him as vulnerable, a precrucifixion Christ rather than a triumphantly risen God. She stands, or tries to stand, between her adored friend and his belligerent wife and traitorous acquaintances, just as she "paint[s] those floors . . . so that never again would [he] have to scrub them."[23] In her memoir, he stands between her and a conventional culture that might judge her deficient in femininity, as well as a bohemian subculture that might judge her weak to the extent that she is feminine. In shielding him, she shields the part of herself that submits to patriarchal demands.

Lawrence's housewifely skills did not always make him weak in Brett's eyes, however; sometimes they simply mitigated the inherent threat of maleness. In an extraordinary, early section of her memoir, she dwells on women's anger and attempts to understand Lawrence's relationship to it. She sets the scene in the Lawrences' cabin in Taos where she is visiting, and she begins by retelling the account Lawrence gave of a fight he had just had with Luhan. " 'She got so mad she threatened to hit me with her stick. I dared her to try. . . . She didn't dare,' " he says, laughing. Brett then gives us Frieda's repetition of the famous tale of how she broke a stoneware plate on Lawrence's head. According to Brett, Frieda spoke with "relish and pride" and "exuberant joy in what she had done." Brett says that she herself then reminisced about her own habit, at fourteen, of throwing china candlesticks at her governess's head. Brett tells us that Frieda then confessed her fear of Lawrence's masculine strength, " 'when he is in one of his rages.' " Lawrence, who was sewing a button on his pants, answered, " 'You had better be!' " Whereupon [they] all laugh[ed], and [Brett] marvel[led] at the neatness of [his] sewing."[24]

In each of the stories Brett retells, violence is connected with sexuality and efforts at control. Prior to telling his anecdote, Lawrence admitted to feeling "a certain amount of physical attraction" to Luhan, but struggling with her for dominance. His struggles with Frieda have a similar cast for, as jealous Brett is honest enough to show, Lawrence continued all his life to see Venus in Frieda's image. Brett herself, awakened from compliance by puberty, rebelled against the one whom society decided should govern her. Brett's struggles with her governess were apparently resolved by her attainment of maturity and so independence, but the other women show anxiety about their own ability to attain power in relation to Lawrence because of the superior strength his gender gives him. But, in Brett's text, at least, a woman can ultimately laugh at his threats because she can see in him "something more nearly akin to herself" than in the ordinary man who insists on a separation of labor on gender lines.[25] Lawrence's anger and violence seem, in his observers' eyes, as much identified with as against woman. Fighting with him seems to represent fighting with oneself about issues of gender, sexuality, and power. He is reconstructed as masculine or feminine in accordance with the text's diverse representations of woman as adversary, friend, or good daughter and Brett's varying degrees of identification with these roles.

The remarkable frequency with which the same basic pattern was repeated in women's responses to Lawrence seems to say as much about the psychology of his female contemporaries as it does about his own. With the end of the Victorian era and its cult of domesticity, intelligent women generally seemed to feel pressured to enact two rarely compatible roles. On the one hand, they were to be good, traditionally feminine wives and mothers. On the other hand, they were to be interesting, because intellectually developed, individuals. This problem was exacerbated for most of Lawrence's female friends; while they longed to have a decisive impact on the world of the arts, they lacked the specific talents necessary for artistic success. They were more often seen as bohemians than artists, and they saw themselves more often as domestic failures than triumphant individualists. While those who played the ordinary female roles, like Lawrence's mother and Chambers's, could feel simple gratitude for Lawrence's participation in their activities, his less conventional female friends seem to have needed his participation in their chores to reassure them of the dignity of the work that absorbs some of almost every woman's energies.

Luhan thought about these matters. Like many of Lawrence's biographers and critics before and after her, she saw Lawrence as "double, split in two," but unlike most others who have written about Lawrence, she connected his doubleness to an ambivalence in women themselves, rather than in his attitude about them. As Luhan puts it:

> He was the Son—the second person of the Trinity—but (God help all women!) though we tried to overcome and possess him, yet secretly we always wanted him to be the Father! . . . He perpetually strove to adopt for his own the difficult and lonely role of Father, and as often he slid back to the shelter of the Beloved Son. Everything conspired against him. The women who loved him seemed to be impelled to hold him back, even when they themselves most greatly needed his attainment. The vacillation went on forever.[26]

Luhan departs here from the usual Freudian interpretation of Lawrence's life. Lawrence's vacillation comes from external not internal pressures. He does not retreat from mature sexual life into playing the role of a son; rather, he must act like a son in order to enjoy the love of women. The role of father, according to Luhan, would be lonely. In what is probably the most influential psychological discussion of Lawrence, H. M. Daleski connects Lawrence's duality to his female-role playing. He goes on to make the same point explicitly that Luhan's "Plum" does implicitly: Lawrence has a "fundamental identification with the female principle." But whereas Luhan regards Lawrence's responses to the women he loved as shaping forces of his behavior and art, Daleski explains that Lawrence's doubleness originated with desire for his mother and was perpetuated by his unhappy recognition that "he was more strongly feminine than masculine" and that he could not "reconcile the male and female elements in himself."[27]

There is no reason to regard Luhan's and Daleski's explanations of Lawrence's doubleness as mutually exclusive, however. It is clear from Lawrence's letters, *Sons and Lovers,* and many early poems that his attachment to his mother was so intense that it greatly affected his development. Surely it led him to attempt to please her by imitating her behavior and attitudes, and his imitation of what have traditionally been considered feminine values and pursuits led to his being rejected by other males and consequently becoming unusually dependent on females (whom he attempted to please, as he had his mother, by playing the role of helpful and compliant son). As Daleski points out, Edward Nehls's *D. H. Lawrence: A Composite Biography* is full of examples of Lawrence's early femalelike behavior and the responses it drew from his contemporaries. What emerges again and again from the women's accounts is the ambivalence that Luhan discusses. And whatever forces, Oedipal or otherwise, created the actual Lawrence, it seems important to keep in mind that

these early, ambivalent female responses contributed heavily to the creation of the textual Lawrence.

For example, Jessie Chambers's older sister, May Chambers Holbrook, tells an anecdote about Lawrence lecturing her on groceries; she
ends by defending him against the grocer's accusation that he is "not
right in his head" because he will "stand and talk *like a woman* about
groceries" and is never seen "with a gang o' lads," but with "two, three
girls." Lawrence, "well aware" of the general opinion that he was men-
tally ill for preferring the company of girls, defends his choice by saying
" 'Girls are ever so much nicer.' " Holbrook returns his compliment by
imagining, when he is teased by the other boys, that "he had lots of fight
in him" and was only held back by his poor health.[28] Like Lawrence's
later female friends, she enjoys his allegiance to a female mode of being,
but rewards him by trying to project onto him a virtue coded as male.
Consequently, Lawrence is written by both Holbrook and Nehls as the
locus of an inharmonious meeting of femininity and masculinity.

An odd situation developed between Lawrence and the majority of his
female admirers. A male creative genius's choice to do housework was
an affirmation of the work's value and also a reassurance that domesticity
and art were not incompatible pursuits. But as work defined the worker,
as much in terms of gender as of class, Lawrence's interest in housework
could not avoid marking him as effeminate. An effeminate man's interest
in women's work could in no way improve the self-image of women
who wanted freedom from their own class without being exiled into the
silences of the lowest one. Consequently, they seem to have felt compelled to urge him to demonstrate that he was a normal male. Yet, as
Luhan notes, Lawrence's female friends tended to withdraw from him
and withhold their affection when he behaved in a traditionally male
manner, since they disliked and distrusted conventional men.

This pattern of drawing close through shared feminine interests and
then springing apart because of the woman's distaste for Lawrence's
masculinity is closely connected to the dominant pattern in women's
attempts to write in collaboration with Lawrence. In artistic endeavor, as
in ordinary life, Lawrence had authority and power because of both his
talents and his maleness. Lawrence's female friends often seemed to want
their creative efforts dignified and improved by his participation, but
they clearly wanted him to participate in the spirit of a son. That is, they
wanted him to help them as a subordinate rather than a savior, to use his

talents to express their ideas. His alacrity both to write about female experience and to accept guidance from women readers seems to have encouraged his women friends to trust him with their work, but whenever he asserted his male authority they withdrew mistrustfully. Only Frieda worked creatively with Lawrence throughout his life.

The frequently told story of Lawrence's early relationship with Jessie Chambers reveals a great deal about what the women he worked with expected from Lawrence, what he wanted from them, and why all his creative partnerships except the one with Frieda eventually failed to provide the women with the intellectual support they had expected to gain. In her biography of Lawrence, Chambers appears as a martyr to a genius who cannot reconcile the pleasures of the mind, which attract her, and the urges of the body, which repel her. It has long been the fashion, among Lawrence's critics, to accept Chambers's depiction of Lawrence as more or less accurate. It may be more useful, however, to look at some of the ways Chambers's biography of Lawrence is shaped by autobiographical imperatives.' A. J. Bramley, who provides an introductory essay for the second edition of Chambers's *D. H. Lawrence: A Personal Record,* analyzes the failure of Lawrence and Chambers's engagement in the following characteristic manner:

> It was a cruel dilemma for both of them, and there is not the slightest doubt that at this period the physical and spiritual side of Lawrence's nature became involved in a dichotomy which was to leave him scarred for the rest of his life. He began to overemphasize the importance of sex, to make wild proposals to Jessie that she should remain his spiritual bride while he sought elsewhere for a woman he could embrace and make the mother of his children, and to show all the symptoms of a person who is suffering from a severe conflict.[29]

Some of these assertions can be accepted without "the slightest doubt": Lawrence did seem to be suffering from conflicting emotions, and his attempts to resolve his problems with Chambers did create a "cruel" situation for both of them. But Lawrence's insistence, when he was past twenty years old, that he must have an outlet for his sexual feelings does not seem an overemphasis of the importance of sex. Emile Delavenay chivalrously claims that Lawrence's insensitivity kept Chambers from reciprocating his desire.[30] Such judgments are consistent with Chambers's own pronouncements about the affair. She says over and over that she was a normal, healthy young woman with natural feelings and that Lawrence was deeply disturbed. She continually contrasts his "funda-mental" error with her own wholeness and asserts her resistance to "this division of love into the spiritual and the physical."[31] Her accounts of her behavior with Lawrence do not always support this coherent self-image, however. Harry T. Moore claims that "her own fundamental Puritanism keeps revealing itself in the narrative."[32] But the basis for Chambers's treatment of Lawrence often seems to be recoil from sexuality rather than general moral strictness. This almost compulsive rejection of sexuality, which goes against her stated belief in the wholesomeness of free love, is an indication of how trapped she was by her society's increasingly complex and contradictory demands on women.

Chambers was anything but a prim, old-fashioned girl. She often showed herself eager to transcend her rural background and be seen as a progressive intellectual. She was deeply interested in the feminist move-ment and was also an aspiring novelist. Much biographical attention has been given to the scene, described by both Lawrence and Chambers, in which he offers her a resentful proposal because his mother has said that it is not fair for him to continue seeing her if he does not intend to marry her. Emily Hahn's interpretation is typical; she is not surprised by Cham-bers's response, but declares, "It is Lawrence himself who sounds pecu-liar."[33] Yet it seems somewhat odd that any young woman who was a member of a provincial community in which there was very little differ-ence between formal engagement and keeping company would have a young man for a close friend for four years, spend long periods of time alone with him, and still be able to tell "him with truth that [she] had not thought about love."[34] The contrast between Lydia Lawrence's ordinary concern with the proprieties as defined by her community and Cham-bers's nonconformist desire for a friendship with a man in which gender is irrelevant shows that Chambers was no simple prude. Like the major-ity of Lawrence's subsequent female friends, Chambers struggled against the boundaries her society placed around female behavior. One set of boundaries confined women who enjoyed sex in the lower class. In a dis-cussion of Virginia Woolf, Robinson shows how closely modernist writ-ers connected female sexual pleasure and loss of class status.[35] Women were not only forbidden to write about sexual pleasure, they were likely to be marginalized as speaking subjects if they were known to have experienced sexual pleasure.

Fearing the implications of active sexuality perhaps as much as the act itself, Chambers tried to sustain with Lawrence the presexual life of childhood. She writes of their inhabiting "a world apart" in which they were held together by "a strong feeling of mutual sympathy" that apparently precluded "personal relations." She later deplores what she sees as Lawrence's tendency to regard "love as something purely physical," yet her early conception of the bond between them seems equally purely disembodied. In her writing, he is idealized as a flame of energy while she represents herself as unaware of the sexual facts of life. At twenty, she says, she "was puzzled, feeling in the dark about the whole business," when Lawrence told her about a friend who "had to" get married. Another time, she had "only the vaguest conception of his meaning" when Lawrence rather cruelly told her that she had "no sexual attraction," and, in case the reader mistake her meaning, she makes it plain that it was the word "sexual" that she could not understand; she "thought he was telling [her] that [she] was unattractive in a general way."[36] J. David Chambers says that his sister, as "mother's confidant," learned that sex was categorically an act of aggression against women, objectifying and silencing them.[37] As long as Chambers could see Lawrence as a beautiful force just barely inhabiting an adolescent body, she could safely identify her own vocation with his. What he was she could strive to be. When he, and their determinedly modern social set, demanded that sexuality be acknowledged, she had to split him into a sick sexual body and a healthy mind so that at least some part of him could continue to represent her most enabling self-image.

Chambers's *D. H. Lawrence: A Personal Record* has helped numerous critics argue that Lawrence, owing to his Oedipal attachment to his mother, could not both love and desire the same woman, and that he consequently rejected Chambers because her spirituality was too reminiscent of his mother's. Yet Chambers's rejection of sexuality is not really comparable to Lydia Lawrence's conventionally religious prudishness. A simpler analysis of the situation is possible, however. Lawrence may have been, as he repeatedly told Chambers, unable to desire her because he wanted a woman with strong, aggressively expressed desires— sexual and otherwise. If Chambers wanted to find her voice through identification with an adolescent creative force, Lawrence wanted to find his voice through union with a powerful woman. Helen Corke, yet another woman friend who recorded her memories of Lawrence, believed that Chambers repeated "the error of Lawrence's mother, who with similar insistence had claimed the boy as she herself was now claiming the youth."[38] To Corke, Chambers was guilty of an antisexual possessiveness aimed at keeping Lawrence from attaining manhood. But Chambers possessed Lawrence only as a character in her writing, and it was only there that his pursuit of adult sexual life was blocked. The actual Lawrence left Chambers and wrote himself into another sort of story.

For many of the women in his life, writing about Lawrence was a way of writing about themselves; their relations with him were a means of constructing themselves as authors. For Lawrence, women were equally necessary to the attainment of authorship. Problems arose in his collaborative relationships, however, because his concept of his literary mission made him represent gender difference in a specific way. His goal, like the women's, was self-empowerment. And like them, he wished to achieve it through the creation of an oppositely gendered force that would compel him to write. From his first writings on, his speaking position is always located in relation to a powerful woman. Lawrence indisputably loved his mother with an unusual intensity, and, rather than searching for an utterly different sort of woman to be his partner in life, he gave his love and sexual desire to a woman who, in her egotism, her aggressiveness, and her passion, closely resembled that imperious "little woman" as he represents her in Gertrude Morel.[39] Lawrence describes Frieda and such embodiments of his female ideal as Ursula Brangwen and Connie Chatterley as being "strong enough to bear" contact with adult masculinity.

Lawrence is always careful to show that what he wants of women is not simply that they wholeheartedly accept their men's sexual attentions but that they enter into a creative exchange of gender-determined energies. Lawrence's heroes and heroines strive together to attain their own and acknowledge each other's sexual maturity. For Birkin and Ursula, Connie and Mellors, and the more autobiographical Lovat and Harriet Somers, the question of whether they can successfully make love is inextricably connected to their pursuits of adult identity and purpose. Invariably depicted as more confident and emotionally stable, the women in these couples set a standard of adult strength that the men must reach. In the world of Lawrence's fiction, it is not female acquiescence but female challenge that empowers men. For Lawrence, the endless fight between the sexes, complicated by the conflict between women's demand for male sexual maturity and their opposition to the authority culture assigns it, is the foundation of all living vital art. It was not for nothing that Lawrence called Frieda the Queen Bee. As much as she strove relentlessly to dominate his life, she also ceaselessly demanded that his virility be manifested.

Whether his art would have suffered had he married Chambers rather than Frieda is unclear. Despite his theory of the relationship between sex and art, Lawrence was quite productive during the period when Chambers was the major contributor to his work. However, it seems certain that his work would have taken a different direction. What is often missing in his early fiction is a sense that men and women can achieve a balance of power. In "The White Stocking," love forces the complete surrender of a girl to a man. More frequently, as in "Goose Fair," "The Witch à la Mode," *The White Peacock,* and *The Trespasser,* men are overwhelmed by women's power and can only avoid utter subordination by running away. The retreat of his male characters from their women, like his own retreat from Chambers, seems derived from fear of being kept eternally childlike rather than from fear of sex.

Helen Corke perceptively attributes Lawrence's vacillations toward and away from identification with women to his tendency to look "within his own soul for sanctions," which he then found impossible to reconcile with "those of his day and society."[40] Corke's view of Lawrence as a sort of moral outlaw longing for acceptance but marginalized by his own ethos accords better with what we know of his consistent dependence on women's approval of his work than does the usual view of Lawrence as a divided man in whom the conventionally proper mother's boy is at odds with the demonic, would-be masterful sexual rebel. Lawrence first became a social outcast because of his preference for female company and traditionally feminine pursuits, which pleased both his mother and his first love. It was only later that he developed the interest in sex that annoyed Lydia Lawrence and Chambers, and it was not until he began to collaborate with more sexually sophisticated women, like Corke and Frieda, that he scandalized society with his sexual frankness. His texts were subsequently set apart from those of other male writers not by his misogynous diatribes but by his attempts to depict female experience as something separate from rather than symbolic of male experience, and by his open reliance on women to help him in this task.

In both theory and practice, Lawrence's muse was active and compelling rather than passively inspiring. This way of relating to women (and femaleness) within his texts resembles the revisionist mythologizing that Alicia Ostriker attributes to feminist poets when she claims: "To identify an active, aggressive woman with Truth is to defy a very long tradition that identifies strong females with deception and virtuous females, including muses, with gentle inactivity."[41] And Lawrence was not content simply to represent woman as an active muse, although he often did so; he went beyond representation to give women real power to judge and reshape his writings.

Women participated in Lawrence's work as models for characters and as contributors of verbal and written source materials, but their major role in relation to his work seems to have been as critics. Lawrence appeared to be uneasy whenever his writings failed to please the women who were important to him, and often female disapproval caused him to discard or extensively revise his work. Chambers reports that, when they were young, Lawrence said that he wrote for her, "and of his poetry he said, 'All my poetry belongs to you.'"[42] Hilary Simpson notes that Lawrence had "an almost obsessive need" for Chambers's "seal of approval."[43] This was evidenced when he responded to her criticisms of the manuscript that was to become *The White Peacock* by "immediately" rewriting it. During the composition of both *The White Peacock* and *Sons and Lovers,* Lawrence "passed the manuscript on" to Chambers, for her responses, "a few sheets at a time." As he became aware that she was infuriated by his depiction of her (as Miriam), Lawrence "left off" visiting Chambers but continued to mail her installments of his manuscript. She and her sister May both felt that Lawrence was extremely disturbed by Chambers's dislike of the novel, although anyone who has read it can hardly be surprised by Chambers's reaction.[44]

Lawrence also sought advice from other women from the very beginning of his career. In a letter typical of his communications with women friends, he tells Louisa Burrows (whom he would begin courting three years later), "Write me your opinions and criticisms—your advice if you like—I shall like it."[45] Philip T. Smith, who was the headmaster at the Davidson Road School when Lawrence and Corke taught there, writes that Lawrence "consulted her [Corke] on the merits or otherwise of both *The White Peacock* and *The Trespasser* before publication."[46] Corke herself says that when Lawrence was making the final revisions to the manuscript of the former novel, he asked her "to read it and *to cut out any prolix passage.*"[47] He was no less intellectually submissive to women much later in his career. Although he was not on good terms with Luhan at the time, when she expressed annoyance with an essay he wrote about the Hopi snake dance ("Just Back From the Snake Dance—Tired Out"), Lawrence meekly promised to "try and do another one" that she would like. He succeeded in writing "The Hopi Snake Dance," which she found "wonderful, deeply understanding."[48]

None of these women exercised as strong an influence on his writing as Frieda did. After he broke with Chambers, Frieda became and remained his most attentively heeded critic. In her biography, she claims, "I read every day what he had written." Of *Sons and Lovers* she says, "I lived and suffered that book, and wrote bits of it." According to Frieda, this working relationship continued all Lawrence's life. He even asked her whether he should publish *Lady Chatterley's Lover.*[49] One anecdote from *Lawrence and Brett* (substantiated by Frieda) illustrates the amazing extent of Frieda's influence on Lawrence's work. Asked by Lawrence whether she likes *The Boy in the Bush,* Brett says that she does except for the ending, which seems to her out of character. In her opinion, Jack, the hero, should have died. Lawrence responds, "I know . . . I know. That is how I wrote it first; I made him die—only Frieda made me change it."[50] This story is rarely commented on by Lawrence critics, yet where else in the history of literature is there such an incident? Frieda was poorly educated and, unlike Lawrence's earlier female advisors, had no literary pretensions, but she made her husband revise his work in a way that he felt destroyed its artistic integrity.

One possible explanation of this extraordinary responsiveness to women's judgments is persuasively presented by Anne Smith in her Freudian "Biographical Overview" of Lawrence's relations with women. In Smith's view, all Lawrence's relations with women were determined by his need to be "safe as a child" protected by a powerful mother. Of course, Lawrence's life had often been similarly analyzed, perhaps beginning with Middleton Murry's *Son of Woman.* What makes Smith's biographical essay so compelling is that she sees Lawrence's marginality as the cause of his inability to achieve a relationship with women that was essentially different from the one he had with his mother. As Smith points out, the view of Lawrence, in his hometown Eastwood, as effeminate began not because of his unusual attachment to his mother but because of his physical weakness. Lawrence was set apart from the beginning because "it was one thing for a middle-class boy to be physically weak and emotionally precocious, and another thing altogether for a working-class boy—especially a working-class boy in a mining village at the end of the nineteenth century, where physical strength and hence potential earning power were the measures of manliness." His exclusion was reinforced later because "the men he knew . . . were more different from him than he was from women, so . . . he had to define himself against a background of women"—a background that, as we have seen, later took form as a body of women's biographical texts. Yet Lawrence's determined retention of many of the values he had learned in Eastwood made impossible his successful translation into any narrative informed by bourgeoise values. For Lawrence as well as his biographers, there was no social text that could give him coherent identity. Smith astutely notes that "the middle-class intellectuals of his adult experience could never have conformed with an image of men and women based on his working-class childhood," and Lawrence could not so completely reject his earliest impressions as to accept the familial roles of the middle-class as normal. Instead, he remained drawn to strong women who, like his mother, "assumed many of the more traditionally masculine functions in [the] family in the working-class way described in *The Rainbow*."[51] Because these surrogate mothers were experimenting with new gender roles, however, they could not share Lydia Lawrence's confidence in her gender identity. Their own liminality demanded that Lawrence take a complementary position. In response to their conflicting needs for the feminization still necessary to women's self-esteem and for the freedom from femininity necessary for literary authority, and for him to both model feminine creativity and give patriarchal authorization to their writing, Lawrence vacillated between genders and classes, in and out of the central speaking position.

Because working-class writers have regularly enjoyed success since the early part of this century, it is easy to underestimate how much Lawrence's class set him apart from the companions and acquaintances of his adult life. Ford Madox Ford was particularly pleased by his discovery of Lawrence because "everyone at that time was eager to find working-class writers, but nobody yet had succeeded in doing so. Gissing and Wells were not really working-class, only lower-middle." As the literary history of the modern period began to be written, Lawrence was classified as "a different animal," "a rare specimen," and he would remain one all his life because he could not break such connections between himself and his class as his Midlands accent, his belief in the intrinsic value of manual labor, and his predilection for living alone with his wife in a little house that the two of them maintained.[52]

Nonetheless, Lawrence was set apart not simply by class, but also by the vicious circle that continually returned him to his unusual dependence on and identification with women. He was weak and fragile, so he grew abnormally close to his mother. Like his mother, he preferred activities assigned to females, so he developed friendships with girls and was more loved and accepted by them than he could be by males, with whom he shared few interests. When he left behind his working-class friends and met intellectual men with whom he might have shared much, he alienated them by his adherence to standards of behavior they could not understand and excited their contempt by his "immature," working-class attitudes toward women. As R. W. Connell has argued, gender is defined differently for different social classes, and working-class masculinity has emerged from negotiations with a longstanding "working-class feminism." The latter often wins the "marital power struggle" in individual families while, to maintain the status quo of all the men in the group, a "facade of men's authority" is maintained.[53] In the middle-class milieu Lawrence had entered, his seemingly empty assertion of his own patriarchal dominance was seen as pathetic wishful thinking.

In addition, Lawrence's homosexual inclinations (exhaustively discussed in Delavenay's *D. H. Lawrence and Edward Carpenter*) undoubtedly made many heterosexual men uncomfortable with him, while his determination to channel his sexual energies into a marriage that would provide a foundation for all his endeavors made Lawrence reject the company of openly homosexual men. His inability to be accepted as a man caused him to become increasingly insistent that he was male and thus increasingly uncompromising in his definitions of maleness and femaleness, thus further isolating himself from more conventional men whose social privileges made it possible for them to show noblesse oblige toward women.

By comparing Lawrence's situation as a writer to that of his contemporary James Joyce, one can see how unusually marginalized Lawrence was. As writers and as men Lawrence and Joyce had much in common, including problems like poverty and chronic illness. They lived most of their lives in partially self-imposed exile and were further alienated from their countrymen by the banning of their books in Britain. And both were known to be excited by sexual activities commonly considered perverse. Joyce, however, was able to define himself as a man in ways that Lawrence could not. Despite his ill health, Joyce was not exiled from the world of men; according to both his autobiographical writings and Richard Ellmann's biography, the majority of Joyce's friends and companions (of which he always seemed to have many) were male. With them he enjoyed traditionally male pastimes, such as drinking in pubs, and his work usually reflects his interest in men's relations with each other. Consequently it seems that Joyce could devote most of his energies to demonstrating that he was an artist, while Lawrence never seemed able to transcend his need to define himself first as a man.

Early in his career Lawrence was apparently so eager to be accepted as an artist and so used to being perceived as effeminate that he was able to be amused that *The White Peacock* "was taken for a woman's [work] in several quarters."[54] That it was also quite successful must have contributed to Lawrence's complacency. Later, as it must have become apparent to him that he would not win easy acceptance as either an artist or a man, Lawrence concentrated on establishing himself as the latter. Brett effectively conveys his preoccupation (as well as her own) with his masculinity. The first words of his that she remembers are, " 'Ah no, Brett, I am not a man . . . I am MAN.' " About their trip to Mexico City, she writes, "A special banquet is given for you by the P. E. N. Club. . . . On your return, we ask you what you said in your speech. 'I don't remember,' you say, 'Except that I said that the most important thing to remember, was that we are all, first and foremost, men together, before we are artists; that to be a man is more important. But they didn't understand. They one and all protested that it was more important to be an artist.' "[55]

To explain these remarks as indications of Lawrence's male chauvinism, his valuation of masculinity over femininity, is to ignore the difference, which he himself points out, between his attitude and that of his audience. They know that they are men and can speak with him as such, but they want to be recognized and spoken to as artists. Lawrence must begin by asserting that he is a man and waiting for acceptance as one before he is able to deal with the issue of art. As his insurmountable marginality decreed, however, Lawrence could not receive reassurance that he was male from other men; he had to seek affirmation of himself as a man in those magnifying mirrors, women's eyes.

Lawrence not only submitted his writings to women he knew, he also seemed most often to think of the reader of his published work as female, as is strongly suggested in *Kangaroo*. *Kangaroo* is unique among the fictional works Lawrence intended for publication in the amount of material it contains that is directly addressed to the reader. This reader seems to be female. We are early made to know the narrator as one who believes "himself entitled to all kinds of emotions and sensations which an ordinary man would have repudiated," and who, thus, frequently finds it easier to talk to women than to men.[56] The chapter in the middle of the novel, "Harriet and Lovat at Sea in Marriage," which summarizes the central conflict the characters face, takes the form of a lecture directed at young married women complete with their (imagined) derisive interjections. At this point Harriet's voice seems to merge with the imagined reader's just as Lovat's voice has periodically drifted into conjunction with the narrator's. Lovat learns about life from his wife, and at the end of the book he speaks "very gently, like a woman" (*Kangaroo,* 343). It is suggested that speaking to a woman brings about speaking like a woman, understanding passes quickly into identification, and the male speaker who allows a female voice to enter his discourse soon both possesses and is possessed by it. This process paradoxically makes it possible for him to speak with authority, for he has incorporated the voice in which he has invested the power to judge.

The parallel between Lawrence's relationships with actual women and his concept of his relationship to the reader is further clarified by the second section of *Mr. Noon*. After the main characters, Gilbert and Johanna, have their first quarrel, the narrator drops his archly urbane mask and continues the fight with the reader, beginning, "And so, gentle reader—! But why the devil should I always *gentle-reader* you. . . . Time you became rampageous reader, ferocious reader, surly, rabid reader, hell-cat of a reader, a tartar, a termagant, a tanger. —And so, hell-cat of a reader, let me tell you, with a flea in your ear, that all the ring–dove sonata you'll get out of me you've got already, and for the rest you've got to hear the howl of tomcats like myself and she-cats like yourself, going it tooth and nail."[57]

One could hardly say that Lawrence is courting the reader, but one must recognize that he is attempting to meet her honestly, stripping away all the artificial conventions that make understanding between men and women impossible. If the reader is "detestable," and a "sniffing mongrel bitch" with a "psycho-analysing nose," she is also the "fiery one" whose released anger can "consume the flabby masses of humanity, and make way for a splendider time" (*Mr. Noon*, 205). The unleashing of her power licenses the release of his own. She is the supreme goddess of his fictional cosmos; her attention to his work makes possible his creation of the new heaven and earth.

Another impulse is also at work in this exchange, Lawrence's representation of the female reader includes both difference and identification. By identifying the narrator with the male character, and thus displacing the fight between husband and wife with a struggle between narrator and reader, he redefines his narrative project as an attack on the Other, who is to be forced into understanding. But then his anger with the dominant discourse's forms of address ("gentle reader"), implied audience ("flabby masses"), and authorizing pre-texts (psychoanalytic theory) is attributed to his female ideal reader. Consequently his project is identified with her. Here Lawrence's situation could be considered analogous to Zora Neal Hurston's in *Mules and Men*, as described by Barbara Johnson. Faced with the problem of revealing to a white audience a black folk-culture to which she is an outsider, Hurston focuses on "the dialogic situation" in which the "inner life" of the culture must be represented.[58] Hurston refocuses the folk tales she retells, in order to comment on the narrative that includes them, just as Lawrence stylizes the criticisms he had received from his actual female readers, in order to comment on his narrator's concept of gender difference and the "master text" that frames it. The author seems to flicker into presence at the places where the text turns in upon itself. In both cases emphasis is moved from the opposition between inside and outside, identification and difference, to the dialogue between these unstable positions. Difference remains vitally important, but it eludes description.

Because of this insistence on the necessity of a female reader, Lawrence's fiction must be considered part of the body of literature written with women's responses as one of the author's major concerns. Because Lawrence's fiction is generally not merely descriptive of women's experience but prescriptive, it could also be placed in that subcategory of male tradition consisting of novels written by men for the edification of women, such as Richardson's *Pamela*. But Lawrence finds teaching women readers of secondary importance to reproducing, as faithfully as he can, their real voices (which necessitates emphasizing their anger and resistance to his ideas); he thus places his work in a different category entirely, one that could be judged to consist of his works alone. If there is any literary tradition to which Lawrence can be said to belong, it is not the dominant one in which male experience is depicted simply as experience and female experience is seen as a side issue, a symbol for male concerns, or a blank space to be filled in with men's fantasies or teachings; rather, it is the tradition of women's literature as a record of marginality and ambivalence.

Lawrence's place in women's literature is anything but obvious; in two basic ways, however, his texts and the circumstances of their production seem connected to women's literary traditions. First, Lawrence's situation in the world shaped his work in a manner almost identical to that in which, according to classic texts on female literary traditions, social conditions have influenced women's writings. In fact, when we look at Lawrence through the filter of these texts, a monstrous shadow sister appears. In *The Madwoman in the Attic,* Sandra Gilbert and Susan Gubar catalog "phenomena of 'inferiorization' [which] mark the woman writer's struggle for artistic self-definition and differentiate her efforts at self-creation from those of her male counterpart"; these phenomena also describe the attitudes that set Lawrence apart from the fathers and sons of patriarchal literary tradition. Lawrence's "urgent sense of [his] need for a female audience" is clear from both his dependence on his female acquaintances' responses to his work and his vision of the ideal reader as female. The accompanying "fear of the antagonism of male readers" can be seen in almost every reference he makes to the reception he anticipates is awaiting each of his manuscripts.[59] Lawrence seems to have believed that, as Patricia Meyer Spacks says, "differences between traditional female preoccupations and roles and male ones make a difference in female writing," and consequently that, because his own writing reflected his predilection for the female role, it was more likely to be deemed acceptable by female than male readers.[60] These attitudes are important not simply as identifying characteristics of certain writers, but as motivational forces that cause these writers to form the literary alliances that bring their texts into a relationship generative of its own traditions.

This relationship has, according to Gilbert and Gubar, been marked by women's anxiety about the propriety of literary creation. As Angeline Goreau has shown, publication has been seen for centuries as a violation of feminine modesty analogous to becoming a public woman or prostitute.[61] Because women playing masculine roles are seen as both unnatural and indecent, female authorship can simultaneously threaten a woman's sense of her self as good and her sense of gender identity. Obviously, in the modern period, as violation of sexual decorums increasingly signified authorial seriousness in texts with male signatures, the threats writing posed to female status and identity increased proportionally. For similar reasons, Lawrence seems to have felt threatened by his own impulse to write. He had received his first lessons in appropriate gender behavior by observing a mother who wrote essays and poetry and a father who called poetry "pottery" and "couldn't read well enough" to realize that he was being insulted in *Sons and Lovers*.[62] Lawrence's desperate insistence that other men consider him, not as a writer, but as a man, indicates that he could not dismiss the early standards that would later lead the representative "anonymous Eastwood miner" to "put him down as nowt."[63] One could say Lawrence felt anxiety about invention because he connected it with femaleness. Moreover, he could not resolve this problem with the sort of literary transvestism that Elaine Showalter deplores, by "masking" his male power with a female voice in order to enjoy the triumphs first of proving that he could be a better woman than a biological woman could and later of proving that he need not be a woman at all. Unlike the writers Showalter criticizes, Lawrence shows "anxiety of authorship that is related to his own cultural position."[64] His identification with and dependence on women apparently left him feeling that he had no triumphant masculinity to reveal. With each sexual revelation, he seems to have felt that he had further embedded himself in a female tradition and further eroded his masculinity.

Like the female writer whose "most potent fear is likely to be of abandonment, her most positive vision of love," Lawrence seems to have experienced as a source of shame what society defines as an overvaluation of sexual love and marriage."[65] Moments of self-exposure in his texts, as in those of women, show forth not phallic power but naked, gender-determined need. Love affairs and marital problems are depicted as the central, most important aspects of life. Sexual experience is evaluated almost entirely according to how much emotional satisfaction it provides. The tone in which he presents these themes is rarely confident. From the poem about his first weeks with Frieda, "Humiliation"—the title of which expresses perhaps all that can be said about Lawrence's feelings about his dependence—to "Strife," a paean to "twoness" in *Last Poems,* Lawrence's autobiographical poetry reveals his unhappy realization that he can feel he exists only in relation to a woman. His own "ambivalence about the self-revelation necessary in fiction" is evident throughout his writings, but nowhere is it more fully revealed than in his explanation to Edward Garnett about the Foreword to *Sons and Lovers*: "I wanted to *write* a Foreword, not to have one printed. . . . I would die of shame if that Foreword were printed."[66] If his most positive vision (as it is articulated in the Foreword) was of woman's approval, his most potent fear seems to have been of being abandoned by her to face the disapproval of men who would read him as effeminate and so inferior.

In the same letter to Garnett, Lawrence claims, "We have to hate our immediate predecessors, to get free from their authority." This might be seen as indicative of manly combativeness and anxiety of influence rather than what Gilbert and Gubar call "dread of the patriarchal authority of art," if Lawrence were the sort of man patriarchal art generally depicts as valuable.[67] But Lawrence was marginal to the world of men because of his class, his habits, his preoccupations, even his personality. As a man "not of the universal kind," he stood in the same relation to his male predecessors as women writers, who, as Myra Jehlen says, "must deal with their situation as a *pre*condition for writing about it." In his identification with women, Lawrence was "outside any of [his culture's] definitions of complete being," hence the popularity of views of him as emotionally deficient, psychologically unbalanced, weak, and immature. He was very unlike the male rebel who "stands fully formed within the culture, at a leading edge."[68] Despite his aspirations to be a leader of men, which he expresses in such novels as *Aaron's Rod* and *The Plumed Serpent,* all of Lawrence's gestures toward leadership ended with swings back to high valuation of marriage, such as he expresses in *Women in Love, The Lost Girl, Kangaroo,* and *Lady Chatterley's Lover.* In rejecting male predecessors, Lawrence is not merely asserting the worth of his own vision; he is denying, just as a woman writer must, the values that form our culture and that would deny him, as a non-man, the authority to write.

That Lawrence's situation as a writer can be considered analogous to that of women writers in all of these ways would suggest only that his work belongs to some category analogous to the one we might call women's literary tradition, were it not for the second major link between Lawrence's work and that of women writers. Gilbert and Gubar stress, in discussing the Victorians, "the loneliness of the female artist, her feelings of alienation from male predecessors," that lead to "her need for sisterly precursors and successors."[69] And, in discussing the moderns, they emphasize the female artist's sensitivity to sexual conflict, which may compel her "affiliation" with "maternal traditions."[70] Lawrence's literary connections seem to have formed in the same way. Because his work as a whole is marked by his deliberate acceptance of the influence of female predecessors and his eagerness to engage in dialogue with their texts, it belongs to that tradition which is characterized by a preoccupation with the interests and problems of women, especially as they have been articulated by the most famous female writers. Any close comparison of Lawrence's fiction to that of the women writers he read and praised early in life will reveal that, like a woman writer whose gender and its prescribed role seem to predestine her work to a peripheral relationship to the dominant literary tradition, Lawrence meditated on and responded to the work of women who were able to write themselves out of marginality and into the center. In the texts of the Victorian women writers whom the dominant literary community had approved, he found strong mothers to bid him speak.

"*You Are the Call and I Am the Answer*": Lawrence's Responses to His Female Precursors

MANY THEORISTS OF INTERTEXTUALITY, even those like Harold Bloom who closely examine the responses specific texts make to each other, vehemently distinguish between their approach and what they dismissively deem "source-hunting."[1] Semioticians, stressing what Jonathan Culler calls the literary text's "participation in the discursive space of a culture,"[2] frequently assert the insignificance of the author's own existence as a subject and focus on the text's responses to cultural codes rather than its responses to identifiable prior texts. Each of these positions strategically resists literary criticism's past tendency, condemned as naïve, to celebrate individual creativity or expose borrowings as sites where authorial deficiency is revealed. Yet we need not choose between ranking authors according to originality and treating authorship and the distinctions between individual texts as complete fictions. Indeed, both choices should be unacceptable to feminist critics. Because of the historically greater prestige and availability of texts produced by men, to take the former position necessarily means devaluing the majority of women's literary works. But to take the position that authorial agency counts for nothing perpetuates the disempowerment of women as readers and writers, as Nancy Miller points out, "prematurely foreclos[ing] the question of identity for them."[3] To keep open that central feminist question, the question of the relationship between gender identity and the development of literary traditions, we might consider the places where texts seem to touch or overlap as records of interaction between actual, gendered beings participating in their own highly individual ways in the creation of systems of meaning.

As Judith Fetterley has shown, in order to respond as women, female readers must often engage in aggressive interactions with texts because of the general presupposition of a male reader.[4] For feminist critics such interactions have taken a variety of forms, ranging from reading oneself into the text, through identification with a female author or character, to reading for the textually repressed "woman"/feminine. In opening a dialogue about gender between ourselves and whatever text we have chosen, however, we sometimes seem in danger of oversimplifying the communication that has always existed between men's and women's fictions. This interchange should be of special interest to feminist critics because wherever one text responds to another the distinction between reader and writer dissolves and power relations are, consequently, unfixed. Here, if intertextuality crosses gender lines, we can see the writer-as-reader bringing her or his own concepts of gender difference and literary tradition into dialogue with those of the other author. In Lawrence's responses to his female precursors this dialogizing process becomes particularly complex.

We might return, for a moment, to the metaphor of the palimpsest and envision the interactions between male and female voices in Lawrence's texts as existing in separate layers. We have looked at a layer in which Lawrence attempts to ventriloquize the voices of his female acquaintances and friends, as representative of the voice of woman, and at a layer in which these same women write themselves into his texts through revisions. We have also looked at a layer that is reflected, as it were, from women's memoirs of Lawrence onto the surface of his texts where it alters our reading of his intentions. Beneath all this, we might uncover a layer in which Lawrence quotes and responds to prior texts by women. But the analogy can be of only momentary usefulness because the dialogues between male and female voices in Lawrence's texts are not really separable. Unlike the layers of writing in a palimpsest, they cannot be ordered chronologically and they have no independent meanings. Instead, Lawrence's gendering of voices is always profoundly intertextual, so that a female voice may be marked by traces of Jessie Chambers's journals, Frieda's editing, and Emily Brontë's and George Eliot's novels, traces that are visible only in relation to each other. Therefore, I will examine Lawrence's responses to his female precursors as integral parts of his project to write for woman and for specific women, a project that has woven his texts into women's literary traditions.

The tone of Lawrence's response is generally angry, as might be expected since a certain amount of hostility is intrinsic to the acceptance of influence. This must have been especially true in the early modern period, when evidence of influence was read as a sign of inferiority.[5] But some of the anger Lawrence shows toward his female precursors seems specific to his own unusual situation as it derives from his values and intentions. Having decreed that woman's truth must be the standard for his utterance, he forces himself to submit to women's judgments. This must have been onerous enough when the judging women were his friends, but at least he had the compensatory knowledge that he also played an important role in their creative lives. And, perhaps, beneath his sonlike pose, he was aware that the women in his life had power over him only to the extent that he granted it. They were his editors at his request. No exterior power structure reinforced the license he gave them to revise his work. His relationship to famous Victorian women novelists was quite different, however. The literary world that he wished to enter had already given their texts some authority.

By the time Lawrence began to think of himself as a writer, earlier women writers such as Fanny Burney, Mary Shelley, and Jane Austen had received considerable critical attention. But the Victorian women writers stood out. The almost unprecedented seriousness with which they took their roles as writers did much to change women's literary traditions. Elaine Showalter sees women's "literary subculture" as beginning with "the appearance of the male pseudonym in the 1840s."[6] This appropriation of the male authority to speak inaugurates an era in which women treat their writing as a vocation rather than an avocation and show their desire to be read as seriously as are male writers. Their intentional blurring of the lines between their language and authoritative discourse (which *they* associated with male authorship) would be deepened for Lawrence by their gender because of his belief in the primacy of the female. In addition, the status that both the dominant literary establishment and the newly emerging community of women writers gave certain Victorian women authors augmented the oracular quality they already had within Lawrence's personal belief system.

Lawrence's relationship to their texts was necessarily marked by the uneasiness that accompanies the urge to question what our ideology decrees we must accept as law. According to Mikhail Bakhtin, "the authoritative word demands that we acknowledge it, that we make it our own; it binds us, quite independent of any power it might have to persuade us internally; we encounter it with its authority already fused to it." Such speech is static; it "can not be represented—it is only transmitted."[7] But Lawrence could not be satisfied, despite his stated intentions, to limit his texts to transmission of what women had previously written. Instead, while leaving intact the authority of the writers themselves, he represented their texts as cryptic, and so as dependent upon his hermeneutics. This strategy allowed him to affirm the authority of the female voice while revising its utterance.[8] But it did not allow him to resolve the ambivalence he felt about his position in relation to woman. Instead his strategy provided a channel into which he could divert both his anger on behalf of woman as the figure for his feminized self and his anger against woman as the one upon whom his meaning depended. Thus his entrance into women's literary traditions, like his entrance into the creative processes of his women friends, was structured as both affirmation of and resistance to women's words.

Lawrence early read many novels by Victorian women and all his life alluded to them in his own texts, as F. R. Leavis, H. M. Daleski, Keith Sagar, Daniel Schneider, and Harold Bloom, among others, have noted.[9] George Eliot, Charlotte and Emily Brontë, and Olive Schreiner are frequently discussed as influences on Lawrence. Nonetheless, obvious thematic similarities between Lawrence's novels and Victorian novels by women have never been taken as evidence that he was intentionally connecting his work to women's literature and its traditions. Yet not only was he deliberately linking himself to a woman's tradition, he was also above all responding to *Wuthering Heights,* as we can see by comparing the interpretive revisions of that novel, in Lawrence's fiction, to those of *The Story of an African Farm, Jane Eyre,* and *The Mill on the Floss.*

Lawrence rarely mentioned *Wuthering Heights* directly, but his few recorded comments on the book reveal both his admiration for Brontë and his view of her as the medium of purely female discourse. In his introduction to M. G. Steegmann's translation of Grazia Deledda's *The Mother,* Lawrence refers to Brontë as giving voice to a transhistorical, transcultural, "sheer female instinctive passion." To him, the novel's presentation of female essence seems to set a standard for "a great book."[10] In "Blessed Are the Powerful" he gives Brontë the highest praise he knows—"Emily Brontë had life."[11] Signs of Clifford Chatterley's emptiness and failure as a man, in *John Thomas and Lady Jane,* are his lack of interest in *Wuthering Heights* and his refusal to allow himself to be

"stimulated" by it.[12] Brontë's "bare and stark," uncompromisingly female depiction of gender relations without "any of the graces of senti-
ment" provided, for Lawrence, the antithesis of Chatterley's feebly
moralistic materialism (*Phoenix, 265*). Brontë's novel exemplified what
Lawrence saw as essential female energy in its apocalyptic assault on the
gender-related conventions of the social world. It cleared space for him
to present his own vision.

Lawrence's construction of a new world begins, in *The White Peacock*,
with the reconstruction of the major themes of *Wuthering Heights*. His
voice is, thus, possessed by a specific female voice and generally feminized in its concerns, since, for Brontë, female experience is the touchstone of meaning. In close parallel to *Wuthering Heights, The White
Peacock*'s main narrative depicts a woman's vacillation between two
suitors, one of whom represents nature and the other culture. Both
Brontë and Lawrence draw a thick line between male and female, despite
Cathy's famous cry, "I *am* Heathcliff." This delineation of difference is
not a reinscription of conventional fictional representations of gender,
however. Heathcliff is (as Cathy continues) "always, always in [her]
mind," as a symbol of nature, freedom, and essential self, "as my own
being."[13] While Cathy, and Lettie, the heroine of *The White Peacock,* are
dialogic subjects divided between social and natural selves, both authors'
male characters are pure symbolic representations of the contending
forces always, always within woman. In a reversal of the usual order,
masculinity and maleness are understood only as symbolic statements in
relation to woman.

In *The White Peacock,* Lawrence initiates the practice, which will carry
over into much of his subsequent fiction, of creating a male character,
like Heathcliff, who seems in some ways a nature spirit, but who is
denied a male voice. Annable, the keeper in *The White Peacock,* who
appears to the others "like a devil of the woods," is this sort of figure.
Annable tries, almost pathetically, to speak as a man against woman,
whom he perceives as antinatural. But he is repeatedly forced by circumstances into traditionally feminine situations—and silence. His first wife
courts him, gives him "a living," uses him sexually, and generally
controls him until she tires of him.[14] It is, ironically, only in the context
of the feminine that Annable has any meaning at all, and that meaning is
in contradiction to the very concept of a male subject. But, although
Annable's marginal and dependent situation in the world recalls Heath-

cliff's, these characters are most alike in functioning as expressions of the wild half of woman. Cicio in *The Lost Girl,* Count Psanek in *The Ladybird,* Henry in *The Fox,* Don Cipriano in *The Plumed Serpent,* and Parkin in *The First Lady Chatterley* also share Heathcliff's demonic power to represent nature. All are like Heathcliff in that their wildness, the essence of their own beings, is not posited as specifically male but is, instead, a displaced aspect of the heroine.

These men are objectified by their identification with nature. In this respect, Lawrence's vision of woman's relation to the symbolic is the reverse of that which such psycholinguistic feminist critics as Margaret Homans attribute to male writers.[15] Because no women in either Lawrence's fiction or *Wuthering Heights* represent nature or are objectified in this way, both authors can be considered to approach the problem of gender through a proto-feminist reversal of signs. Like Heathcliff and Hareton, Lawrence's men attain individual presence, are brought up out of the landscape, through being contemplated and used by women. In return they revitalize women by representing for them the voice of nature—in Susan Griffin's words, "the roaring inside *her*"—that is muted for women by the socialization process that creates a second self.[16]

Lawrence also takes on attitudes and tones implicit in *Wuthering Heights* in his use of a male as a figure for culture. Both authors conflate female soçialization (with its inherent fragmentation of the self) and marriage. Cathy Earnshaw makes a fatal mistake in marrying. It is only through marriage that she will finish being "converted . . . into . . . the lady . . . the wife of a stranger; an exile, and an outcast, thenceforth, from what had been [her] world" (*WH,* 107). Edgar, as a representative of civilization and its laws, must, ultimately, insist on his rights as her master and try to make her bow down to the Law of the Father.[17] This law demands the death of her true being. In Brontë and in Lawrence's first novel, marriage appears as a social disease, in every sense of the term, which can only infect women. The males, parasitic in their dependence on the women to give them meaning, have no immanent presence to be attacked. Their role within marriage as symbolic husband figures does not block their self-expression. Surface meaning, determined by their relation to woman's quest for an integrated self, is their all.

Brontëan or Lawrencian woman, in contrast, can be understood through the model of two concentric circles. Both writers envision the feminine as a socially constructed shell around the innate female. Marriage augments the shell to such an extent as to destroy the living essence within it. Indeed, only one woman in *Wuthering Heights* survives her husband, and she, Catherine Linton, has an unconsummated marriage to a dying boy. Lawrence's description of Lettie after three years of marriage evokes Brontë's depiction of the delirium that leads up to Cathy's death. "Like so many women she seemed to live, for the most part contentedly, a small indoor existence. . . . Only occasionally, hearing the winds of life outside, she clamoured to be out in the black, keen storm. She was driven to the door, she looked out and called into the tumult wildly, but feminine caution kept her from stepping over the threshold" (*WP,* 331). In both passages, female freedom is equated with fresh air, and marriage (as feminine socialization) with suffocating enclosure.

Both Brontë and Lawrence, in their revulsion against the socially constructed feminine, create male monsters. Of all the writers presumed to have influenced Lawrence, Emily Brontë is the only one who apparently shares his ambivalent attraction to pathologically antisocial characters. Lawrence's depictions of Annable, Cipriano, and Romero (in "The Princess") are all comparable to Brontë's depiction of Heathcliff as justifiably contemptuous of law and convention, though excessively violent. Even Mellors's harshness toward his daughter is reminiscent of Heathcliff's offhand cruelty to that pale, diminished version of Cathy who is her daughter. In each case the man's violence is ostensibly directed against the affectations that are called femininity. Lawrence's women protagonists are often completed by male halves who can knock away the mask of the angel in the house, as Heathcliff does to Isabella. In both writers' worlds such violence seems necessary. When they are free from Heathcliff's abusive presence, Isabella and Catherine Linton try to enact the social roles they have been assigned in Edgar's world, behaving as if there were nothing in them beneath the veneer of ladylike sweetness, as if no power could come from them but the fairy/angel/mother magic that polishes the "rough diamond" to reveal male value (*WH,* 90). It is only in reaction to Heathcliff, as Françoise Basch has pointed out, that their lady selves are deconstructed and they discover primal, oppositional rage.[18]

Lawrence's most interesting translation of this vision of gender relations into his own terms is perhaps in *Women in Love,* where the end result of Birkin's continual battle with Ursula's sentimental pretensions and feminine posturing is her discovery of an incisive female voice that repeatedly and authoritatively undercuts his pronouncements. Because Birkin's voice is, to a large extent, aligned with Lawrence's, this is, as in *Kangaroo,* a seemingly undesirable outcome, a loss of authorial gender identity. But in Lawrence's fiction the absorption of the male into the female is presented as positively as Heathcliff's final merging with the ghostly Cathy who has always possessed him and determined his utterance.

While Lawrence's later works abundantly show Brontë's influence on him, *The White Peacock* also comments obliquely on his attitude toward that influence. It is along this oblique line of connection that the complexities and contradictions in Lawrence's renunciation of male selfhood appear. By pointedly modeling the partially autobiographical narrator Cyril on Lockwood and by naming Cyril's sweetheart "Emily," Lawrence suggests the psychological significance of his adaptation of Emily Brontë's story.[19] Lawrence's need to imagine a connection between himself and Brontë was first manifested in his idea that she was like Jessie Chambers. What Chambers saw as "a clumsy probing into [her] personality" was probably also Lawrence's awkward first attempt to understand the woman writer whose work charted his own emotional landscape of incestuous longings, ungovernable anger, rejection of conventional gender roles, and intense identification with wild nature.[20]

Lawrence's choice to identify himself with Lockwood, rather than with Lockwood's creator, points to a desire to be contained within Brontë's vision and so to have his meaning created through her expression of it. But this desire to enter into and become part of Brontë's fiction is problematized by the exigencies of his own production of texts. To fulfill his chosen mission of writing for women, he must write the female voice as well as be written by it. And as a creative writer, rather than a scribe, he must reshape his precursor's words, not simply repeat them. He seems to have begun by attempting to construct an Emily Brontë that comes from and through himself.

The Emily in Lawrence's novel very much resembles Miriam of *Sons and Lovers* and is clearly derived from Chambers in many ways, but she can also be seen to represent Lawrence's vision of a sensibility that is passionate and yearning toward wild rebellion yet made awkward and frequently inexpressive by a timid acceptance of the rules of Christian society. If Lawrence's idea of Emily Brontë was formed by both *Wuthering Heights* and the 1850 "Biographical Notice" Charlotte Brontë attached to it, he would probably have believed not only that she had such a nature, but also that "an interpreter ought always to have stood between her and the world."[21] Emily Brontë herself provides two such interpreters in *Wuthering Heights*, Lockwood and Nelly Dean. Lawrence expands the role of the former and, by making the narrator a significant actor in the drama, uses him as a vehicle for self-revelation. His revelations seem to be concerned as much with his relationship to women's literature as with his relationship with any individual woman. The narration emphasizes Lawrence's uneasiness about his role as an interpreter of the female voice. Lawrence does not make Cyril, his narrator, a parallel character to Lockwood; rather, he uses Cyril to join Brontë within her story and to comment on his literary relationship to her even as he recreates her and (re)interprets her tale.

That Emily Saxton, the girl Cyril courts, is meant to represent Emily Brontë is made clear by Lawrence's inclusion of a famous incident from Brontë's life. By 1909, Lawrence had read both Elizabeth Gaskell's *The Life of Charlotte Brontë* and Charlotte Brontë's *Shirley*.[22] Gaskell's biography includes an account of Emily being bitten by an apparently mad dog and, because of "her nobly stern presence of mind, going right into the kitchen, and taking up one of Tabby's red-hot Italian irons to sear the bitten place, and telling no one, till the danger was wellnigh over, for fear of the terror that might beset their weaker minds."[23] The story also appears in *Shirley*, where Charlotte modifies the incident to make her heroine's behavior more conventionally feminine than her sister's. The changes she makes are consistent with Shirley's character and do not seem meant to minimize her sister's heroism. Lawrence's alteration of the anecdote is another matter. It virtually recasts Emily in the role of enemy to nature. There is no suggestion that the dog which bites Emily in *The White Peacock* is mad; he is simply wild. She is not trying to help him, but to kill him. This distortion of the actual behavior reported by Gaskell suggests that Emily Saxton is meant as Brontë in the authorial persona that most confused and disturbed Lawrence, a persona, however, that also allowed him to feel justified in speaking as her interpreter.

Having defined maleness as a viruslike state, characterized by a lack of any essential self, and marriage as the medium that allows maleness, in its deadly social form, to close off the female self, Brontë could not possibly show Heathcliff and Cathy marrying and living happily ever after. Heterosexual union, in the novel, is only satisfactory when achieved outside the material body, which inevitably connects us to the social body. Although Lawrence seems to have been fully receptive to the tone of the story of Cathy and Heathcliff's passion, he resisted Brontë's narrative resolution of it. Because of the importance of the physical to Lawrence, he could not accept a consummation placed outside bodies and mortal life. He seems able to understand such a resolution only as cowardly fear of the natural world. Consequently, Emily Saxton is shown as perpetually shrinking from nature and physical experience.

He associates this shrinking with the feminine by changing the genders in his rewriting of one crucial scene of *Wuthering Heights*. In *Wuthering Heights*, Cathy is bitten by a bull dog, tended by the Lintons and socialized/feminized in the process. In *The White Peacock*, Annable's son, Sam, is bitten by a bull dog and tended by Emily, who sets about taming him. She teaches him to read, and one of the first sentences in his lesson is "shoot the fox"—foreshadowing the action that marks Henry's transformation from natural to social man in *The Fox*. To Lawrence, maleness, with its unselfconsciousness and, indeed, apparent lack of inner content, allows a man to be passively filled by nature. Conversely, the female who allows femininity to define her self must draw back from nature's violence and raw materiality. Literacy and fiction are the means by which Emily puts nature at a remove, and the means by which Lawrence creates a vision of Brontë's fiction making as a specifically feminine complicity with cultural myths against nature.

The point of Lawrence's depiction of Emily seems to be that women are complicitous with cultural fictions, if they become fiction makers because they shrink from the pain unavoidable to feeling beings in contact with wild nature. He implies not only that *Wuthering Heights* falsifies reality in implying that people are divided into passionate wild creatures whose affinities are with nature and passionless beings who belong indoors, but also that Brontë creates this fiction because the femininity she accepts (wrongly) as her self puts her in opposition to nature. Lawrence violently rejects *Wuthering Heights'* resolution of the conflict between passionate wildness and socialized deadness in Hareton's transformation into a gentleman. Lawrence bitterly shows, through Annable's miserable scramblings to inhabit the "sloppy French novel" his first wife makes of their marriage and George's lost bumblings in Lettie's Pre-

Raphaelite dream, that Hareton made into a gentleman is just the despised Edgar recreated (*WP,* 179).

In the midst of his acceptance of its influence, Lawrence shows distrust of Brontë's fiction making, as he generalizes it to represent woman's fiction making. As he presents it, the voice that comes from the feminine constitutes a real danger, but its threat is no greater than that posed by failure to hear and respond to the female voice so often covered by it. Lawrence continually links his narrator's attraction to and recoil from women to the need of all the male characters to understand the demands made by the female voice in order to prosper or even to survive. In *Wuthering Heights* the male characters paradoxically project onto the women meaning as both vital shelter and the wild unknown, hence not only Lockwood's extreme terror when he dreams that a girl is trying to come into his room in the night but also the penalty he pays for rejecting her. Unwilling either to risk contact with the demanding but enigmatic and contradictory feminine he himself has literally dreamed up or to respond to Cathy's transcendent female presence, Lockwood is left outside, his hearth cold. In *The White Peacock,* George's destruction comes about because he draws back from Lettie's confusing desperation; he fails to interpret her veiled demands that he free her from marriage. George prefers dreaming of Lettie as the Lady to confronting the reality of her social entrapment. Heathcliff, Lockwood, and George all fail to hold the women who could save them. Because they shy away from understanding the women, the men cannot act decisively to free women from their unnatural and oppressive social lives. Consequently the men cannot gain meaning and wither away. Cyril is equally unable to free Emily, and within his anxiety, which pervades their contacts, we can read Lawrence's anxiety about his own failure to bring into prominence what he saw as the female voice in Brontë, that which speaks the value of woman against her valuation by society.

That Lawrence was not satisfied with his first interpretation of *Wuthering Heights* is indicated in numerous details in his characterization of Emily Saxton that express an anxious realization that he is failing to speak as if from female experience and failing to evoke a female essence. In Cyril's first scene with Emily, he tries to rouse her out of her habitual irritation into real rage by articulating her feelings himself—"It makes you wild," he says—but he can only make her show "nervous passion" (*WP,* 18). Later Cyril is unable to teach Emily to dance. Like Emily

Brontë, according to Charlotte's account, she is "powerless in the tumult of her feelings" (*WP,* 117). But when Cyril's sister, Lettie, takes over, the two women dance well together. Just as Charlotte Brontë's introduction attempts to give a more genteel and feminine cast to her sister's self expression, Lettie's lead tames Emily's passionate movements into feminine prettiness. Lettie and Charlotte Brontë's gender enables them to bond with the less socialized woman and thus shape and direct (interpret) her self-expression so that her female passion is represented within the limits of feminine decorum. Without some source of interpretive authority, Lawrence knows that he must leave women's literature to the women, just as Cyril must stand and watch Lettie lead Emily in the dance.

Characteristically in Lawrence's fiction, women seem a far more self-sufficient group than they do in *Wuthering Heights.* Brontë's women have little to say to each other, and Nelly, who stands as the nexus of all communications, is always ready to betray what she has learned, to turn speech into pain. What is suggested of an untrammelled and triumphant femaleness is seen in peripheral communications directed to no sister, but simply released into the void: Cathy's writings in the margins of religious texts, the negation of Edgar and Heathcliff written into the son Isabella names after them and thus marks for destruction. When men fail to read the female through the feminine in *Wuthering Heights,* the female remains untouched in her sublime solitude, though the woman's body may die. If men are hurt in the process, Brontë seems unconcerned. Brontë's power comes to her directly from what her text identifies as the female within. The femaleness of her text is most strongly manifested in its resistance to interpretation. As Bette London has shown, *Wuthering Heights'* narrative structure, in which each new speaker or text-within-the-text comments on the previous one, calls into question the implicit hierarchy on which interpretation is based; "it challenges the possibility of a stable primary text to be glossed."[24] The female and the literary are, thus, both associated with resistance to the systematic determination of meaning.

Lawrence, however, as a male author writing for women, is dependent upon hermeneutics because of his need to connect to what is female in his woman precursor. He is as dependent as Cyril on understanding woman and so releasing the essential female power that will give his existence meaning. His only means to power, in the literary territory he wishes to inhabit, is through interpretation of the female voice. Cyril's future is foreshadowed by the lives of his natural father and Annable, who briefly acts as a father to him. Cyril says his mother "turned away" from her husband "with the scorn of a woman who finds that her romance has been a trumpery tale" (*WP,* 4). Annable's wife, too, turns away from marriage when the "Romance of a Poor Young Man" that she creates to contain her passion begins to bore her (*WP,* 177). Both men are incapable of replacing their wives' feminine fictions with anything more satisfactory, so they lose their wives, who were finally too strongly female to be contained themselves by the pretty stories society allowed them to tell. The cast-off husbands go into declines and die. Cyril's only real hope, the novel suggests, would be to create a story that could satisfy a woman by expressing her full nature. Instead he is only able to create the brief homosexual shelter of the idyllic episode called "A Poem of Friendship." While this "poem" delights him, it can do nothing to structure his life or give it significance. In the next chapter, its mood gives way to those created by a book by "the squire's lady" and Emily's "legend," both of which work together to determine the futures of the main characters (*WP,* 260, 268). These metafictional references to the task of writing show Lawrence's awareness of his inability "to transcend Cyril's vision."[25] The inclusion of the failed attempt to unite with Emily shows his recognition that he is still unable to join his work successfully to Brontë's. His voice remains masculine and capable of full communication only with men, a voice which, in a stunning reversal of patriarchal values, Lawrence ranks hardly higher than the silence of death.

Since Lawrence chose to give away the authority of voice that his gender conveys, seemingly in the hope of speaking from the female center of truth he found embedded in *Wuthering Heights,* it is unsurprising that his failure to comprehend the book fully made him angry at the author as a woman. Lawrence seems enraged that the same woman who creates an untamable Heathcliff and holds him up to us as the living embodiment of nature's force turned in adoration toward woman can then dispose of him to make way for the advent of a more manageable indoor version. In diminishing Brontë into a type of Jessie Chambers, Lawrence seems to be avenging himself upon her for allowing conventionality the apparent victory in a novel that would otherwise have been a tribute to uncompromising fierceness, for giving her readers a glimpse of the heaven in which male passion and female passion meet and fully natural life is attained, and then denying that it is possible in life after childhood. In the simplest psychological terms, she figures the with-holding mother.

Lawrence's railing against such mothers in *The Lost Girl* illuminates his own understanding of the Oedipus myth as a description of the male condition: "Wretched man what is he to do with these exigeant and never-to-be-satisfied women? Our mothers pined because our fathers drank and were rakes. Our wives pine because we are virtuous but inadequate. Who is this sphinx, this woman? Where is the Oedipus that will solve her riddle of happiness and then strangle her?—only to marry his own mother!"[26] Here Julia Kristeva's psychoanalytic description of interpretation as representing "appropriation, and thus an act of desire and murder," seems particularly apropos.[27] Jane Gallop's comments on this idea in reference to literary responses to prior texts are also il-luminating. She points out that interpretation always involves trans-ference, the unconscious granting of parental authority to another speaker or ideology, as it is represented in a text.[28] When the transference is so complete that the violence inherent in reading/interpreting is dis-avowed, what Bakhtin calls "dead quotation" results.[29] To Lawrence, the only way to bring the mother's oracular language back to life is to be swallowed up by it. In Lawrence's revision of the Oedipus myth, the aggressiveness of his interpretation is acknowledged. Interpreting the sphinx is the foreplay to killing her. But, as in *Kangaroo,* understanding forces union, and the man who sets out to make the withholding mother yield must end by entering/marrying her.

In literary terms, the question Lawrence puts to the sphinx is not What do women want? but What do I mean in her language? The primary intention behind all of Lawrence's work seems to be the solution of the riddle of how the female voice assigns meaning to men, but ironically, like the Oedipus in his complaint, he fights with his (literary) mother only to return to her. Having wrested away the authority to define her and so himself, he nervously gives it back to find out if that was what she really meant (and meant him to mean). In his reworkings of material from *Wuthering Heights,* he vacillates between locating his own voice in relation to the meanings Brontë seems to assign to each gender and trying to speak in her voice to say what he wishes she had. Throughout his vacillations, he momentarily reorients phallocentric myths that at-tempt to define man, so that, in his versions, the definitions reaffirm his vision of the inescapable primacy of woman.

In her insightful article "Potent Griselda," Sandra Gilbert demonstrates Lawrence's preoccupation with the myth of the Great Mother who is served by Dionysus. She discusses his mixed feelings about "both real mothers and Great Mothers," but might have added comment on his similar feelings about literary mothers.[30] Ambivalence about Emily Brontë is evident in the novella to which she devotes most of her attention, *The Ladybird*. Parallel descriptions of characters immediately suggest *Wuthering Heights,* although the dynamics between the characters are stylized to answer questions Brontë raises.

Male access to language is foregrounded. Count Psanek, who returns to Daphne against his will—just as Heathcliff returns to the married Cathy—and becomes her "vicar in wrath,"[31] has the eloquence Heathcliff lacks. Heathcliff is taciturn even with Cathy. Psanek "can't stop talking" to Daphne, and even tells her, " 'I speak for me and you' "(*LB,* 58, 63). Psanek's ability to express Daphne's unconscious thoughts is Lawrence's solution to the romantic problem Brontë poses. Because Cathy's feminine socialization so blinds her to the connection between sexuality and love that she cannot understand that it is imperative to her own sanity and Heathcliff's that she not give herself to Edgar, she never directly gives Heathcliff the authority to save her. Psanek speaks as (rather than merely symbolizes) the fierce female spirit hidden in woman. Unlike Heathcliff, he can, as he promises Daphne, " 'always be in the darkness of' " her, while still communicating freely with her conscious self (*LB,* 104). This is necessary not just for Daphne's good but because, as Gilbert shows, Psanek is no more of an autonomous individual than Heathcliff. Like Heathcliff, Psanek exists through the woman he loves; she must come to him "else he would die" (*LB,* 102).

Lawrence implies Psanek is Daphne's weaker half. The mythic and fairy-tale levels of *The Ladybird,* as Gilbert observes, refer to tales of female power to create men or bring them back to life, including the stories of Isis and Osiris, Demeter and Dionysus, Theseus and Ariadne, and Grimm's six swans and their sister.[32] Alienated Psanek, "like a little ghost," scarcely seems to exist outside the dark connection Daphne allows him to have with her (*LB,* 97). On the story's mythic/symbolic levels, he seems to be a magic creature called into being by her need. In the same sense that Heathcliff is the fairy-tale answer to Cathy's request for a whip,[33] Psanek is the answer to Daphne's desperate subconscious call, as Lawrence's repeated references to calls and summonses at the story's climax suggest. Psanek, in turn, like the forgotten wild part of herself, calls her "into the underworld" of their dark, silent communion, the subconscious world in which she finds her soul (or female essence) and so peace (*LB,* 103–4).

Like Heathcliff, Psanek acts as the agent for what is repressed in his beloved. Daphne "remains silently master," forcing Psanek to express her secret anger to her father and husband (*LB,* 95). Lawrence rejects the realistic level of *Wuthering Heights,* in which Brontë shows that the world will not allow female wholeness, only to adhere more tenaciously to the spirit of Brontë's novel: her assertion that, despite the world's demands, female passions are infinitely valuable, are the only transcendent things on earth. As Psanek is the answer to Daphne, speaking what she cannot, Lawrence tries to make himself act as an answer to Brontë, in his characteristic polemical style asserting the worth of female passion and expressing female rage against the conventional world.

Here his ambivalence emerges. The two main narrators of *Wuthering Heights,* behind whom Brontë glides evading interpretation, are put aside. Lawrence offers a revision that reduces *Wuthering Heights* to myth and ignores its many comments on specific crimes against women in a particular time and place. Cathy's and Heathcliff's rage against the world is separated from its economic and political causes and presented *only* as protest against woman's eternally reenacted entrapment in a socially constructed femininity. Moreover, Daphne, unlike Cathy, cannot express her anger directly. Man, who is often little more than an artistic convenience to Brontë, becomes an existential necessity to woman in Lawrence's interpretation of Brontë. Thus, Lawrence becomes a rather self-important answer to a call that he himself projects as coming from Brontë. But this mythologizing of the battle for narrative power cannot resolve all the problems Lawrence faces in interpretation of the mother-text.

As Lawrence's familiarity with women's novels must have caused him to understand, he was not the only writer to attempt to interpret *Wuthering Heights* and to give that interpretation in the form of another novel. For example, it seems apparent that George Eliot was thinking of *Wuthering Heights* when she wrote *The Mill on the Floss. Jane Eyre* and *Wuthering Heights* are obviously similar in many ways. And Olive Schreiner's *The Story of an African Farm* so closely resembles *Wuthering Heights* that its influence seems indisputable.[34] Clearly, then, Lawrence's novelistic responses to Emily Brontë are part of a cluster of intertextually related dialogues. And his sense that he must confront his female rivals and prove his right to lead Emily in the dance is often apparent. His responses and allusions to *Wuthering Heights* rarely occur in isolation. Instead they appear in texts that also include references not only to Schreiner's, Eliot's, Charlotte Brontë's novels but also to *their* responses to *Wuthering Heights*. Thus it would be misleading to think of the intertextual relationship between Lawrence and any one of his female precursors as involving only two voices. Their voices come to him blended or in contiguity, always in conversation with each other prior to his framing of them within his own fiction.

This situation could only increase Lawrence's anxious sense of his own marginality. As Joanne Feit Diehl shows in her study of Emily Dickinson's relation to Romantic traditions, the writer who invests the generative power of a muse in a "composite precursor" has created an "internal adversary" whose authority both compels a dialogue and threatens to drown out the writer's own voice.[35] Obviously, such a mythic monster, half superego half demon-lover, is more likely to be created by a female than a male writer, power relations and their eroticization being what they are. But here, again, Lawrence seems aligned with women's literary tradition by his fear that he will be negated in advance by harmonizing voices from the past. Like a poststructuralist feminist critic, he defends himself against what he initially took to be authoritative discourse by foregrounding its disharmonies and internal conflicts. This process is easiest to see in Lawrence's responses to writers whose authority he ultimately rejected, like Olive Schreiner.

In two interesting influence studies, Christopher Heywood has pointed out many thematic and stylistic correspondences between *The Story of an African Farm* and Lawrence's *Sons and Lovers, The Rainbow,* and *Women in Love*.[36] He is especially persuasive in arguing that Schreiner's novel must have been a source for *Women in Love*. A clear understanding of the relationship between the two texts requires an investigation of their connections to *Wuthering Heights* as well, however.

The Story of an African Farm seems at times like *Wuthering Heights* retold without any ambiguity. The heroine Lyndall resembles both Catherine Linton in her delicate beauty and arrogant independence and Cathy Earnshaw in her selfishness and inability to "bear this life," but she is presented to the reader completely uncritically.[37] Her moral superiority over all her would-be oppressors is repeatedly stressed. Her male other self, Waldo, resembles Heathcliff in his stoical suffering of the abuses that are heaped on orphans in Victorian fiction, but he always remains pure of heart. Lyndall's rejection first of "the stranger," whose brutal strength arouses her sexually, and then of life itself, are treated as spiritual triumphs. Lawrence recognized the book's considerable emotional power; he wrote Chambers, "It will wring your woman's heart when you come to read it."[38] But Lawrence could not long admire a *Wuthering Heights* in which Cathy (Lyndall) loves Heathcliff (Waldo) because their shared intellectual interests make him a bodyless spirit to her (*SAF*, 200). The main characters' complete renunciation of passion was also bound to grate on Lawrence as his own attitudes about the life-affirming function of fiction developed. Lawrence often alludes to *The Story of an African Farm* in contexts that contradict its conclusion that "a man's soul can see Nature" only when no "passion holds its revel there" (*SAF*, 301).

One borrowed trope is a case in point. Lyndall, rejecting the stranger's marriage proposal, says, "Your man's love is a child's love for butterflies. You follow till you have the thing, and break it" (*SAF*, 231). Heywood correctly points out that "Gudrun provides a near-echo of Lyndall's image" when she thinks, in similar circumstances, that Gerald "tore at the bud of her heart . . . Like a boy who pulls off a fly's wings, or tears open a bud to see what is in the flower."[39] Nonetheless, Lawrence revises Schreiner's figurative language to introduce a new idea. Lyndall's point is that men are destructive because they are possessive; she continues, "If you have broken one wing, and the thing flies still, then you love it more than ever, and you follow till you break both; then you are satisfied when it lies still on the ground" (*SAF*, 231). Lawrence's topic is not the perversity of men, but the cruelty and dangerousness of forcing natural things. Gerald and Gudrun are both "torn open" and "tortured" (*WL*, 437). He is like "an open flower" but in agony because he is "incomplete, limited, unfinished," while she fears that he will "destroy her as an immature bud, torn open, is destroyed" (*WL*, 437). This is the sort of naturalistic love language Schreiner parodies when Lyndall mocks Gregory by imitating the speech in which he claims "[t]here are as many kinds of loves as there are flowers" (*SAF*, 221). Lawrence, however, sincerely equates human love and natural cycles. Far from depicting passion and closeness to nature as mutually exclusive states, Lawrence, like Brontë, stresses their interdependency. This is particularly evident when, after an argument, Ursula brings Birkin a sprig of heather and their shared appreciation of nature removes "the complexity" from their love, releasing "a hot passion of tenderness" that culminates in their most important sexual experiences (*WL,* 302).

Lyndall dies because neither nature nor love can offer her something to worship. As Gilbert and Gubar observe, she is killed by her own feminism, which afflicts her with an insatiable desire for the power to fight injustice,[40] a desire that nature itself conspires with culture to frustrate. She is a wonderful creature, but life fails her. Cathy dies because she has deliberately turned her back on passion and nature by purposefully divorcing herself from the Heights and so the integration of passionate and natural life it represents. She dies like the "handful of golden crocuses" Edgar puts on her pillow, because "the soil of his shallow care" cannot nourish her, but she chose to uproot herself, as Brontë reminds us with Heathcliff's tirades. Lawrence was bound to be more attracted to this explanation of women's unhappiness than to Schreiner's vision of nature and female sexuality in conflict.

From his first novel, which begins with George unfolding the wings of and inadvertently crippling just-hatched "pretty field bees" to "torment them into flight," Lawrence remains fascinated by the idea that natural development cannot be forced. And from the beginning, he agrees with Brontë in seeing the opposition between the concept of the lady and the development that makes possible a full flowering of passion. Lawrence's early uses of elements of Schreiner's novel, which he apparently read only a few years after reading *Wuthering Heights* (around 1909), may represent an initial leaning toward her philosophy of despair; certainly the ending of his first novel is bleak. But by the time he began "The Sisters" (the first version of *The Rainbow* and *Women in Love*) Lawrence seems to have decided to show that the wholeness through passion that Brontë depicts is attainable in real life. The theme of frail women crushed by relentless nature no longer seems to have attracted him. "The Sisters" moves in the opposite direction from *The Story of an African Farm,* toward celebrating, rather than bewailing, the connection between man, woman, and nature. In that his agreement with Brontë's attitude about nature supersedes his attraction to Schreiner's, there is a progression in Lawrence's acceptance of influence from the two writers. But this sort of progression is not typical of Lawrence's pattern of response to his precursors. Lawrence's allusions to *The Mill on the Floss* and *Jane Eyre* are more consistently and combatively revisionary. He insistently reworks material that they share with *Wuthering Heights,* always favoring Emily Brontë's vision of woman as naturally and heroically defiant.

George Eliot is generally regarded as the first and strongest female influence on Lawrence's fiction—and with good reason. As U. C. Knoepflmacher shows, Lawrence's "heroines, characters like the sisters Ursula and Gudrun Brangwen or like Connie Chatterley herself, resemble George Eliot's creations in their intense search for a new 'worldly' morality able to accommodate their physical vitality as well as their spiritual enthusiasm."[41] The immediately apparent similarities between Eliot's and Lawrence's novels suggest his long contemplation of and struggle with her most fundamental ideas. Lawrence began his writing career with the expressed intention of following Eliot's "plan," and his early enthusiasm for her work left obvious marks on his own, as Chambers has demonstrated.[42] F. R. Leavis's comparison of Lawrence and Eliot in *D. H. Lawrence: Novelist* seems to have had a powerful impact on professional readings of Lawrence; hardly any book-length study of Lawrence's work written after 1956 fails to mention Eliot. But H. M. Daleski goes furthest in his argument "that George Eliot was the major initial influence on Lawrence, and that indeed, he found himself through her."[43] When Brontë is recognized as an influence at all, Lawrence is often seen as moving toward alignment with her work from a prior emulation of Eliot.[44] His responses to both *The Mill on the Floss* and *Wuthering Heights* comment on Eliot's use of Brontë, however.

Like most readers, Lawrence probably recognized many similarities between *The Mill on the Floss* and the first part of *Wuthering Heights.* In both novels, the heroine's failure to fit the patriarchal definition of femininity is stressed. Although Cathy Earnshaw is much more aggressive than Maggie Tulliver, both are notably robust and spontaneously unconventional. Each has a frail, prim foil (Lucy and Isabella) and is heavily criticized in childhood for being different. Maggie, generally considered wicked, can count on no one but her father to "take her part," and even he is convinced that her frequent, irrepressible revelation of intelligence is "bad."[45] Cathy, "too mischievous and wayward to be a favorite," is rejected even by her father (*WH,* 40). Each heroine, on reaching physical maturity, is attracted to the young man whom her older brother (and guardian) most detests. Each encourages this young man's love only to neglect him, later, in favor of a more handsome, polished man. Both Cathy and Maggie regret these choices when it is too late to honorably change their minds, and subsequently ruin their lives with scandalous vacillations. Finally both women die young without having resolved their conflicting desires.

If Eliot was thinking of *Wuthering Heights,* her attitude seems to have been critical. The major differences between the texts could be read as attacks on the attributes of *Wuthering Heights* that seem to have pleased Lawrence most. Brontë's depiction of the young Heathcliff and Cathy shows that passionate people can enjoy completely satisfying intimacy, at least in childhood. Eliot removes the third child soul mate (Heathcliff) and shows us brother and sister in unresolvable conflict from the beginning. As Gilbert and Gubar say, "Eliot could be said to be retelling Emily Brontë's story to undercut that early vision of gynandrous bliss."[46] Eliot denies the possibility of wholeness through union for Maggie by making her suitors an unattractive cripple with whom she must suppress her normal physical responses and a handsome fool with whom she would have to forget both her moral seriousness and her hunger for knowledge. In addition, as Daleski notes, "Eliot evades a full confrontation of the issues her fiction has raised" by freeing Maggie, with death, from ever actually having to enact the self-repression and denial she chooses.[47] Eliot also passes quickly over the unhappiness Maggie causes the other characters. Like *The Story of an African Farm, The Mill on the Floss* stresses woman's victimization by exterior forces. In contrast to Maggie, Cathy Earnshaw may appear unattractive to us because Brontë dwells in agonizing detail on the consequences, for all the characters, of her foolish marital choice.

Perhaps the greatest difference between the two stories, however, is that Brontë begins by positioning Cathy at the very periphery of culture where females can exercise some power to define themselves and name their own desires. Although the temptation to sell her limited freedom for a place in the Grange, storehouse of civilization's riches, proves irresistible to Cathy, Brontë insistently tells us, through Heathcliff's voice, that Cathy could have chosen otherwise. For Maggie there are no choices outside the world men have made to benefit themselves; single at home, single in service away from home, or married to either of her suitors, she will always be denied expression of her true self. Maggie's loyalties are split between the family and the world that together define her. As long as Cathy lives she can find herself with Heathcliff in nature; in every sense of the word he functions *as* Cathy's nature. He is the objective correlative of her power, her sexuality, her defiant existence as a being unlimited by the Father and culture's rules. But Maggie's access to her own hidden essence, briefly found in the "red deeps," can only be interrupted by men. In Maggie's sexual economy, as in that described in Luce Irigaray's "This Sex Which Is Not One," female solitude is both pleasure and wholeness which male presence undoes. As a revisionary response to *Wuthering Heights, The Mill on the Floss* is an assertion of essential femaleness martyred because of male inadequacy.

In *The White Peacock,* with physically attractive George who is eager for intellectual improvement, Lawrence reintroduces Brontë's idea that males and females can complement and complete each other. And, like Brontë, Lawrence denies the reader the satisfaction of seeing this promising union realized and instead concentrates on the tragedy that follows the woman's rejection of it. Moreover, he almost always refuses his heroines the release of death and so goes much further even than Brontë in his attention to the pain caused to herself and others by the woman who chooses as society dictates. "A Modern Lover," "The Witch à La Mode," "New Eve and Old Adam," "The Shades of Spring," "The Shadow in the Rose Garden," "A Sick Collier," "Odour of Chrysanthemums," "England, My England," "Fannie and Annie," "The Princess," "The Woman Who Rode Away," "None of That," and "The Blue Moccasins" all feature men who awaken either from the life of the mind or simply from stolid, unfocused physicality to intense yearning for sexual fulfillment but are rebuffed by women who seem compelled first to flirt with passion then to retreat into propriety. In some other short stores, "Second Best, "You Touched Me," "In Love," and "Mother and Daughter," and in five of Lawrence's seven short novels, *Love Among the Haystacks, The Ladybird, The Fox, The Captain's Doll,* and *The Virgin and the Gipsy,* the same conflict is depicted but is at least partially resolved when the woman yields or begins to yield to a trancelike sexuality and feels, like Maggie, "absorbed in the direct, immediate experience, without any energy left for taking account of it" (*MF,* 516). In order to preserve her heroine's moral authority and to let us understand how lowering marriage to shallow Stephen Guest would be, Eliot must make Maggie's conscience awaken her. In Lawrence's fiction, as in *Wuthering*

Heights, the problem is not that nature draws woman into a somnam-
bulistic union with imperfect man, but that the demands of society and
culture wake her up again.

Lawrence answers Eliot's vision of male-female relations with his
many depictions of the woman who torments her lover because she is
unable to submerge her conscious mind in her instinctual sensuality. One
short story in particular seems to be an intentional response to Eliot's
novel. Despite its similarities to *Middlemarch,* which various critics note,
Lawrence's "The Daughters of the Vicar" seems derived from *The Mill
on the Floss* by way of speculations about what might have happened to
Maggie had she lived to marry Philip Wakem. Tall, self-sacrificing,
high-minded Mary with her "queenly" coiled hair is very reminiscent of
Maggie.[48] Although her husband, cold Mr. Massey who "lack[s] the full
range of human feelings," is hardly the emotional equivalent of Philip
Wakem, they are parallels in smallness and malformed frailness ("DV,"
145). Mary's embittered awakening, through the birth of her son, to the
demands of her body could have been suggested to Lawrence by Eliot's
description of how Bob Jakin tries to arouse Maggie's interest in life by
putting his "two months old baby" into her arms (*MF,* 615–16).

However, Lawrence does more than extend and develop Eliot's ideas
when he associates her heroine, who chooses to honor her mind and
higher sentiments at the expense of her instinctual needs, with the
problem of obsessive motherhood. He recalls one of the most unusual
ideas in Brontë's novel, its virtual assault on the values ordinarily associated with maternity. In *Wuthering Heights* motherhood need not be
obsessive to be bad. If mothers are not shadowy and ineffectual, like the
senior Mrs. Earnshaw and Mrs. Linton, they are the prime agents
of incapacitating socialization. Frances, Isabella Linton, and Nelly, the
mother of them all, teach weakness, vanity, and affectation. These surrogate mothers' attempts to separate Cathy from Heathcliff somewhat
overschematically represent the mother's role in severing the connection
between natural woman and her soul. For Brontë's characters less moth-
ering means more freedom, more self.

Eliot's vision appears to be just the opposite. In *The Mill on the Floss,*
Mrs. Tulliver is bad to the extent that she is deficient in maternal
instincts. Her foil, Gritty Moss, whose only vocation is to be a "child-
producing woman," is an exemplar of intrinsic female value that gives
the lie to her market-economy based culture (*MF,* 139). Her maternity is

an economic drain and a spiritual and emotional fountainhead. Generally in Eliot's work, mothers are unlikely to be criticized for taking an active interest in their children's lives; they are far more likely to be negligent than domineering. Moreover, the tragic situation of the motherless person is a characteristic feature of Eliot's work, playing a prominent part in *Adam Bede, Middlemarch, Daniel Deronda,* and *Silas Marner.*

In her discussion of *Silas Marner* in "Life's Empty Pack: Notes Toward a Literary Daughteronomy," Sandra Gilbert examines Eliot's attitude toward the problems of motherhood in a way that illuminates Lawrence's response to Eliot's work. Gilbert argues that Eliot repeatedly dramatizes a "Daughteronomy" that commands, "You must bury your mother; you must give yourself to your father," and is based on our cultural insistence that women function not as inheritors but as the things passed on between men.[49] Lawrence seems to agree that women inherit nothing, neither power nor self-confidence, and because of this deprivation give themselves up to the unequal and so unfulfilling marriages that the culture privileges. But he adds to Eliot's material in order to illustrate his own belief that wives who merely act out their cultural and biological functions are potential devouring mothers.

This response to Eliot is evident in *Sons and Lovers.* Lawrence deals with Walter Morel's family history in a sentence, but describes Gertrude's early life at enough length to emphasize both her disassociation from the unnamed mother, who she "favoured" and "loved . . . best of all," and her hopeless emulation of her father.[50] Like her father, she becomes "proud and unyielding," "puritan," and "stern" (*SL,* 7, 10). Faced with her first frustration in love, she can only think of what she would do if she "were a man" (*SL,* 8). Seemingly trying to play out the father's role, she chooses to marry a man who is "different: soft, non-intellectual, warm" (*SL,* 9). When Morel disappoints her, "she [is] her father now," reacting as he would (*SL,* 13). But, because she has not inherited the father's masculine authority, she cannot force her husband to conform to her standards and must, instead, adapt to the ordinary life of a collier's wife. Her next attempt at power is made through her sons. It is as if Lawrence were to say, in response to Eliot, "Yes, you are right that the daughter who would obey cultural commandments must renounce her mother and ally herself with the patriarchy, but she will become not simply a matriarch in the sense that she is symbolically the father's bride, but one who is furiously power-hungry and perverse because she has sacrificed her true self. Her deference to men will lead to a compulsion to destroy them." This principle is exemplified by both Lettie, who trims away her sensuality to fit into Leslie's cool, fashionable world, and Mrs. Morel, who constricts her intellectual ambitions to survive in Morel's mining town. Whereas Maggie is so lovably gentle that Eliot must act out the anger we feel on her behalf, women who suffer unfulfilled conflicting desires in Lawrence's work express their own rage as directly and forcefully as Brontë's women do.

According to Gilbert, and most other feminist critics writing on women's traditions, a shift in focus from woman's victimization to her furious reaction to it is typical of modern women's revisions of their Victorian female precursors' themes. Here, again, Lawrence's interests seem to parallel those of women writers. Like most of his female contemporaries, Lawrence has good, although different, reasons to emphasize women's anger more than their sadness. First, to depict women submitting with gentle resignation to the demands of a male culture would have violated the truth of his own experience with his forceful mother, his aggressive wife, and his defiantly bohemian women friends—a truth Brontë's vision affirmed. Second, Lawrence's identification with women and his desire to create female characters "from the inside" seem to have caused him to endow them with many of his own traits. Consequently, his female characters tend to rage against social limitations and other people's will to dominate as much as he does. Finally, and most importantly, Lawrence seems compelled to revise Eliot because the "Daughteronomy" she reinscribes finds its mirror image in his own situation.

As his contemporary biographers reveal, Lawrence's early life was more like that of a daughter than of a son. As an adult, he took on his mother's role as house manager, moralist (although with a very different system of values), and defender of domestic virtues. Because of his enactment of the feminine sex role and his need for continual reiterations of female approval, he was treated by women as a child (albeit a brilliant one) or at best an equal rather than as a powerful male. Lawrence is like the daughter who, in Gilbert's words, "inherited an empty pack and cannot *be* a father"; his literary voice could only steal, not assume patriarchal authority. And like the novelist daughters, when Lawrence speaks "*for* the father," he reveals ambivalence about this humiliating task.[51] In *Women in Love* as in *The Mill on the Floss,* union with the dominant male causes a drift toward death.

What makes Lawrence's situation a *mirror* image, a reversal, rather than a copy of a woman writer's is his sense of the mother's power, rather than the father's, as inescapable. Unlike the daughters, both writers and characters, that Gilbert discusses, he cannot bury the mother. Homans, working from the same Lacanian model of the development of language (and hence authorial voice) as Gilbert, theorizes that male and female writers differ in their attitudes toward this cultural imperative. For males, the loss/killing of the mother is a positive experience because it brings full separation, a triumphant sense of individual power. For females, separation can never be complete because the sense of self is bound up in identification with the mother.[52] The absence of the mother is a sort of death of the self. From *Sons and Lovers* to *The Man Who Died,* Lawrence's works suggest this very (female) attitude: the individual is present and viable only to the degree that he is connected to a living, speaking Magna Mater.

Under the cover of articulating the "Law of the Father," Eliot can rebelliously impart feminist messages. By supporting, at least overtly, patriarchal culture's values, Eliot gains authority and so becomes, in a sense, a matriarch—what Gilbert calls a "culture-mother." Thus, she is a double agent of meaning, both for the Father and for herself. But Lawrence's ambivalence cannot find the same sort of subtle subtextual expression Eliot's does, partly because of differences in his temperament and style, but mostly because of his concept of his literary mission. Both Maggie's choice of submissive Liebestod with the patriarch ("Tom Tulliver . . . was master there now" [*MF,* 611]) and Eliot's choice of subversively rebellious creativity are closed to Lawrence because he does not feel inadequate in relation to the male voice but in relation to the female. To him the Father is more properly called the Mother; the Father as authorizing principle is a hollow myth. Oscillating toward and away from the seductive but terrifying figure of the literary mother, who is never for a moment absent and always seems to bid him speak, Lawrence can only retell Eliot's story of the "inadequacies of a daughter's estate" from the position of that daughter's son, who always recognizes that, although she is divided and so denied full being, woman can truly be neither a submissive, pitiable daughter nor a coldly rational, "culture-mother" but is, no matter what part of herself she represses, one woman held together by anger and a will to power.[53] Whereas Eliot achieves authority by representing herself, as narrator, in the service of patriarchal culture, Lawrence, to remain true to his sense of woman-as-truth, must stay subordinate to woman as she appears through texts with a female signature, fragmented but struggling toward unity.

This vision of woman, derived not simply from Eliot's work but from Lawrence's understanding of her relationship to it, as its creator, informs almost every piece of fiction Lawrence ever wrote. Daleski's observation that Lawrence, in his early works, had the same aim as Eliot, to "put woman together again" and portray her "achieved wholeness of being," seems accurate but understated.[54] To describe his situation as author more precisely, one could say that Lawrence took, as one of the main goals of his fiction, the continuation of Eliot's (and Brontë's) examination of the personality and behavior of woman under the social pressures which lead her to suppress half of herself. He seems to be forever laboring to leave his battles with women authors and go inside the psyche of an individual female character, as Eliot does with Maggie, without losing, in the alienating maze of culturally determined meanings that would govern her thoughts, the suggestion of an untouchable core of wildness that Brontë gives her more opaque heroine.

Lawrence's responses to his female precursors' revelations of ideology are very different from what we might expect from a self-proclaimed male supremacist, so different, in fact, that they must serve to contextualize his claims to speak for women. If Eliot sometimes seems to share Maggie's internalization of cultural values that we might rather see her call into question, she certainly remains distant enough from her male characters. While Brontë so carefully delineates the cruelties committed against Heathcliff that she often seems to be defending him against the reader's judgments, Eliot lavishes unexplained, stereotypical male faults on her men. Except for the comic Bob Jakin, they are all selfish, arrogant, competitive, ungrateful, and insensitive to Maggie's pain. Lawrence, however, seems less disturbed by Eliot's depiction of men as inferior to and consequently destructive of women than he is by her idealization of renunciation, which ultimately leads her to celebrate Maggie's self-repression. Surprisingly Lawrence himself questions the existence of men good enough to complete the best women, in *The Rainbow,* which ends without Ursula having met her match, and in *St. Mawr,* where Lou, after searching for a mate through England, Europe, and America, chooses celibacy because she is "weary of the embrace of incompetent men."[55] But the Christian resignation that somewhat consoles Maggie for male inferiority is anathema to Lawrence, as he shows in the vast majority of his works. *The Rainbow, Women in Love, The Plumed Serpent,* and *The Virgin and the Gipsy* all deal extensively with the failure of Christianity to provide its adherents with an adequate ethical system, and in "The Daughters of the Vicar" Lawrence directly challenges Eliot's morality as it is expressed in *The Mill on the Floss.*

Of course, it would be a mistake to read the morality of *The Mill on the Floss* as identical to Eliot's own, even leaving aside the issue of her cohabitation with Lewes. In *Middlemarch* Dorothea's unhappy marriage to Casaubon is the result of misguided self-renunciation, and in *Daniel Deronda* the admirable Mirah rejects her brother's insistence that "women are specially framed for the love which feels possession in renouncing."[56] But Lawrence's responses to *The Mill on the Floss* suggest that he read the doctrine of renunciation Maggie "wrestles" her way toward as reflective of Eliot's response to both *Wuthering Heights* and *Jane Eyre.* If so, his reading is in line with later feminist discussions of the intertextual relationship of Eliot to Emily and Charlotte Brontë. As Showalter expresses it, "Brontë's Jane Eyre is the heroine of fulfillment; Eliot's Maggie Tulliver is the heroine of renunciation."[57] Eliot does swerve violently away from the ideology of female self-assertion so often forcefully expressed in the Brontës' novels. Cathy Earnshaw and Jane Eyre both achieve union with the men they love because both are capable of considering nothing but their own best interests. Cathy's "infernal selfishness" makes her haunt Heathcliff until he comes to join her in death (*WH,* 133). Jane triumphs over Rochester and her circumstances because, as she asserts, "*I* care for myself."[58] None of Eliot's heroines have such victories.

Lawrence's need to feel authorized to speak by a female command or call ill-suited him to champion renunciatory heroines—or the authors who created them. It was inevitable that, when he brought women's texts into dialogue in his own work, he would come down on the side of the writers who celebrated woman's aggressiveness, just as he had preferred self-assertive Frieda to meek Jessie Chambers. With Emily Brontë, Schreiner, and Eliot, the choice was clear, but Charlotte Brontë presented Lawrence with a more difficult problem, as his direct discussions of her work show.

Lawrence did become critical of Charlotte Brontë as he grew older, but less so than is suggested by his most frequently quoted comments on *Jane Eyre* in "Pornography and Obscenity."[59] He says he "must admit" that *Jane Eyre* is "much nearer to pornography than is Boccaccio," and that in both works, "titillations are slightly indecent," because "sex excitement" coexists in them with "a desire to spite the sexual feeling, to humiliate it and degrade it."[60] As the tone of this passage implies, Lawrence makes this judgment reluctantly. Earlier, Lawrence implies that he did not find *Jane Eyre* repugnant, but lovely. He writes, "Titian or Renoir, The Song of Solomon or *Jane Eyre,* Mozart or 'Annie Laurie,' the loveliness is all interwoven with sex appeal, sex stimulus, call it what you will" ("Pornography," 173–74). It seems that, if Lawrence felt compelled to condemn his early favorite on moral grounds, he was unable to dismiss it.

Both Lawrence's admiration for Charlotte Brontë's work and his competitiveness with her is understandable if we consider that almost all of Lawrence's fiction has the same major theme as *Jane Eyre*: a woman's struggle to achieve fulfillment against social expectations and men's demands. While it seems unlikely that Lawrence had Charlotte Brontë's work continually in mind while he wrote, it is equally unlikely that he forgot a book that was not only one of his favorites but Frieda's "favorite novel that she read continuously" while at school.[61] It seems impossible that Lawrence could have missed the connections between *Jane Eyre, Wuthering Heights,* and *The Mill on the Floss,* which constitute a discourse on the topic of how woman, in order to reach fulfillment, might position herself in relation to man, the cultural edicts of Christianity, and nature. In fact, one motif that appears in all three novels reappears frequently in Lawrence's work in the context of gender relations, where it seems to authorize not only his writing but also his representation of women's voices. The motif is a call and answer involving supernatural forces.

In both *Jane Eyre* and *Wuthering Heights* the central love affair culminates in a supernatural call. Heathcliff is summoned by Cathy's ghost. Jane begs heaven for a sign of what she must do and, (as if) in response to her secret desire, hears the "loved, well-remembered voice" of Rochester calling her back to him (*JE,* 369). Both Brontës present these calls and responses explicitly in opposition to traditional Christian religious experience. Although Rochester's call is made in the midst of sincere prayer, his religious attitude is hardly orthodox; he asks not for moral improvement but for reunion with Jane in either life or death (*JE,* 393). Jane is called away from a future as a missionary through what she believes is the agency of "nature . . . roused" (*JE*, 370). This confirmation of her desires allows her to "assume ascendancy" over St. John, who has been her "hierophant," and pray "in [her] own way—a different way to St. John's" (*JE*, 370, 368). Heathcliff "pray[s] one prayer": that Cathy will haunt him and so remain with him (*WH*, 139). He refers to union with Cathy in death as "*my* heaven" and rejects Nelly's advice that he seek Christian instruction by saying, "that [heaven] of others is altogether unvalued and uncoveted by me!" (*WH*, 259, 263). In both novels, heaven is relocated literally in the call and response between man and woman, and thus (hetero)sexual passion is represented as religious ritual, an idea Lawrence toys with much more explicitly in *The Rainbow,* *The Plumed Serpent,* and *The Man Who Died.*

Lawrence's two favorite Eliot novels, *The Mill on the Floss* and *Adam Bede,* also featured mystical calls from one lover to another, but Eliot's use of this motif is not as compatible with Lawrence's ideology as the Brontës', even though Eliot uses it to reinscribe the subordination of woman as divinely mandated. In *Adam Bede,* the call is climactic. At the sound of Adam's voice, which Dinah at first takes for a "purely spiritual monition," she goes to him and consents to become his wife.[62] Because Dinah's marriage marks the end of her independence and authority as a preacher, Eve Sedgwick seems right to see Dinah's confusion about the source of the call as "chillingly" significant. Adam's voice replaces God's for Dinah, and consequently she changes from a powerful priestess into a silently receptive wife.[63] Whereas in the Brontës' novels the call heralds the triumph of nature and a natural female essence against the Law of the Father, Eliot imagines a call to womanly submission.

Stephen's letter to Maggie and her reaction to it comprise the most powerful and succinct evidence that Eliot meant to question the Brontës' depictions of the path to fulfillment. Like Cathy and Jane, Maggie feels homeless and "unspeakably, sickeningly weary" at her most intense moment of moral crisis (*MF,* 646). Stephen's "passionate cry of reproach: an appeal against her useless sacrifice of him—of herself" echoes Heathcliff's "*Why* did you despise me? *Why* did you betray your own heart, Cathy?" (*MF,* 646; *WH,* 134). Stephen's reference to "that long look of love that has burnt itself into [his] soul, so that no other image can come there" is even more evocative of Heathcliff's complaint to Cathy that "all [her] words will be branded in [his] memory, and eating deeper eternally," and his later confession to Nelly that he is so "surrounded with [Cathy's] image" that it obliterates everything else (*MF*, 647; *WH*, 133, 255). Stephen's plea that Maggie return him "to life and goodness" and his explanation that "I am banished from both now," seem a paler version of Rochester's furious response to Jane, "Then you snatch love and innocence from me? You fling me back on lust for a passion—vice for an occupation?" (*MF*, 647; *JE*, 279). Stephen's demand, "call me back to you," is reminiscent of both Heathcliff's and Jane's prayers that they be summoned back into their heavens (*MF*, 647). Like them, Maggie mystically experiences the presence of her lover. "She did not *read* the letter: she heard him uttering it, and the voice shook her with its old power" (*MF*, 647–48). But she meets this strange force with conventional religious faith and prayer, renounces selfish pleasure in the name of Christian virtue, and is granted her "final rescue" from further temptation. Rather than yearning for deathless union with a lover, "[h]er soul [goes] out to the Unseen Pity that would be with her to the end" (*MF*, 649).

Lawrence's use of this call and answer pattern in *The Ladybird* is remarkably similar to the Brontës', but his inclusion of flood imagery to represent the rescuing force suggests that he was thinking of Eliot as well. The argument between their texts is represented within Lawrence's through symbolic characters and acts and also in dialogized indirect speech. He begins his story with a description of the exemplary Christian Lady Beveridge. Her way represents a possible future for Lady Daphne, should she not answer the call of the pagan deity whom her own need has called into being (*LB*, 43, 93). Throughout the story Lady Beveridge's Christian values are opposed to Psanek's creed of passion and rage. Lawrence seems to be quoting both *Jane Eyre* and *The Mill on the Floss* when Daphne thinks of "this dark, everlasting love that was like a full river flowing forever inside her" (*LB*, 107). Eliot's vision is transmitted only to be refuted, however. Maggie is carried to God the Father and her own innocence and light by the upsurging of (her own) nature, but Lawrence's heroine is carried by the same force down into the darkness that lies outside the Father's law for (re)union with the male who signifies her own defiant power.

In his unwavering belief in the value of dark passion and in the necessity of man's carrying it back to socialized woman, Lawrence aligns himself with Emily Brontë not only against Eliot but also, often, against Charlotte Brontë. His utopian and apocalyptic leanings would not allow him to accept the compromises with reality in the second half of *Wuthering Heights*. Instead he tried repeatedly to rewrite the story as an unmitigated affirmation of the importance of Heathcliff's and Cathy's union. Nonetheless, his rewritings of Emily Brontë's novel are more in the nature of didactic intensifications than contradictions of Brontë's ethos. Even so, his treatment of the Victorian women writers who share Emily Brontë's preoccupations is generally critical and revisionary, as can be seen if one examines his responses to Charlotte Brontë's and George Eliot's treatments of women's anger.

In Emily Brontë's world view, as in Lawrence's, people cannot be cured of their anger, and women seem particularly endangered by the social forces that push them to suppress it. Cathy's ultimately fatal convulsions of frustration, and Catherine's reversion from intimidating witch back into a "little lady" who must depend on her man to fight her battles indicate that Emily Brontë, like Lawrence, believes in the necessity not only of releasing rage but of acknowledging its continual regeneration. His concept of history as composed of alternating periods of love and anger, which he propounds in *The Ladybird, The Plumed Serpent,* and *Movements in European History,* resembles *Wuthering Heights'* chronological structuring in which Heathcliff's era of rage and ecstatic defiance gives way to Nelly's era of civilized love and compromise. In declaring, as he often does, that the era of love has ended, Lawrence is in no way opposing Brontë's vision since the decorous, recognizably Victorian, period that begins with Catherine's reformation of Hareton can be considered to have been ended by World War I. Lawrence's attitude toward anger is not so compatible with those of Eliot and Charlotte Brontë.

Anger is a major issue in both *The Mill on the Floss* and *Jane Eyre*; "Jane Eyre's problem, like Maggie Tulliver's, centers on what to do with her feelings," especially her "womanly rage."[64] By splitting her heroine into an identically named mother and daughter, Emily Brontë is able to set the romantic/heroic fulfillment of defiance (Cathy with Heathcliff) against the mundane fulfillment of compromise (Catherine with Hareton). But Eliot and Charlotte Brontë each choose to dramatize only one path to fulfillment. While Eliot allows Maggie no alternative except to sublimate her anger in an exalted renunciation, Charlotte Brontë resolves Jane's problem in the storm of poetic justice that ends *Jane Eyre*.[65] Gilbert and Gubar's discussion of Charlotte Brontë's use of fire imagery shows all the intricate connections between the "ridge of lighted heath, alive, glancing, devouring" that is "a meet emblem of [Jane's] mind" in her childhood rages and the fire that removes Bertha and reduces Rochester to harmless dependency.⁶⁶

The most striking differences between Charlotte Brontë's concept of womanly rage and that of Emily Brontë (and Lawrence) is that the former, in *Jane Eyre,* allows compromise not only with reality but with Victorian morality. Emily Brontë illustrates both society's demand that women repress their anger or die *and* the evil that results from obeying that demand; Charlotte Brontë intercedes for her heroine and thus strongly suggests that suppression of anger will be rewarded with a kind of divine intervention. The circumstances of the resolution of Jane's romantic problem imply that submission to socializing forces must precede the successful call and even that woman's anger must be transferred outside herself and destroyed before fulfillment can be achieved. When Jane learns to "regulate [her] mind," providence takes her part and releases her mind's fires (*JE,* 316). It is not simply to allow Jane's marriage that Bertha is destroyed. As many critics have noted, Bertha is Jane's double in that she incarnates the furious rebelliousness against patriarchal control that Jane learns to repress as she matures. Before Jane can achieve her happiness, her anger, exteriorized as both Rochester's rejection of Christian morality and Bertha's entire being, must be killed.

Although it is clear from a great many of Lawrence's poems and essays that he was attracted by the idea of curing women's rage into quiet submissiveness, he seems unwilling to dramatize such a resolution in his fiction. Even when he sets the stage to show a woman's taming, the conflict between the sexes is projected beyond the novel's closing; the angry voices of his women seem likely to continue being heard. Ursula in *Women in Love,* March in *The Fox,* Hannele in *The Captain's Doll,* Harriet in *Kangaroo,* and Kate in *The Plumed Serpent* never give in to their lovers' demands for their submission. In "Mother and Daughter" and "The Woman Who Rode Away," which depict heroines who do submit, the specific acts of female submission paradoxically express anger and rebellion. Through her engagement to the fatherly Arnault, Virginia Bodoin is finally able to strike back against her mother, who has always treated her as her *"alter ego,* her other self."⁶⁷ The woman who rides away is in furious rebellion against just such a husband as Arnault. "Like any sheikh," he isolates her, "sway[s] her, down[s] her, [keeps] her in an invincible slavery" until she, realizing she is "dead already," allows the Indians to sacrifice her in a ritual to destroy the white man's world.[68] When Lawrence gives up the idea of male leadership and organized revolt, he also seems to give up this idea of a woman rebelling against one patriarchal system by surrendering to another, and when he deals at great length with *Jane Eyre,* in the second version of *Lady Chatterley's Lover,* he seems determined to show that Jane should have been mated to the signifier and agent of female anger, Heathcliff, rather than buried in Victorian niceness with the safely crippled Rochester. Lawrence's re-writing of Charlotte Brontë's story reveals that what really disturbed him about *Jane Eyre* was the taming of Jane through resolution of her rage, not the maiming of Rochester through which her rage was re-solved.

The figure who represents Jane's rage is given an important role in the second version of *Lady Chatterley's Lover, John Thomas and Lady Jane.* Higdon has convincingly demonstrated that Lawrence's Bertha Coutts, the estranged wife of the gamekeeper, was derived from Bertha Mason.[69] Their lives, habits, and attitudes are remarkably similar, and Bertha Coutts is even described as being "like a mad-woman" (*JTLJ,* 298). But, while *Jane Eyre* tells us very little that can excite sympathy for Bertha Mason, Connie blames Parkin's insufficiencies for driving her rival "evil-mad" (*JTLJ,* 298). Connie's musings about the marriage-maddened Bertha recall Cathy Earnshaw, who also "fought against even the love in her own soul" (*JTLJ,* 299). Lawrence, like Emily Brontë (and Jean Rhys), finds the explanation of the wife's insanity in her situation as wife—in the situation of any wife—subject through marriage to the demands of a patriarchal order that denies her femaleness. Moreover, Lawrence, like Brontë, keeps this specter of female rage alive. If Bertha stands in for Cathy's angry ghost, Connie is no civilized and repressed Catherine Linton. Like Cathy (or Jane in her childhood), the Connie of *John Thomas and Lady Jane* exults in her own rage. Her anger, again like that of both heroines, arises from her condition as a woman. "She [is] angry, angry at the implied insult to womanhood" not once but often throughout the novel (*JTLJ,* 333). Like Jane and Cathy she finds an angry, rebellious lover, but unlike them she understands that his fury is "part of her own revolt" (*JTLJ,* 275). The intermingling of angry voices destroys the false "Paradise of wealth and well-being" available to Con-nie at Wragby Hall, but destroys nothing in the two lovers except artificial gender identities built up around their true selves by society (*JTLJ*, 345). Yet the Eden is still contained within the male order; its existence seems to depend on open female revolt against that order.

Lawrence's responses to *Wuthering Heights* and the novels he felt were influenced by it suggest that to him the tragedy in their shared theme adheres not in woman's (or man's) circumstances, but in the cultural inscription of repression and denial of uncivilized female passions, as if anger, fierceness, and violence could be separated out of sexual relations by the simple addition of sweet femininity. To Lawrence, Cathy represents the aspect of Brontë (he might call it her daemon—her essential self) that needs the body, no matter how imprisoning marriage and pregnancy make it seem to her, to make possible revitalizing contact with the natural world through man. He interprets Cathy's longing for death as the mark of Heathcliff's failure to bring her fulfillment and so creates Heathcliffs of his own who can better answer the call that he heard in women's fiction, that he imagined coming from her core self.

Lawrence's impulse to rewrite *Wuthering Heights* was naïve. Brontë's discontent is of another sort than that which proposes worldly solutions. Despite her enumeration of injustices in property laws, she seems ultimately above concern with social change, although not above gender chauvinism. In *Wuthering Heights,* she values woman's natural passions above all else, and disdains everything, including woman's own fertility, that interferes with the expression of those passions. What gives Cathy her stature is her refusal to accept any compromise, her refusal to control herself in any way. For Brontë such refusal necessitates death, although the tone of *Wuthering Heights'* conclusion reveals her regret that this must be. Olive Schreiner and George Eliot (at least in *The Mill on the Floss*) fatalistically value death as the only possible release from the conflict between the demands of passion and civilization, a conflict that rends humans in two. Charlotte Brontë seems to believe that the death of anger is a possible solution and proposes killing it by killing male power.

Lawrence, however, sees the male consciousness as the ground on which female wholeness can be achieved. If *Wuthering Heights* is the wild female call, he cannot see the assertions of feminine victimization and virtue presented in *The Story of an African Farm, The Mill on the Floss,* and *Jane Eyre* as valuable answers. To Lawrence, man "alone of the two, perhaps, can dimly apprehend the whole of the dream" of passion; woman, who can only appreciate man as her "pure ecstatic servant," does not understand that his effectiveness in that role depends on his ability to "read" her (*JTLJ*, 136, 135). Consequently, Lawrence's high valuation of female passion is always accompanied by implied or explicit exhortations to men to interpret it for the women who feel it. His ideal union depends on both the woman's anger ("like discernable fire"), which energizes sexuality, and the male's "higher understanding," which makes her "acknowledge him as a sort of fate, her own fate" (*WL*, 141–42).

Lawrence begins to move back across the border between gendered texts when he goes from finding an ideology through Brontë to speaking as or for her. In apparent reaction to his recognition of the necessity of the female voice and audience to his own existence as an author, he insists on the necessity of man to woman. If his women generally found their female voices issuing from the throats of men and asserting men's importance, as Daphne does, Lawrence would make us understand Brontë's femaleness only by contrast. The confrontation between their texts would have the look of war and its crossfire would show us the hard outlines of a textual gender specificity without shading. Instead, Lawrence's virtual compulsion to give voice to female anger that resists appropriation and undercuts his assertion of the value of man, even as he speaks it, makes the border waver. Although in this respect Lawrence's new heaven and earth have in common with the old ones dependence on a masculine hermeneutics, the world of Lawrence's fiction is almost always a return to the world of *Wuthering Heights* before the first sighting of the Lintons: female anger and revolt flourishing in the interstices of patriarchal power.

"We Should Rise Braced and Purified": Responses to Lawrence from Some Shapers of Modern Women's Literature

THE RECORD OF LAWRENCE'S failure to help his female followers achieve an enabling sense of themselves as writers is inscribed in the Lawrence figure their memoirs created. This Lawrence always appears in feminist criticism as a two-faced, or two-voiced, betrayer. He is, in Kate Millet's words, "the most . . . fervid of sexual politicians [but] the most subtle as well, for it is through a female consciousness that his masculine message is conveyed."[1] In such feminizing descriptions of him writing somehow from "a female consciousness," Lawrence's authorship closely resembles what Alice Jardine refers to as the modernist "becoming woman," a process through which binary concepts of gender and traditional concepts of subjectivity are broken down, but only when woman is "the *first* to disappear," abstracted into a female principle.[2] This is the negative Lawrence, whose continual appropriation of the female voice places him in feminist criticism as an adversary of women's creativity. But a positive Lawrence figure was also created textually, one who often resisted the paranoid urge to absorb woman and her knowledge, and instead made his texts the medium for an affirmation of the authority of specific women's writings.[3] Both Lawrences appear in the texts of several of his famous female contemporaries. There and in his own texts, he is placed in relation to female intertextuality not only as an intruder but also as a participant in the development of women's traditions.

As Lawrence recast the manuscripts of Helen Corke and Mollie Skinner and accepted influence in the forms of written and oral contributions

and detailed criticism from Frieda, Jessie Chambers, Mabel Dodge Luhan, Catherine Carswell, Dorothy Brett and other women, he worked
their ideas into the complex fabric of his responses to and revisions of
some of the most highly respected novels written by women in the
previous generation. Through the intermediary of Lawrence's fiction,
the women who sought his help in articulating their own visions entered
into a relationship with women's literary traditions. His preoccupation
with answering Victorian women novelists brought the later female
contributors to his texts into a dialogue with their precursors. However,
by no means all of Lawrence's female contemporaries needed him (or
anyone else) to save their ideas from obscurity or to connect them to
women's traditions.

Just as Lawrence began his literary career, liberalization of concepts of
women's thought, emotion, and behavior made it possible for women to
write about their own and other women's experiences more freely and
with higher hopes of being understood than had previously been possible. Some women were well suited to take advantage of these changes
both because of their own experimentation with new gender roles and
because they successfully communicated their originality in their writing. Unlike Lawrence's female followers, these women found themselves as speaking subjects in relation to what they recognized as woman-
centered literary traditions, and they achieved enough recognition as
writers to bolster their sense of themselves as speakers with an audience
rather than figures for male interpretation. Nonetheless, the number and
quality of references to Lawrence in the works of such innovative female
modernists as Virginia Woolf, Katherine Mansfield, H. D., and Anaïs
Nin indicate that his attempts to speak for women were difficult to
ignore even for women writers who had no need of an intermediary to
connect them to their own literary heritage.

The responses of Woolf, Mansfield, H. D., and Nin to Lawrence's
work are often mentioned by critics, but generally only in the context of
discussions about the differences between the women's personalities and
his. That all five writers shared a sense of themselves as continuing and
modifying women's literary traditions has been ignored. Yet in Woolf's,
H. D.'s, and Nin's writings about Lawrence and in Mansfield's literary
allusions to him, one is constantly reminded of their awareness that they
are engaged with him in the creation of a body of modern literature for
women. Woolf's literary relationship to Lawrence seems the most mis-

understood. Many misapprehensions about Woolf's readings of Lawrence's work can be corrected simply by attention to what her implicit comparisons of Lawrence to other writers reveal. But Mansfield's and H. D.'s more complicated understandings of Lawrence are only fully disclosed in their fiction. Nin's assessment of Lawrence, which has become more interesting with the development of language-based feminist criticism, is most clearly articulated in her book *D. H. Lawrence.* Consequently, I will have more to say about Mansfield's and H. D.'s fiction than Woolf's and Nin's, and I will look more closely at the latter two writers' literary criticism than at Mansfield's and H. D.'s nonfictional writings. Consideration of Woolf's critical comments on Lawrence may help illuminate Mansfield's more oblique responses, H. D.'s quasi-autobiographical approach, and Nin's tentative proto-feminist criticism.

Woolf's connection of Lawrence to women's literary traditions should be especially important to feminist critics who are engaged in tracing such traditions, because Woolf's own literary criticism often relies on and encourages a gynocentric approach in which references to men's texts function only to stress the value of authorial techniques and attitudes that are associated with women. In *A Room of One's Own,* female creativity and discourse are very obviously privileged in this way, but the same position, based on comparativism, is in evidence in many of the other texts Woolf produced, including her letters and diary. These private writings often convey the sense that, sometimes against her will, Lawrence slipped across the border between the genders in Woolf's mind. Like all figures who threw stable gender identity into doubt, Lawrence interested Woolf, and, no matter how frequently his ideas and style annoyed her, she could never quite dismiss his work.

It was also almost inevitable that Woolf would devote careful attention to Lawrence's work, not because she immediately recognized his attempts to participate in women's literary traditions, but because she was urged by many friends, throughout her life, to acknowledge his genius. Although Lawrence reacted against Ottoline Morrell's and David Garnett's efforts to integrate him into the artistic and intellectual community of Bloomsbury, he retained admirers and defenders there, including such close friends of Woolf's as E. M. Forster and Clive Bell.[4] Lack of direct contact with Lawrence allowed Woolf to come to his work with greater emotional detachment than his friends could achieve. Rather than treating him as a disappointing alter ego, as they so often did, Woolf made many attempts to uncover for herself the value that critics she respected saw in his texts. In her written record of these attempts, Lawrence often appears as a positive participant in women's literary traditions, but her representation of him is seldom without ambivalence.

Woolf's comments about Lawrence in her letters generally reflect her uneasiness about her own annoyance with his work. At first this uneasiness appears to arise from a desire not to condemn her friends' taste. When writing to Molly MacCarthy, who was not one of Lawrence's advocates, Woolf makes fun of *Women in Love* saying, "balls are smashed on every other page—cats—cattle—even the fish and the water lilies are at it all day long. . . . I get a little bored."[5] Five days later, she wrote to Lawrence's ardent defender S. S. Koteliansky, "I am reading Women in Love. . . . I can't help thinking that there is something wrong with Lawrence that makes him brood over sex, but he is trying to say something, and he is honest, and therefore he is 100 times better than most of us" (LW, 2:476). The pressure Woolf was under to agree that Lawrence was a genius is evident in later letters. Nonetheless, Woolf does not seem to be equivocating when she tells Dorothy Brett, "I can't get hold of Lawrence; I like and dislike" (LW, 5:202). The need she expresses "to read him through," is more than a concession to Brett (LW, 5:202). At the time the letter was written, 1933, Woolf had already begun to think seriously about Lawrence's fiction. After Lawrence's death in 1930, she read, in the space of a year, *Sons and Lovers, The Man Who Died,* and her friend Aldous Huxley's edition of Lawrence's letters.[6] She then began to develop an attitude about Lawrence that was more than just a reaction to her friends' enthusiasm for his work. This new attitude is articulated in her diary and in two of her essays, "Notes on D. H. Lawrence," written in 1931, and "The Leaning Tower," written in 1940.

What Woolf saw in Lawrence, when she gave him her full attention, was the last thing that her readers might have expected: a writer with whom she had "too much in common."[7] Robert Keily points out the similarities between Lawrence's and Woolf's positions as writers working outside "the center of the literary establishment" and taking on, as a "moral responsibility," the task of generalizing the very imaginings that separated them from the dominant culture, translating the alienating and alienated personal into "universal experience."[8] Nonetheless, most feminist critics now take the position, powerfully argued by Rachel Blau DuPlessis, that Woolf and Lawrence belonged to what might be called utterly opposed branches of modernism. In DuPlessis's view, the literature produced by both branches attacks "bourgeois culture," but, while the woman modernist "invents a new and total culture," such male modernists as "Eliot, Pound, Yeats, [and] Lawrence" promote a "revolution from the right" to (re)establish an idealized patriarchal past.[9] Not all of Woolf's female contemporaries, however, saw literary modernism as so neatly divided. As Bonnie Kime Scott points out, Rebecca West found Lawrence and Woolf comparable in their resistance to dominant modes of understanding and representing human experience.[10] And, while Woolf knew that she shared more with other women writers, an awareness that she and Lawrence had some goals in common seems, from time to time, to have teased at her mind, affecting her concept of literary traditions.

Woolf's recognition of Lawrence's marginality and its effect on him as a writer is apparent in "Notes on D. H. Lawrence." In this essay, she praises the freshness of *Sons and Lovers* and attributes this spontaneity to Lawrence's social situation. In Woolf's view, because Lawrence must disconnect himself from his own personal past, he is also disconnected from the dominant literary tradition. She writes, "one feels that he echoes nobody, continues no tradition, is unaware of the past, of the present save as it affects the future."[11] But, because Woolf also describes women writers—notably the Brontës—in this way, one may assume that she sees Lawrence as connected by circumstance if not intention to women writers. She feels she understands his approach, that "Lawrence writes his books as I write this diary" (DW, 4:95). His work has the freedom from predetermined form and received ideas that Woolf increasingly both valued and associated with women's writings.

That Woolf identifies with Lawrence as a writer excluded from the dominant tradition is strongly suggested in "The Leaning Tower." In discussing writers who began to publish before 1914, Woolf says, "They have all been raised above the mass of people by a tower of stucco—that is their middle-class birth; and of gold—that is their expensive education. That was true of all the nineteenth century writers except Dickens; it was true of all the 1914 writers, save D. H. Lawrence." But it is true neither of herself nor of the four women she has mentioned in her discussion of literary precursors: Austen, the Brontës, and Eliot. Her list of " 'representative names' " of her own generation also includes no women.[12] This striking omission of all women, together with her designation of Lawrence as an outsider, implies more than Woolf ever directly says about Lawrence's relationship to literary women. Woolf knew that Lawrence, like most women writers, saw the world from beneath the tower. Not only was his education deficient in the same way as almost all women's, his financial position was as insecure.[13]

Perhaps such circumstances should not affect a writer's style, but Woolf understood that they often do. Consequently, it seems more than coincidental that Woolf criticizes Charlotte Brontë's writing style in the same terms as she does Lawrence's. Both writers' awareness that they have been denied privileges which would have enhanced their fiction gives them an angry self-consciousness Woolf sees as antithetical to art. Like Lawrence, Brontë "will write in a rage where she should write calmly."[14] But if their shared marginality causes them to mar their work with outbursts of anger, it also endows them with an attractive intensity. Woolf believes such writers have "in them some untamed ferocity perpetually at war with the accepted order of things," which can raise their prose above the limits held to by more conventional writers.[15] Carolyn Heilbrun goes so far as to say that the propaganda in Lawrence's work may have suggested to Woolf the possibility of expressing her own anger, denied as long as she held to the conventional impersonality of "the great art of the patriarchy."[16] Certainly Woolf made clear that she believed women writers and male writers like Lawrence, by virtue of their circumstances, should present visions opposed to those of the more typical middle-class male author.

In Woolf's view, only the writer who has been excluded from the dominant tradition can, as a member of "the immense class to which almost all of us belong," create a unifying vision that embraces "the two worlds." In theory, then, Lawrence and Woolf were engaged in a struggle with a common literary goal. Indeed she ends "The Leaning Tower," which was originally a speech to workingmen, with an exhortation that stresses the shared goals of all marginal writers: "Let us trespass at once. Literature is no one's private ground."[17] As we have seen, however, Woolf's actual attitude toward Lawrence was less comradely than distrustful, her recognition of his genius far less jubilant than annoyed. In fact, when Desmond MacCarthy speculated that Lawrence was the model for *A Room of One's Own*'s celebrated novelist and smug inheritor of educational and financial privileges, "Mr. A," whose female characters are ciphers, Woolf responded that Lawrence "was not in [her] upper mind; but no doubt was in the lower" (LW, 4:130).

A popular explanation for Woolf's ambivalent response to Lawrence's fiction is that she was disturbed by his emphasis on sex.[18] This view would seem more plausible if Woolf had ever criticized Lawrence for a lack of decorum in treating sexual matters, but she did not. She even complained about a lack of sex in one of his novels. In her review of *The Lost Girl,* she playfully confesses to reading "nervously, for we always dread originality, yet with the sense that once the shock was received we should rise braced and purified."[19] To Woolf, one of the most rare and pleasing qualities of *Sons and Lovers* is that "[t]he only thing we are given to rest upon, to expand upon, to feel to the limits of our powers is some rapture of physical being."[20] As when she writes to Koteliansky about *Women in Love,* Woolf demonstrates her understanding that Lawrence's concentration on sex contributes as much as his social class does to the freshness of his vision. Rather than being shocked by Lawrence's sexual frankness, Woolf seems to have hoped that it would be a force against conventionality in prose and so help the cause of those marginal writers who were undermining the tower from without.

However, although Woolf and Lawrence both wrote under what she calls "the same pressure to be ourselves," they responded to that pressure in significantly different ways (DW, 4:126). Woolf's early works show both her recognition of her peripheral position as a woman writer and the uncertainty this position gives her. In *The Voyage Out,* Helen Ambrose believes it is her duty to enlighten her motherless niece Rachel about life.[21] Helen's position can be considered analogous to Woolf's in that both have taken on the task of acquainting others with reality, both are trying to reveal truths about life. But what Helen terms seeing life is distinct from experiencing it (*Voyage,* 98). Because she is a woman, Helen can bring Rachel no nearer to experience than their position as observers in the darkness outside a window; correspondingly, Woolf removes Rachel by death from the constricting ignorance demanded by her social role instead of giving her freedom to experience life knowledgeably. This trope of the window as the boundary between female ignorance and male education appears again in *Jacob's Room,* where the narrator herself stands outside. As Alex Zwerdling has shown, Woolf dramatizes her own deeply felt sense of distance from the university and the masculine power structure it represents when she describes the private conversation of the men in Simeon's Cambridge rooms as inaudible to the narrator.[22]

Still, Woolf continued to write, keeping her fiction true to the vision of an outsider. The structure and content of her novels were conceived in opposition to the dominant novelistic tradition, even as it had been followed by many of her female precursors. Love affairs were pushed out of the center; marriage lost its place as the resolution. As Woolf matured, as her experience with writing from the outside of what the majority deemed the important world increased, her show of uneasiness about her peripheral position diminished. Although the window trope reappears in many of her later texts, it is more and more often used to mark the boundary between a valuable interior that is coded as female and an exterior world of empty male activity, as in *A Room of One's Own* where true creativity is pushed, with the narrator, into the enclosed female space while men posture around the grounds of Oxbridge enforcing the idiotic misogyny they have inherited without question. Here the elevated window is redefined as a place of female vision. Jane Marcus has speculated that Woolf's faith in "the power of one's inner voices" developed as a "defense" against her lack of the sort of education that confers authority.[23] Bonnie Kime Scott suggests that Woolf found within an intentionally feminist, fragmented mode of discourse a superior linguistic space outside the traditional and thus controlled and static language of male hegemony. From this vantage point, which Woolf shared with other women modernists, she could deconstruct patriarchal fictions and reconstruct in their place a more fertile and vital articulation of human experience.[24] Both *To the Lighthouse* and *Between the Acts* dramatize the unique ability of the outsider to pull together fragmented impressions of life—disparate consciousnesses—into a coherent statement. Lily Briscoe and Miss La Trobe understand, because of their own exclusion, that life cannot be represented by one person's or, as is so often the case in fiction, one couple's story. Paradoxically, their understanding of the disunity and disharmony of human experience makes possible their unifying visions.

In addition to recognizing the power to comprehend the world that her position as an outsider gave her, Woolf also realized that those excluded from the dominant literary tradition are not excluded from all literary tradition. Woolf's impulse as an artist is toward inclusion rather than compartmentalization; in urging women, working-class people, and all whose visions are alien to those of the "tower dwellers" to write, she is not advocating the formation of separate literary schools but calling for the loosening of old conventions, the broadening of tradition to admit diversity. She stresses the importance to women writers of their own, separate tradition, however (*Room*, 108). Woolf's awareness that she shared a common literary cause with all writers who could not observe life from the tower did not prevent her realization that she also belonged to a subdivision of that massive group, one that she names as a class daughters of educated men.[25] In text after text, Woolf makes it plain that it is from this class that she draws her inspiration and that it is only within the transgenerational literary community that centuries of these daughters have made that her own speaking position becomes that of an insider. But her feeling that "[o]ur class is the weakest of all the classes in the state" probably contributed to Woolf's emphasis on the shared interests of all marginalized writers, for there is strength in unity (*Guineas*, 13).

Lawrence's most obvious response to his own marginal status was bound to annoy Woolf because it threatened such unity. Excluded from middle-class privilege and the dominant literary tradition, Lawrence, like the "Old Adam" he mocks in his fiction, tried to replace the hierarchical system that demanded his expulsion with a new one that he could control. Unwilling to be a follower himself, he dreamed of a utopian community, Rananim, peopled with his own disciples. Lawrence's followers tended to be women, and his leadership often took the form of demands for female submission. In his fiction this pattern does not prevail. As Cornelia Nixon has shown, Lawrence's "leadership period" is characterized by a concentration on hierarchical relations between men.[26] Male leader-rebels like Lilly in *Aaron's Rod* and Ramón in *The Plumed Serpent* receive much more deference from men than from women and are balanced by female counterparts in other novels, like Ursula in *The Rainbow* and Lou in *St. Mawr*. But Woolf, who was all too familiar with Lawrence followers like Dorothy Brett, must have felt that if he had to make his own path, he then expected others, especially women, to follow it, and for Woolf "to follow submissively in his tracks seemed an unthinkable aberration."[27]

Her objection to Lawrence was not simply that he was misogynistic but that he wished to eradicate the freemasonry of the marginalized and put in its place yet another system that would privilege some and exclude others. In her estimation, he was always "giving advice on a system," condemning others when they failed to conform to his rigid rules, while she longed for "a system that did not shut out" (DW, 4:127). Even worse, the rules for living he outlines in his later works do not seem unconventional to Woolf, as she indicates in *Orlando*. When the heroine at last sits down to complete the poem that has been her life's work, Woolf writes:

> Surely, since she is a woman, and a beautiful woman, and a woman in the prime of life, she will soon give over this pretence of writing and thinking and begin to think, at least of a gamekeeper (and as long as she thinks of a man, nobody objects to a woman thinking). And then she will write him a little note (and as long as she writes little notes nobody objects to a woman writing either) . . . and the gamekeeper will whistle under the window— all of which is, of course, the very stuff of life and the only possible subject for fiction. . . . love—as the male novelists define it—and who, after all, speak with greater authority?—has nothing whatever to do with kind- ness, fidelity, generosity, or poetry. Love is slipping off one's petticoat and—But we all know what love is.[28]

What Lawrence saw as a return to tenderness, with *Lady Chatterley's Lover,* was also a return to conventional novelistic plotting and values, as Woolf shows. The story of Connie Chatterley, beginning with her recognition of her loneliness, moving quickly to her first meeting with Mellors, and ending with her pregnancy and their plans to marry, is "the only possible subject for fiction," as the most banal novelists have always believed. The story departs from standard form only in its language and depiction of sexuality. Woolf minimizes the novel's shocking elements with her cool comment "[b]ut we all know what love is." Her repetitions of the phrase "nobody objects" stress the conventionality of Lawrence's heroine; though she breaks society's law (by committing adultery and crossing class barriers), still she is an unobjectionable woman, cast in the same mold as thousands of other fictional heroines, each of whose "show of emotion and excitement" is always dependent on her relations with a man (*Orlando,* 268). Woolf's sarcastic tone indicates how little regard she has for the smug authority of novelists whose visions are determined by such egotism and limited imagination. Her contemptuous reference to definitions given by the male novelists groups Lawrence with all of them and so with the dominant tradition.

Woolf would return to Lawrence's work but with her expectations shadowed by her knowledge that, at the end, he betrayed his early promise of acting as an artistic force against the received ideas she believed poisoned fictional portrayals of women. Although for many years she made sporadic attempts to reach a decision about Lawrence, her writings indicate that she remained ambivalent. In one sense, Woolf's criticisms of Lawrence are not unreasonable. What she seeks in his novels is the minimum she requires from all art: a fresh, open-minded view of the diversity of life. Where she finds instead complaints, self-aggrandizement, and affirmation of stale and limited concepts of gender, she criticizes. If by Woolf's standards Lawrence's novels fail, it is because he could not make a virtue of marginality but instead succumbed to what she believed were the worst temptations facing a nonprivileged writer. But Woolf herself seems to have been unable to resist all of those temptations. Her high valuation of female writing and traditions, and indeed her need to discuss them in contrast to male practice suggest the particularly feminist type of essentialism that defiantly reads (and reinscribes) female difference as superiority. To the extent that Lawrence's texts exemplify the literary practices that she associates with a female principle, she is willing to group him with women writers, but when he subsumes women's voices into a totalizing representation of true woman, Woolf must distance herself from him.

If identification with Lawrence presented problems for Woolf, it much more severely threatened the women who knew him best as a person rather than as a voice within his fiction. Never having met Lawrence, never having suffered his attempts to write for his female acquaintances, and, apparently, never having recognized his audacious revisions of famous women's novels, Woolf could treat Lawrence's work relatively calmly. Although clearly interested in discussing him, Woolf rarely seems disturbed by Lawrence, which is understandable because of her deeply felt sense of primary connection to other women writers. With the one exception I have mentioned, Woolf does not write Lawrence into her fiction as a subject for her authorial control. Even in *Orlando,* Woolf's relation to him seems almost exclusively what Gérard Genette calls metatextual.[29] That is, some of Woolf's texts provide a commentary on Lawrence's, but no revisionary impulse is manifested. When Woolf alludes to Lawrence's material, she satirizes rather than reenvisions the situations and emotions he depicts. In *Orlando,* and possibly in *A Room of One's Own,* Woolf emphasizes her narratorial distance from his writings by presenting them as quotations from a male Other in contrast to whom the female author/text can be better understood. Her direct references to Lawrence, which are almost always part of a discourse on tradition, never have an argumentative tone or betray anxiety. In short, no matter how Woolf vacillated about him, she always constructed her Lawrence with serene detachment, in accordance with high modernism's demand for objectivity.

Her friend Katherine Mansfield was not so fortunate in her relationship to Lawrence or to his work, and so could not maintain a similarly exemplary unemotional position. She knew Lawrence personally as a rival for John Middleton Murry's attention and as her self-appointed advisor and spiritual guide, and she seems to have seen her texts' relationship to his in the same terms as her relationship to himself. To Mansfield, Lawrence was a rival with whom she was compelled to struggle and a powerful thinker whose dangerous philosophy she must refute. Her confrontations with Lawrence and his work within her own texts form a complicated, multi-toned intertext that Mansfield herself recognized was out of control.

The difference between Woolf's and Mansfield's approaches to Lawrence's fiction is most immediately evident if one compares Mansfield's notes for a review of *The Lost Girl* to Woolf's review.[30] The tone of Woolf's discussion is complacent. She concludes with the nicely qualified observation that "though the novel is probably better than any that will appear for the next six months, we are disappointed."[31] In contrast, the emotionality of Mansfield's notes reveals how threatening she found the book. Her diction suggests her desire for a morality-based legal struggle against the book. Although she wisely decided that her anger with Lawrence made her an unsuitable reviewer of his novel, Mansfield nonetheless feels that it "ought not to be allowed." Her reasons for wanting the book stopped seem to fall into two categories. On the one hand, she finds it "[a]ll false." Yet, on the other hand, she condemns it for (presumably realistically) depicting as admirable what she deems evil characters and behavior. She believes "the hero and heroine are non-human" and concludes that "this is life when one has blasphemed against the spirit of reverence."[32]

What Mansfield thinks Lawrence should have revered is unclear, but her most persistent complaint gives a clue. Mansfield finds the heroine Alvina's sensuality extremely objectionable. She refuses to believe that

Alvina could love the Italian countryside as Lawrence says she does, for Mansfield sees Alvina as nothing but an animal. She finds Lawrence's description of the physical sensation that tells Alvina she is pregnant "a kind of sinning against art," because "it is *not on this plane* that the emotions of others are conveyed to the imagination." Lawrence's sin against art seems to be that he creates a female character who experiences life physically despite her emotional sensitivity. Mansfield apparently wants Lawrence to have reverence for the spirituality of female experience and perhaps also for its tragic nature. His vision is of triumphant female sexuality, an intelligent woman's life built around sexual fulfillment. Mansfield's response is, "I feel a horror of it—a shrinking." This, she admits, is "not criticism," but it is a comprehensible response from a woman more interested in depicting the dangers than the triumphs of female sexual experience (*Scrapbook,* 183).

Such an agenda was fraught with risk for any woman writer who accepted impersonality as an artistic goal. Mansfield, like Woolf, feared that her condition as a woman might debase her art. Because maleness and universality have traditionally been equated while femaleness has been read as trivially personal, textual emphasis on women's experiences has often threatened a loss of literary status. To conventional readers, a woman writer's focus on women's sexual problems has virtually guaranteed that she would be read into her text and the text would be considered a veiled confession of the very failure as a woman that, within the patriarchal system, has explained women's rebellious desire to write. Fictional representations of women's sexual experiences were safest when they either conformed to conventional moral standards or affirmed the value of heterosexuality, as it has traditionally been socially constructed. But only when a female character lost specificity, possibly even becoming the figure for man, could she signify more than her female author's (stigmatized) tendency toward autobiography. Mansfield often stated her determination to purge all traces of her personality from her writing.

As Antony Alpers shows, Lawrence "almost certainly" influenced Mansfield's aim to go beyond the personal, but their visions of the impersonal in human life and in art differ markedly.[33] For Lawrence, the fundamental answer to personal problems could be found in sexual communion that transcended individual personalities. In contrast, Mansfield agreed with the Victorian notion that, for women especially, "suffering must become Love. . . . [one] must pass from personal love to greater love."[34] To Mansfield, impersonal love was the most universal of emotions, "greater" because it is given to "the whole of life," "*all* things."[35] Throughout his career, in such works as *The Ladybird, Women in Love, Kangaroo, The Plumed Serpent,* and *The Man Who Died,* Lawrence represents impersonal/universal love as a false value that leads to dangerously unhealthy repression of instincts. He often opposes it to a sexual connectedness that he considers impersonal because the participants are not interested in each other as individuals but as vehicles for deified male and female energies. For example, in *The Man Who Died,* the hero can only truly be reborn when, realizing that the chaste, universal love he asked of his disciples was "the corpse of their love," he desires physical contact with a woman through whom he touches Woman.[36] At least in theory, such sexual experiences are as impersonal as universal love, but Mansfield's own life and the ideology that she adopted to aid her depersonalization of it into fiction must have made her skeptical about the effects any sexual experiences could have on a sense of female identity.[37]

Devaluation of all types of adult sexual activity is pervasive in Mansfield's stories, in which fragile, dreamy, unworldly girls abound. These child-women cannot grow up into full participation in life, because the world of Mansfield's fiction offers no safety to women, as "The Little Governess" shows. Mansfield may well have been thinking of *Jane Eyre* while writing this story; certainly the title brings it to mind. Mansfield's story is a refutation of Brontë's, however. Mansfield's heroine is excessively punished for the sort of innocent empathy that repeatedly saves Jane by winning her the respect of those who can help her. A childlike, sensual joy in simple diversions makes both young women desirable, but desirability, which is both a boon and a danger to Jane, is simply the ruin of Mansfield's little governess. Mansfield implies that women must be sheltered in the seclusion of the Ladies' Cabin, away from the real world, or they will be destroyed by men.[38]

Mansfield cannot refute Lawrence's ideas as easily as she did Charlotte Brontë's because she and Lawrence had a great deal more in common with each other, as writers, than either had with Brontë. This becomes apparent if one follows Keith Cushman's lead and compares Mansfield's "Bliss" to Lawrence's "The Shadow in the Rose Garden," and the novel which seems to have inspired both stories, *Jane Eyre.*[39] All the three texts dramatize the disillusionment of characters who, at what should have been a time of romantic triumph, discover a prior sexual and romantic claim that cheats them out of the anticipated pleasure. The depictions of love, sex, and marriage in the two short stories are almost identical. Lawrence's and Mansfield's attitudes are similarly comparable to Brontë's.

In *Jane Eyre* the spoiling of Jane's wedding proves ultimately to her advantage because the revelation of Rochester's wife, and the events which follow, equalize Jane's and Rochester's positions. This is consonant with the general optimism of the novel, which emphasizes the gradual improvement of Jane's situation as she matures. In contrast, "Bliss" and "The Shadow in the Rose Garden" are testaments to bitterness and despair. Neither Mansfield nor Lawrence can read marriage as the resolution of conflict between men and women. While the flower-filled field in which Jane and Rochester are united symbolizes renewal and redemption, the blossoming pear tree in "Bliss" and the rose garden in Lawrence's story represent natural paradises from which the modern writers' characters have permanently fallen. Love as spontaneous, natural blooming is something they can observe or remember but not partake of. Charlotte Brontë diminishes Rochester's power and pride so that he and Jane can unite; Mansfield and Lawrence stress the illusory quality of union and the cruelty of marriage, which must be based on that illusion. Lawrence's couple submit stolidly to disillusionment, "shocked so much, they [become] impersonal, and no longer [hate] each other."[40] Here Lawrencian impersonality is not a value to strive for, but a tragic fate.

Had Lawrence's vision of life always been expressed as it is in "The Shadow in the Rose Garden," Mansfield might never have been moved to revise his texts. But "The Shadow in the Rose Garden" differs from the majority of Lawrence's stories and novels in its pessimism. Lawrence seldom describes bad marriages without prescribing ways they could be made more fulfilling. These prescriptions are founded on beliefs about sex that Mansfield found intensely upsetting because they went against her own view that sex disappointed and demeaned women, and also because Lawrence placed sex above universal love, which she made the touchstone of female identity. Like Woolf, Mansfield saw Lawrence swerve abruptly from transgressive attitudes she shared to conventionally misogynous pronouncements that she despised, and in response she moved from aligning herself with him against female precursors like Charlotte Brontë to adopting certain traditional female writing strategies as part of her revision of his texts.

Mansfield, annoyed by her perception that Lawrence's concept of female sexual experience was incompatible with hers, was subjected to the further irritation of seeing details of her own life incorporated into Lawrence's fiction. It is not surprising, then, that Mansfield felt compelled to respond to Lawrence's fiction in her own much more extensively than Woolf did. Three of her stories, "The Daughters of the Late Colonel," "The Garden-Party," and "At the Bay," seem to contain detailed responses to specific texts by Lawrence. All of these stories were completed during a period when Lawrence must have been frequently in Mansfield's thoughts. On 7 February 1920, when she was ill in a nursing home, Lawrence sent her a vicious letter in which he is said to have called her "a loathsome reptile" and told her "I loathe you. You revolt me stewing in your consumption. . . . I hope you will die."[41] Mansfield's reaction was equally extreme. She wrote to Middleton Murry, "the desire to hit him was so dreadful that I knew if I ever met him I must go away *at once*."[42] At the end of that year Mansfield struck back against what offended her in Lawrence's work, certainly with her notes on *The Lost Girl* and probably also with "The Daughters of the Late Colonel," which she finished the same month, December 1920.

In her notes on *The Lost Girl,* Mansfield refers to "the rotten, rubbishy scene of the woman in labour" (*Scrapbook,* 182). The woman is Mrs. Tuke, whom Lawrence introduces with a description of her collection of odd household objects.[43] As Mrs. Tuke endures her labor pains, she is attended by the nurse Alvina, who is being serenaded by her lover, Cicio. Mansfield seems annoyed that Lawrence depicts Mrs. Tuke as so fascinated by the sexually charged situation that she asks to have Cicio brought to her bedside to distract her. In Mansfield's story, the Colonel's daughters, Josephine and Constantia Pinner, are distressed by a nurse's hearty appetite for sensual pleasures. She tells them that she enjoyed working for "Lady Tukes" because " 'she had such a dainty little contrayvance for the buttah. It was a silvah Cupid . . . holding a tayny fork. . . . he bent down and speared you a piece.' "[44] The nurse and her employer's name might be coincidence, but the ridiculous cupid and the greed for butter strongly suggest that Mansfield is making fun of Lawrence. The toy cupid and his little spearing fork, she seems to say, not the feral Italian and his passion, are the frivolous rich woman's and sensual nurse's concept of "quite a gayme" ("Daughters," 466). For Lawrence, desire overcomes all considerations of class and national differences. Mansfield's nurse's desire is structured by her bourgeois aspirations; she seeks her fulfillment in luxury foods and dainty contrivances, not unrestrained sexual activity. Mansfield puts her view of purely sensual life as a vulgar buffoonishness in complicity with consumerism against Lawrence's vision of self-surrender to sexuality as mysteriously beautiful and destructive of social hierarchies.

Mansfield's conflation of Alvina-as-repressed-daughter with the old-maidish housekeeper Miss Pinnegar in the characters of the Pinners says much about her fatalism. Like *Jane Eyre*, *The Lost Girl* is essentially optimistic. In this novel, environment, time, and habit count for nothing against sexual energy. Freed by her father's death, Alvina transforms herself from a thin, nervous, aging girl to a "handsome, reposeful woman" (*LG*, 300). Mansfield's Constantia and Josephine Pinner also long for adventure and fulfillment but find only ironic answers to their questions about what will happen "Now? Now?" ("Daughters," 483). The future will be an even emptier version of the past. Josephine's childlike belief that a feather boa in a photograph is a "a snake that had killed their mother" hints at a symbolic truth ("Daughters," 482). The coils of impoverished gentility are inescapable; constricting lives kill. But since all men in Mansfield's texts uphold the Law of the Father, which alone can confer power and meaning, release from the patriarch just means being cast adrift.

A second set of details in Mansfield's story also suggests its connection to Lawrence's fiction. The title "The Daughters of the Late Colonel" is reminiscent of "The Daughters of the Vicar," Lawrence's reworking of themes from George Eliot's *Mill on the Floss*. The families in both short stories are very much alike in their poverty, pretensions, subjugation to an irascible father, and lack of social contact with any other men except clergymen. The two younger sisters particularly resemble each other; Constantia, like Louisa, is sensual and seems formed for a better life. The major difference in the stories is that the sensual daughter's escape is a possibility to Lawrence because of his differing view of the relationship between the sexes. In both stories, the men seem a different species from the women. But Louisa can break through to enigmatic Alfred physically. Their embrace is not only a form of communication; it begins both a bond (their engagement) and the dissolution of bonds (to Louisa's family). In Alfred we might read an idealized version of Lawrence's liminal function for his women followers. Identification/connection with this man disconnects woman from her Victorian gender role and so allows her to find a new, more satisfying self.

In Mansfield's texts inability to communicate verbally cannot be remedied with physical contact, and men cannot figure women's suppressed selfhood. Rather, male presence suppresses the feminine, and linguistic failure condemns women to solitude. Josephine and Constantia comically misunderstand their nephew Cyril and find their father a terrifying mystery, but the incident that seems emblematic of their relations with the opposite sex is their discovery of the illegible note from the mysterious admirer at Eastborne ("Daughters," 482). As in "The Little Governess," and "Je Ne Parle Pas Français," lack of a common language represents an unbreachable barrier between men and women. Marriage is a possibility only when women can read the masculine script and speak the masculine language, but to do so is to lose feminine identity. As in the dialogic novels on which Dale Bauer bases her revision of Bakhtin's theory, in Mansfield's fiction women's failures to understand the dominant discourse or to find an interpretive community able to receive their own speech "defamiliarize the prevailing ideologies" for the reader, exposing the ways they block reciprocal communication between the sexes.[45] If "The Daughters of the Vicar" is Lawrence's refutation of Eliot's pessimism in *The Mill on the Floss,* "The Daughters of the Late Colonel" is Mansfield's reassertion of that pessimism.

It would be an unjust oversimplification of the difference between Lawrence's and Mansfield's narratives to say that she is pessimistic and pragmatic while he is optimistic and mystical. However, when it is in evidence, her optimism frequently seems informed by a somewhat Victorian exaltation of female renunciation. Many of Mansfield's stories show a sense of redemptive mystery very much like George Eliot's. Mansfield sees the material world as the locus of failure and betrayal, but seems to believe in a feminized spiritual realm that transcends these dangers. Calvin Bedient says that to Eliot, "the spirit is identified with duration, the flesh with the ephemeral."[46] In both Mansfield's and Eliot's fiction, spiritual escape occupies the place that escape through sexual communion does in Lawrence's. Mansfield's ideology may seem reactionary if we read her heroines' rejection of sexual life in favor of universal love as an affirmation of the Victorian demand for female selflessness. But Nancy K. Miller has shown that what seems to be a giving up of the self in such women's novels as *The Mill on the Floss* may actually represent the female author's refusal of patriarchy's "division of labor that grants men the world and women [romantic] love."[47] In choosing to reinscribe her female precursors' plot of romantic renunciation, Mansfield often seems to be wholeheartedly rejecting the patriarchal edict that woman's pleasure must come through her love for a man, an edict that Lawrence seemingly accepts, although his texts' resisting female voices defamiliarize it. The difference between Lawrence's and Mansfield's sorts of optimistic mysticism can be understood through a comparison of Mansfield's "Garden-Party" (completed in October 1921) and Lawrence's "Odour of Chrysanthemums" (1911).

Both stories focus on a woman's reactions to a young laborer's accidental death. A scene in which the woman's viewing of the corpse helps her understand life is central to each story. But the relationship between life and death in "The Garden-Party" is antithetical to that in "Odour of Chrysanthemums." Almost every detail of Mansfield's story seems chosen to contradict Lawrence's. Everything natural in the setting of "Odour of Chrysanthemums" is consistent with the despair of the protagonist, Elizabeth Bates: "The fields [are] dreary and forsaken," the leaves are "withered" on the trees, and the chrysanthemums are "ragged" and "pale." Elizabeth and her children sit "almost lost in darkness."[48] Life seems on the verge of being extinguished. In "The Garden-Party," however, the unquenchable resurgence of the golden light/life of summer is forecast in images of brightness standing out from darkness: karaka-trees with "their broad, gleaming leaves, and their clusters of yellow fruit," "two tiny spots of sun" making stars, and the protagonist Laura's "black hat trimmed with gold daisies."[49]

In the "Odour of Chrysanthemums" marriage symbolizes life and divorce death. But despite the emphasis on darkness, loss, and despair the story is not pessimistic. If marriage synecdochically represents ordinary life experience, in its most perfect state it also promises immortality. The old mother-in-law, as mythic wise woman, frames her daughter-in-law's experience as a cautionary tale by suggesting that, had the younger Bateses been "truly" married, their union could have survived death. "The Garden-Party," as Sandra Gilbert and Susan Gubar point out, concerns the felicitous separation of the sexes; Laura gains strength and knowledge from the death both because she does not know the man and, implicitly, because he is a man.[50] His death, which separates him from Laura forever, helps her find a higher sense of commonality and connection. Just as darkness and light represent complementary values rather than irreconcilable opposites in Mansfield's texts, the death emphasizes oneness.

Laura's visit to the dead man resolves the problem of her attraction to workers, which could have introduced tensions into the seemingly presexual rapport between Laura and her twin brother. Although separated by their sex roles, Laura and Laurie are struggling to share perceptions of life. Like Woolf's Rachel and Helen, they remain distant from the world they wish to understand; they go on "prowls" together through the lane of cottages because "one must *see* everything" ("Garden-Party," 542; emphasis mine). The dead man is a worker with whom Laura can experience a truly "marvellous," because purely visual, communion, which can then be transferred to the brother ("Garden-Party," 548). Representations of women attempting to attain subjectivity through turning their gaze on the world of men have received much attention in feminist criticism, especially in film theory where some critics have persuasively argued that, as Naomi Scheman claims, "we [women], somehow, impossible as it may seem, do it [look at others] in creative rebellion, as feminists."[51] Lawrence's story is informed by his belief in the necessity of the male vision and so stresses the urgency of uniting fully since male death ends all redemptive possibility. Mansfield's implies that the death of the man will bring sweet resolution by freeing the woman's "loving" look, which can become all-embracing because of the removal of any threat of degrading sexual embraces and depressing failures at verbal communication across gender lines. Lawrence emphasizes the importance of marriage as a grappling with life; Mansfield reveals the power of death to provide her heroine with a transcendent period of escape from imprisonment by sexuality.

Lawrence's depiction of Mansfield as Gudrun in *Women in Love* harshly criticizes, as simple dishonesty, Mansfield's strategies to make her texts seem impersonal. Gudrun's art is purposefully disconnected from her personality. The miniature, painted wooden figures she produces are amusing because they are odd, quaint in a way that she, with her dramatic clothes and forceful presence, is not. That Gerald supposes them to be savage carving rather than the work of the sophisticated, chic Gudrun is indicative of the hugeness of the gulf between her work and life. When Ursula insists that the artist's work should be a reflection of his life, Gudrun argues: "The two things are quite permanently apart. . . . My art stands in another world, I am in this world." To Lawrence, this attitude is immoral because it makes artists dangerously indifferent to their own and the world's problems. Lawrence believes "the world of art is only the truth about the real world."[52]

It seems worth noting that such claims about the truthfulness of art have been fundamental to the development of feminist criticism. As Jardine points out, "Feminism, while infinite in its variations, is finally rooted in the belief that women's truth-in-experience-and-reality is and has always been different from men's and that it as well as its artifacts and productions have consequently been devalued and always already de-legitimized in patriarchal culture."[53] In demanding that women's art address this problem by narrating truths about the author's own experience, Lawrence anticipates one prescription often made by early feminist critics.[54] In *Women in Love,* however, one of the primary purposes of Ursula's truth telling is to reveal the evil of the false artist, Gudrun, whom Lawrence is (and was) generally considered to have based on Mansfield.

It seems impossible that this attack on her work and the ethics underlying it was not bothering Mansfield as she wrote "At the Bay," a continuation of the family story begun in "Prelude." Lawrence's novel was published in June 1921; Mansfield's story was completed in September of that year. While working on "At the Bay" in early August, Mansfield wrote to Richard Murry and to Brett about *Women in Love,* which had been sent to Middleton Murry for review.[55]

As befits a memoir of childhood, "Prelude" deals primarily with the contrast between childlike and adult perceptions. Mansfield's sympathies are clearly with the former. Little Kezia Burnell's innocence, warmth, and sensitivity to beauty make her the most attractive character, except perhaps for her grandmother, Mrs. Fairfield, who treats all the others as her children and has no identity outside her motherliness. Mrs. Fairfield's daughters, Linda and Beryl, are both most endearing when most childlike. Stanley Burnell's adult preoccupations appear crass in contrast to their delicate dreams. He smugly feels he has "bought the lovely day . . . got it chucked in dirt cheap with the house and ground," while Beryl imagines a young admirer tiptoeing through the flowers and calling her "little girl." Yet, one is never given the sense that maturation must bring corruption and loss. Rather Beryl's vague sense that something "rich, mysterious, and good" lies beyond everyday "false life" allows the reader to hope the younger characters may escape from the coarseness and limitations of a marriage like the Burnells' into something greater.[56]

Mansfield's need to refute Lawrence's ideas makes the life that her characters have entered in "At the Bay" much less promising. "Prelude" and *Women in Love* both create an impression that all of human life is moving toward some renewal. As Lawrence described it, his novel is "end-of-the-world," but "the beginning of the new world too."[57] As in "Prelude," where fresh, affirmative child-vision challenges Stanley's foolish but deathly commodification of life, in *Women in Love,* the survival of Ursula's and Birkin's love and marriage allows for hope. Lawrence voices, as Birkin's thought, the doctrine of immortality only hinted at in "Odour of Chrysanthemums": "Those who die, and dying still can love, still believe, do not die. They live still in the beloved" (*WL,* 471). This concept of immortality depends on a fluidity of identity that would make it possible for one to live on in another. Interestingly, it is not the lover who (conventionally) preserves the memory of the beloved, but rather the beloved in whom the lover remains, as if passion had unsettled the boundaries between the two. Love is represented as a force that disrupts the sense of a unified self and makes possible new configurations of presence. Instead of self and Other, we glimpse one-within-another. In contrast, "At the Bay" depicts a world of fixed identities. Social roles and gender relations seem as old and immune to change as in the pastoral opening, which introduces shepherd and dairy-girl as the figures for male and female.

In *Women in Love,* Lawrence advocates a new mode of being in which partners break each other free from an old and disintegrating world. In "At the Bay," Mansfield answers him that there is no new world and no new way to live. The two paths out of conventional life that Birkin explores, sensuality for its own sake and sexuality as communion, are dead ends in Mansfield's fiction. One must literally look beyond human relationships to find moments of transcendence. In "Prelude," Mansfield uses two opposing modes of perception, child and adult vision, to suggest the possibility of a richer life outside traditional social roles, but in "At the Bay," she sets the female viewpoint against the male to reveal the inescapability of these roles. In *Women in Love*, Birkin and Ursula's love, including their fierce struggles to find new identities through each other, shows that men and women can meet outside their social roles— at least in fiction. Mansfield counters Lawrence's novel's conclusion by presenting antagonism between the sexes as part of the unchangeable comedy of human folly and selfishness rather than as a portent of the collapse of the dominant social structures. The activities of the Samuel Josephs suggest that part of the function of social rules is to contain this natural antagonism. Mrs. Samuel Joseph and her "lady-help" draw up and supervise a daily program of competitions for the children, because otherwise, "like savages," "the boys [pour] water down the girl's necks or the girls [try] to put little black crabs in the boy's pockets."[58] That Linda's and Stanley's passions are restrained by the demands of their (gender-determined) social roles seems beneficial, for they, too, are monstrously selfish.

It is in her depiction of women, however, that Mansfield's response to Lawrence is bitterest. Mrs. Kember and Beryl are evocative of Gudrun and Ursula. An ugly image powerfully connects Mrs. Kember to Gudrun. Gudrun sees herself as the female counterpart of the evil artist Loerke, whom Birkin describes as "a rat in the river of corruption," "the wizard rat that swims ahead" (*WL*, 418–19). Beryl realizes Mrs. Kember looks "like a horrible caricature" of her sinister husband, as she swims "away quickly, quickly, like a rat" ("Bay," 277). Beryl is reminiscent of Ursula not only because of her soft, conventionally feminine prettiness and dreamy romanticism, but because of her feelings about the cynical, outcast Mrs. Kember. Like Gudrun and Ursula, one is somehow played out and beyond development while the other is full of beautiful life and promise. But just as Ursula is "always forced to assent to Gudrun's pronouncements, even when she [is] not in accord altogether," Beryl accepts Mrs. Kember's ethics even though she feels "poisoned by this cold woman" (*WL*, 15; "Bay," 277). Like Ursula, Beryl is shown to be right to distrust her female would-be mentor's advice, but Mansfield's exploration of the consequences of contact between feminine disillusion and feminine innocence again revises Lawrence's vision.

In Lawrence's view, a woman can go into the depths of dissolution, but a man cannot. When Gudrun transfers her attention from Gerald, she enters a realm in which "there were no more *men* . . . only . . .

creatures like Loerke" (*WL*, 443). This acceptance of corruption "blasts" Gerald, "withers [his] consciousness," leaves him "shrivelled as if struck by electricity" (*WL*, 430–31). To Mansfield, it is the woman, Mrs. Kember, who is "burnt out and withered" by the journey into corruption, while Harry Kember has the smooth, masklike indestructibility that Lawrence gives Gudrun ("Bay," 275–76). As Susan Gubar notes, Mrs. Kember reflects Mansfield's apprehension of the corrupting influence on women of "male modes of relating to women."[59] Her perverse machinations blight Beryl's romantic dreams. Apparently in collusion with his wife, Harry Kember entices Beryl into a night in which "the shadows were like bars of iron" ("Bay," 298). Once again, Mansfield rejects Lawrence's idea that it is possible to escape from the falseness of the conventional world into self-realization and fulfillment. Beyond the gate of the confining role her family thrusts upon her, Beryl can only find another cage. By refusing to become another Linda or Mrs. Fairfield, Beryl turns into Harry's "cold little devil" ("Bay," 299). Whether or not Beryl gives herself sexually is not really important; sex and even marriage have not saved Mrs. Kember from spiritual destruction. To Mansfield the dissolute, cold, cynical woman and the blooming, open, hopeful woman are not two sisters, two possibilities, as they are to Lawrence, but two stages in the development of women who leave socially prescribed paths.

Because Mansfield and Lawrence were so familiar with each other's attempts to describe female experience, attacks on the other's vision almost inevitably became part of each writer's fiction. That Mansfield, like Woolf, would counter as strongly as she could Lawrence's insistence on sexual consummation as the solution to women's problems was predictable. Although Lawrence and Mansfield both seem to believe in essential differences between women and men, their concepts of the structuring of these differences is not the same. To Lawrence, female and male are complementary, interdependent, and, to a certain extent, as in Birkin's theory of immortality through love, interpenetrating. Because, according to Lawrence's philosophy, women and men need each other's presence, power, and action in order to find their own subject positions, ideal contact between them is always opposed to traditional gender relations in which woman is objectified. At its best, sexual intercourse is a form of communication between two subjects and thus a radical force against the construction of gender by society. To Mansfield, sexual contact cannot involve real intercourse because she sees gender difference as opposition. In her texts, male activity demands female subjection. Male power is achieved at the expense of woman. It is certainly possible to gender these differences in textual representations of sexuality and so attribute Lawrence's to masculinist ideology.[60] But if we consider Mansfield and Lawrence's disagreement in the context of female traditions, in which they themselves place it through their revisionary allusions to Victorian texts, we can see it as reflective of a longstanding conflict within feminist discourse. For instance, in such self-contradicting texts as *Wuthering Heights* and *Shirley* as well as in the currently ongoing debates among feminists over pornography and politically motivated celibacy, tension is evident between the desire to imagine female sexual experience as, at least potentially, rebelliously deconstructive and the desire to reject it as inevitably constructed by and contributive to patriarchy.

Nonetheless, it was to be expected that both Woolf and Mansfield would be irritated by Lawrence's pretensions to speak for women about sexuality and that they would frequently react to him in a way best characterized as contradictory. After all, he is encroaching on women's literary territory. What might seem remarkable, however, is that Woolf and Mansfield took Lawrence's attempts to articulate women's experience as seriously as they did. Several texts produced by each of the women implicitly recognize Lawrence's connections with female precursors like Charlotte Brontë. Woolf's comments on Lawrence and his work focus on the analogies between his marginalized situation, and consequent challenges to literary conventions, and those of the woman writer. Mansfield's revisionary responses to Lawrence center around their shared beliefs in the failure of language to connect woman and man and in woman's entrapment in constricting social roles. All three have faith in a female essence that is always in opposition to femininity as constructed by male language and the social world it creates. Mansfield and Woolf suggest, by their responses to his work, that they took an interest in Lawrence not because he was their opposite, but because he was a participant in their traditions. If it is difference that makes them "rise braced and purified" from contemplation of Lawrence's vision, it seems to be a sense of literary connection that makes this contemplation so productive and profound.

Because of their literary aims and the reception of their texts, Woolf,

Lawrence, and Mansfield met intellectually, more or less, as equals. Woolf was interested in a separate female literary form (*Room,* 79–81). Mansfield revealed, in story after story, her doubts about women's ability to decode the male language. And Lawrence wrote, "We may speak the same verbal language, men and women. . . . But *whatever* a man says, his meaning is something quite different and changed when it passes through a woman's ears."[61] But, while they might have had more confidence in the understanding of the female reader, they still wrote for men as well as women, as if they believed that both could read the same texts similarly. Despite the innovations in their use of language and narrative structure, their works diverge from the male norm more in theme than form. Like their female Victorian precursors, they treated women's fiction as a thread woven into the whole fabric of literature. While this thread was always recognizable, often because it was colored in contrast to that of the dominant tradition, it was seen only within the pattern made by the whole. This inclusive attitude is shown in the male-female twinning motif in such works intentionally centered on women's experience and perceptions, as *Mrs. Dalloway* and "The Garden-Party." Accordingly, the fiction of all three writers was received by their contemporaries as making noteworthy contributions both to understanding of the increasingly interesting topic of female experience and to the creation of an innovative modernist body of texts. The discourse contained in their responses to each other helped shape modern women's literature in a sense from the outside, because of their view of it as contained within a vaster literary tradition that always contributed to its meaning. In this way they stand in contrast to H. D. and Anaïs Nin, each of whom could be considered a sort of literary feminist separatist because of her efforts to free women's use of language and literature from male systems of signification.

Lawrence's literary relationship with H. D. at first resembled his with Mansfield. Since both H. D. and Lawrence were publishing in *Poetry,* they knew each other as poets before they met, just as Lawrence and Mansfield had known each other as writers of short stories.[62] As had happened with Mansfield, in the beginning they took a friendly interest in each other's work. He gave both large doses of advice. Indeed, his meddlesomeness in regard to H. D.'s poetry was so extreme that Scott deems it censorship.[63] Mansfield and H. D. both handled Lawrence's bossiness by retreating from him, a response he considered devious. His suspicion of Mansfield became so profound that he refused to believe that she was seriously ill, instead considering her a self-dramatizing hypochondriac, until right before her death. Toward the end of his friendship with H. D., he wrote, "Feeling sorry for her, one almost melts. But I *don't* trust her" (LL, 3:308). As with Mansfield, mutual suspicions between H. D. and Lawrence made collaboration impossible and would deeply shade both writers' literary representations of each other. Here the resemblances between Lawrence's relationships with the two women end, however.

From the beginning, the affection between Lawrence and H. D. was much more intense than the tentative friendliness Lawrence and Mansfield offered each other. H. D.'s relationship with Lawrence began on fairly egalitarian terms. They exchanged manuscripts and discussed their poetry, and they shared beliefs in utopian communities, general perfectionism, and a mystical dimension underlying the quotidian.[64] But, unlike Mansfield, H. D. seems almost unambivalently to have wanted a male mentor all her life. She writes of this need extensively in *Tribute to Freud,* where she repeatedly connects Lawrence, Freud, and her father. In 1914, when H. D. first met Lawrence, she was in the process of breaking with Ezra Pound, who had dominated her emotionally and intellectually since her late adolescence.[65] When they met again in 1917, living in the same house on Mecklenburgh Square, her estrangement from her husband, Richard Aldington, was already beginning and she found Lawrence's attentions seductive. Although he might simply have meant to add her to his collection of female admirers, like Brett and Carswell, who compensated him for Frieda's criticism and independence, she rewrote him into her ongoing family romance in which father/lovers lovingly supported her creativity.

It seems necessary to mention here a legend that has developed about Lawrence and H. D. Various critics repeat the speculations that H. D. was the model for the priestess of Isis in Lawrence's novella *The Man Who Died* and that it was written for her. In her critical biography of H. D., Janice Robinson adds, "It seems to have been widely known within her circle but only rarely acknowledged publicly that Lawrence's references to Isis in his writing were veiled references to H. D."[66] Moreover, Robinson theorizes not only that Lawrence and H. D. were lovers in 1914 and resumed their affair secretly in 1918, but that Lawrence was the father of H. D.'s daughter Perdita. In Robinson's opinion,

Lady Chatterley's Lover is a roman à clef about the clandestine love affair of Lawrence and H. D. All of these speculations seem equally unlikely. Stephen Guest, H. D.'s admirer and the nephew of Lawrence's friend Barbara Low, gave H. D. the information about her part in *The Man Who Died*. His idea that she was the priestess of Isis might have been a sudden inspiration or a calculated attempt to please, but it was not supported by any known evidence.[67] Priestess figures appear in *The White Peacock, The Trespasser, Sons and Lovers,* and "Shades of Spring," all written before Lawrence met H. D. Although all of Lawrence's fictions have some autobiographical content, none are true romans à clef. Rather, as he did with Mansfield in *Women in Love,* Lawrence often incorporated his acquaintances' ideas into his texts so that he could debate them.

Lawrence's use of H. D. in *Aaron's Rod* indicates that he ranked her intellectual life much lower than Mansfield's. H. D. was the physical model for Julia, "a tall stag of a thing."[68] Julia's role in *Aaron's Rod* is slight. The brief "ritual dance" in which she moves "sliding, waving, crouching in a *pas seul*" in "worship" of a tree (*AR,* 44), is reminiscent of Gudrun's dance before the cattle in *Women in Love* and Anna's dance to the moon in *The Rainbow.* But whereas Anna and Gudrun experience mystical connection with the objects of their worship, and feel "unconscious sensation," "voluptuous ecstasy," and "rapt trance," Julia's dance seems forced and artificial; rather than hypnotizing or horrifying the onlookers it makes them laugh (*WL,* 159). Unlike Gudrun, who offers the most powerful and successful opposition to Birkin's values in *Women in Love,* Julia is not significant enough to debate Lilly, the prophetic figure in *Aaron's Rod.* She has a bad marriage and "a nervous kind of *amour* . . . based on soul sympaty and emotional excitement," which function like the romantic problems of Halliday in *Women in Love* to show the emptiness of life for fashionable Londoners. While Gudrun's hyperaware intellect makes her a frightening destructive force, "Julia's got no mind"; she is only a silly body indecisively drifting after men whose "art matters" (*AR,* 62, 63, 66). Lawrence struggled with Mansfield's art, but he seems merely to have rejected H. D.'s. He began by thinking, "Mrs Aldington has a few good poems" (LL, 2:203). But, when he became more familiar with her attitudes and work, he mocked her with comments like, "Hilda Aldington says to me . . . why am I not in Love with a tree," and "Hilda Aldington says [some of my poems] won't do at all; they are not *eternal,* not sublimated: too much body and emotions" (LL, 2:645; 3:102).

When he was most fond of her, Lawrence compared H. D. to "Magdalen at her feet-washing," because he felt that she represented a "world of knowledge," "deeper" than that of compartmentalized intellect and sexuality, but in an "unproud, subservient, cringing, bad fashion" (LL, 2:180). Her willingness to join the women who treated him as a prophetic leader pleased him, but the inclination toward dependence that made her do so did not. Lawrence seems never to have understood that the kind of friendship he demanded, based on complete acceptance of his dominance, could only come from the sort of dependent personalities that he despised. While she submitted to his will, Lawrence had an affectionate contempt for H. D. After she escaped from him, with Cecil Gray, he seemed to lose interest in her except as an example of what he would term a lost girl. As an artist, she seems to have ceased to exist for him.

Consequently H. D. had even more motivation than Mansfield to respond to Lawrence's use of her in his fiction, but her self-defense had a different aim. While Mansfield defended herself against the accusation that she was an evil artist, H. D. needed to show that she *was* an artist, not just a confused follower of artists. Mansfield defends her vision while H. D. defends herself. This difference may explain why *Bid Me to Live,* her thinly fictive memoir of her wartime sufferings with Richard Aldington and affair with Lawrence, focuses on the superior artistic sensibility of the heroine, Julia.[69] Like most autobiographical *Künstlerroman,* it is expansive on the topic of the formation of her poetics. Here we can see what Susan Stanford Friedman calls "a self-analysis that paralleled Freud's own in *The Interpretation of Dreams,*" as H. D. writes her way toward repair of her "shattered self."[70] On this level, *Bid Me to Live* is fascinating because of the depth of H. D.'s understanding of how her artistic relationship to Lawrence helped her construct a female artist figure whose creative power was primary and independent.

Therefore, H. D.'s response to Lawrence is, in at least one way, more in line with intentionally feminist literary practice than Mansfield's is. She represents the struggle between herself and Lawrence as a conflict between male and female poetics. The outcome of this conflict is of vital importance because the survival of female creativity depends, in *Bid Me to Live,* on its triumph over male creativity. In H. D.'s novel, men choose their own social and sexual roles and then assign roles to their women.

When Rafe (Aldington) enlists in the army and so becomes "another person," Julia is forced into the role of soldier's wife (*BML*, 16). His behavior makes both her and his mistress, Bella, "simply abstractions . . . WOMAN of the period, the same one" (*BML*, 103). A woman may try to escape, through the "loophole" of art, from the "biological catch" that allows men to make her into a sexual type—"old maid," "affable *haus-frau*," or whore—but, even as an artist, if she remains within the patriarchal system, she will be both "man-woman" and mere woman with a woman's vulnerability to male definition. For instance, in a religious skit, Rico, the Lawrence figure, makes her play the tree of life, so she must run away from him to keep from becoming his "greatmother," the energy source of his work (*BML*, 182). When her lover, Vane (Cecil Gray), tells her to pick a room to work in, he has "particularized her status" and she can write; when he tells the housekeeper that Julia is his sister, he makes her "Nobody" and she loses confidence in her work (*BML*, 161, 171–72, 176).

The novel traces Julia's discovery of how she can be "saved" from the (male) powers that negate or block her art (*BML*, 10). Initially she imagines literary alignment as a part of her heterosexuality. She calls her first lover "her first poet" (*BML*, 41). When she feels happy with Rafe, it is because "[t]hey completed each other" artistically, and "[w]riting letters to [him] and writing poetry go along in the same sort of groove" (*BML*, 34, 44). Other men are easy to escape, but Rico is not, because "[i]f any of them mattered, it was obviously Rico" (*BML*, 86). He is "the true artist" who arranges the others like "dummies" for his show (*BML*, 79, 91). She realizes that she is writing for Rico (*BML*, 51–52, 80). Yet he puts unfair constraints on her art; "Rico could write elaborately on the woman mood, describe women to their marrow in his writing; but if she turned round, wrote the Orpheus part of her Orpheus-Eurydice sequence, he snapped back, 'Stick to the woman-consciousness'" (*BML*, 62). Julia cannot reject Rico because his approval has empowered her, but she cannot coexist with him because his maleness gives him unbreakable authority over her. Her solution is to steal his power for herself by giving him a (subordinate) place in her imaginative but not in her physical life.

Similarly H. D. met Lawrence after his death in a way that she could perfectly control, in her fiction. There she makes his mythology her own. In his book, she is the negligible nervous Julia whom the Lawrencian Lilly scorns, but in hers, she and Lawrence are perfectly, mystically mated.[71] She becomes the heroine of *The Ladybird* and he her "night husband," through her use of that novella's imagery. Like Daphne and Psanek, they are both "burnt out . . . and white." Her comparison of him to the Dionysian "wild-cat" echoes his repeated description of Psanek as a "little wild-cat." She decides he is "Dis of the under-world, the husband of Persephone . . . her husband" (*BML*, 141). But she does not sink under the earth in his grasp. She dominates it as the " 'priestess' as Rico called her" of *The Man Who Died*, a "wise-woman with her witch-ball, the world," experiencing "the sex-union they so vaunted" in "another [superior] element" (*BML*, 147, 148–49). In this element she becomes Lady Chatterley, "waiting for" Lawrence outside "a simple little house in the forest" while he chops wood (*BML*, 173). But this waiting, this separation from male perception and definitive power, is more complete and completing for her than a reunion could be.

Gilbert and Gubar describe this strategy of drawing empowerment from male defeat, absence, or death as typical of women modernists. As in Mansfield's "Garden-Party," "it is as if the vanquished [man's] power had been victoriously transmitted to *her*."[72] The difference is, however, that in H. D.'s novel it is not a male stranger, but the double, the male twin, who must die in order for female vision and language to emerge. In *Tribute to Freud*, H. D. confesses, "I envied these women who have written memoirs of D. H. Lawrence, feeling that they had found him a sort of guide or master."[73] In *Bid Me to Live*, she charts her journey beyond dependence on him to confirm the value of what she believes are the female perceptions that inform her work. Their shared belief that "it is the intuitive woman-mood that matters" is enormously important to her, but her understanding that she must convey that mood in her own way is even more important (*BML*, 62). To "catch [his] mannerisms, [his] style of writing, [his] style of thinking, even" is unacceptable to her (*BML*, 176). But because she cannot entirely leave behind his affirmations of woman's power, she goes "away together" with him in her fiction (*BML*, 183). DuPlessis charts H. D.'s journey from "models of coequality," in which the male retains the patriarchal position and the female is matriarchal in complement, to a concept of her speaking position as that of "a virgin with maternal power . . . who also has access to male power in her person." Within H. D.'s enactment of the role of seduced and adoring daughter, psychoanalytic transference is transmuted into a transfer of power whereby woman's Otherness is redefined as superior authority.[74] *Bid Me to Live* is not only an admission and passionate explanation of Lawrence's influence on its author, it is also the ground on which she brings that influence under her control.

H. D.'s, Mansfield's, and Woolf's responses to Lawrence all give the impression that at various times they saw him as set apart from other male writers. For Woolf the uniqueness of his genius seems to come from the similarity of his situation to that of a woman writer. Because she finds his efforts to describe female experience inadequate, a surrender to received ideas, Woolf cannot believe that he is any more than a brilliant failure. In her work, his failure is depicted as a betrayal of women; he could have helped bridge the chasm between men's and women's literary traditions but did not. In many of the texts in which she refers or alludes to him, one has the sense of Woolf repeatedly turning away from Lawrence and directing her attention back to the women writers whose strategies and innovations she could admire with far fewer reservations. A more complex sense of Lawrence as betrayer emerges from Mansfield's revisions of his writings. It is not that he goes over to the other side, but that he uses his inside knowledge of women's lives to promote what she sees as insanely false teachings. H. D. overcomes her anger at Lawrence's didacticism because she feels that the subjects of his artistic attention are "deified," and she sees this process as connected to his recognition of the supremacy of a great female power (*BML,* 181–82). She brings him into her texts as a show of her own artistic power and the triumph of female creativity. But all three women consider Lawrence's relationship to women's literature so important that they perpetuate it by giving him a place in their writings.

Because they were his contemporaries and they had to fight against the privileging of male speech, they understood differences between their representations of female experience and his as threats to their authority. Even when answering him after his death, they had to meet him within the context of their shared experiences of the world of the twenties and thirties. In the work of H. D., who lived long enough to achieve the greatest historical perspective, reasons that women might like Lawrence's fiction are delineated more clearly than they are in Mansfield's or Woolf's. All three women, however, make their reasons for objecting to Lawrence much more evident than the reasons they found him impossible to dismiss.

Anaïs Nin's *D. H. Lawrence: An Unprofessional Study* is the sort of wholehearted appreciation of Lawrence that could probably have been written only by a woman who became a writer too late to see him as a competitor and too early to hear of him as an acknowledged master. Nin's book was one of the first favorable commentaries on Lawrence's work to appear after his death.[75] Much of *An Unprofessional Study* is devoted to discussion of Lawrence's depictions of women. Although her study of Lawrence is unprofessional in its subjectivity and impressionistic organization, Nin clarifies what she found useful in Lawrence's fictional treatment of women, especially women artists. Nin is particularly impressed by Lawrence's "complete realization of the feelings of women."[76]

Her understanding of Lawrence is opposed to Woolf's; rather than believing that he imposes the system of traditional patriarchal values on his fictions, she declares, "His philosophy . . . is a *transcending of ordinary values,* which were to be vivified and fecundated by instincts and intuitions. . . . Lawrence has no system, unless his constant shifting of values can be called a system: a *system of mobility. . . .* Lawrence's world is liberated . . . from dead ideals." Nin believes that this approach to writing is particularly congenial to women because "[w]omen are intuitive." In Nin's view, many distinctive aspects of Lawrence's fiction come from his intuitive approach and so make his work especially accessible to women and difficult for men. She discusses in detail the similarities between Lawrence's style and what she believes is the mode of perception natural to women, noting not only his "suspicion of the intellect," but also his richly textured descriptions of women's clothes, his close attention to "little occupations of women," and his "sensitiveness" to flowers.[77] Nin, unlike Lawrence, does not seem to distinguish the stereotypical attributes that culture assigns to women from the attributes that culture decrees women must repress. Conventional femininity is represented, in her texts, as an undistorted reflection of female essence. Yet she gives us a profoundly feminized Lawrence.

Nin's discussion of the femininity of Lawrence's style both anticipates a major trend in later feminist theory and raises important questions about the way that theory attributes gender to language and literary texts. Nin's belief that styles of language usage can be classified as masculine or feminine has affinities with French theories of *l'écriture féminine.* Although there are major disagreements within the articulations of these theories, they have in common a focus on the female body and female sexuality as metaphoric representations, or even as the actual sources, of a form of presymbolic language that disrupts "phallogo-centric" discourse. Nin's views are especially close to those Luce Irigaray expresses in *Ce sexe qui n'en est pas un*. Irigaray maintains that the uncentralized multiplicity of women's sensations is reflected in the diffuse structure of feminine writing.[78] Nin believes the same except that she sees Lawrence as transcending the "rule" that "a man's emotions are concentrated, while women's are spread all over their bodies," and therefore "[h]is moments of *blind* reactions strike a response in women."[79] One has only to compare Nin's description of Lawrence's most spontaneous, "careless" work to Irigaray's description of female language to see why Nin feels that Lawrence's style must result from womanlike perceptions.

Irigaray writes that man cannot "discern the coherence of any meaning" in woman's language because:

> In what she says . . . woman is constantly retouching herself. She steps ever so slightly aside from herself with a murmur, an exclamation, a whisper, a sentence left unfinished . . . When she returns to it, it is to set off again from . . . another point of pleasure, or of pain. One would have to listen with another ear, as if hearing *an "other meaning" always in the process of weaving itself, of embracing itself with words, but also of getting rid of words in order 'not to become fixed, congealed in them.* . . . What she says is never identical with anything, moreover; rather, it is contiguous.[80]

Nin believes that men misunderstood Lawrence's writings because, for him, truth "dwelt in chaos and oscillation," and life is determined not by fixed patterns but by need for "connection and flow."[81] Thus, Lawrence's texts take an involuted form, creating meaning in repetitions of sounds that work against connection to an exterior (male) symbolic tradition.

Correspondences are also evident in Nin's descriptions of Lawrence's language and the descriptions of the "nonsymbolic mother-daughter language" that Margaret Homans believes appears exclusively in women's writings. Homans writes of "a literal language," meant to represent the pre- or nonsymbolic order, that provides a "distinctly female . . . pleasure." Homans distinguishes this pleasure from that produced by the reemergence of the first language, which Julia Kristeva calls the semiotic. Kristeva theorizes that, because the semiotic is repressed in the (male) individual's consciousness when he separates from the mother and learns symbolic language, he identifies it with "the 'forbidden' maternal body," and returns to it, as a writer, with a sense that "he violates a taboo." To Homans, the woman writer, on the contrary, returns to nonsymbolic language (or rather a sort of writing meant to represent it) as to the mother from whom she will never completely break. The obscenities Kristeva finds indicative of the male writer's defiant awareness that he is enjoying the forbidden are absent from the female writer's use of this sort of language. For the woman writer, it is a kind of love song contained within female identification in which "words matter as sound, monotonous and rhythmic, issuing from and returning to the [maternal] body."[82] Nin's description of Lawrence's texts challenges the binary nature of this vision, however. The epistemological problems inherent in considering a particular type of language female or male are pointed up when she shows that Lawrence "had repudiated many old symbolic terms and had to create his own vocabulary," and that, consequently, in some of his writings, "The words almost cease to have a meaning; they have a cadence, a flow, and Lawrence gives in to the cadence. That is why there are so many 'ands' and *enchainements,* repetitions like choruses, words that are meant to suggest more than their own determinate, formal significance."[83] Nin finds such language, which both she and Homans consider female, in *Women in Love* and *The Lost Girl.* But Nin's reader is left wondering why this language written by a man is to be read as female, and, in fact, why such language is to be considered female at all.

Irigaray connects the linguistic fluidity she sees as female self-expression to the multiplicity of women's sexual response and even to the infolded, indeterminate form of women's genitals. She does not believe that an individual's biological sex determines his or her language, however; she points out that what she calls female language appears in some male authors' texts. Homans comes closer to linking language and gender, at least as it is culturally constructed. Her psychoanalytic theory of the development of language makes it seem highly unlikely that a male writer could use female language as a woman might. Nin, however, is uninterested in the artist's psychology and linguistic development, and by ignoring Lawrence's biography and even his sex, she is able to define his perception as female on the evidence of his writings alone. Nin treats Lawrence's texts not as (re)constructions of the feminine but as transmissions of female essence.

Unlike Woolf and Mansfield, Nin does not believe that Lawrence betrays the feminine/female voice in his texts by subordinating it to conventionally masculine fictions about women. Nin sees Lawrence's stories, and indeed his pronouncements about women, as neither conventional nor misogynous, because she shares his faith that gender difference is the source of identity and value. It does not matter to Nin that the woman artist "is not provided for in Lawrence's metaphysics," because "the *core* of her is; [*t*]*he core of the woman is her relation to man.*" Despite her interest in a separate and independent female language and literature, she believes, as Lawrence does, that at its best the relation between woman and man is characterized by a "see-saw rhythm" of love and hatred, submission and resistance which "is the basis of strength, of balance, of unison." She considers Lawrence "extremely sympathetic" to "the problems of the modern woman," not only because she agrees with his negative assessment of the patterns men have historically imposed on women's lives, but also because she shares his conviction that living "the man's life" cannot satisfy any sort of woman. His equation of female desire with "vital, impersonal creation and recreation" appeals to her sense of female fertility as a source of artistic vision. Because she believes that women have "a secret, natural connection," which men lack, to "the earth" and "elemental flows," Nin, like H. D., finds Lawrence's "mystical attitude towards the flesh" a tribute to woman as the primary source of both life and art.[84]

Although Nin's reading obviously comes from a high valuation of women and all that has been traditionally associated with women, it has some of the problems of the exclusionary systems that vexed Woolf— and of the theories of *l'écriture féminine* that continue to bother many feminist critics. As Ann Rosalind Jones says of the French concept of *féminité*, "It reverses the values assigned to each side of the polarity, but it still leaves man as the determining referent, not departing from the male-female opposition, but participating in it." Moreover, again like theories of *l'écriture féminine* in Jones's view, Nin's theory excludes as irrelevant to feminine language all female experience that is outside of or in contradiction to one totalizing vision of *the* female body and its sensations, ignoring "the lived differences among women."[85] Unlike Lawrence's uneasy, ambivalent essentialism, which caused him both to theorize about *the* female voice and body *and* to include in his texts the contradictory words and ideas of actual women, Nin's essentialism seems untroubled by a recognition of differences within the body female. Since she sees female characters as comments on Woman, Lawrence's texts appear far more coherent in her responses than in Woolf's, Mansfield's, or H. D.'s.

Woolf, Mansfield, and H. D. were often attracted by what they considered similarities between Lawrence's texts and texts produced by women. One might understand their attraction in terms of the "ideal of permanent alternation or dialectic of gender modes, rather than dominance of either" that Marianne DeKoven finds both in Kristeva's theoretical texts and in some experimental writing. To the extent to which Lawrence's doctrines are undercut within his texts by such antipatriarchal heteroglossia, they do seem to present such a model. As DeKoven points out, however, "successful experimental writing generally requires the presence of articulated meaning in the text," and the need for a certain amount of clarity (always coded as male) limits all textual flights from patriarchal language.[86] Because of this privileging of the masculine voice that seems inherent in language, it is all too easy to overlook the ways Lawrence acknowledges female authority and, instead, to read Lawrence's masculinist diatribes as representative of central meanings in his texts. Like many subsequent feminist critics, Woolf, Mansfield, and H. D. often read Lawrence's texts as univocal, and when they do so they are repelled by his many unpleasant narratorial comments on female characters who refuse or cannot achieve sexual union with a man.

In contrast, whether Lawrence judges a character like Gudrun good or evil is unimportant to Nin, as is his apparent hostility to the idea that women might find fulfillment in diverse ways. What interests her is his depiction of the superficial and material as "the man's world—the outside" and the inner, "untouched core" of both individuality and artistic perception as female. If the raw experiential material of art is female because of its impersonality, disorganization, and fertile contiguity, artistic expression is also female in its opposition to the utilitarian values of man's world. Nin sees Lawrence's agreement with what they both consider female sensibility as his instinctive "truthfulness" and believes that it prevails in his fiction over his more conventional and "rationally" determined attitudes. His work pleases her, as a woman artist, because of its ubiquitous emphasis on the necessity of a defiant, unsubmitting female to the maintenance of the balance that nourishes both life and art.[87] Nin clearly does not care what Lawrence has his female characters actually say, let alone what his male characters or masculine narrator say about them. She seems satisfied that Lawrence's desire to interpret and speak for women artists was overpowered by his conviction that their self-expression was of primary importance to the articulation of his own experience and the novel's truth.

In her attitudes toward and interpretation of Lawrence, Nin is a transitional figure. Lawrence's work is a part of literary history to her; he cannot answer or challenge anything that she writes. Yet, for the first part of her life, she inhabited the same world he describes. His depictions of that world are of paramount importance to her both because his vision of women coincides with hers and because his sensibility fits her definition of femininity. He seems to play two roles in her creative imagination. She identifies with him as an outcast, intuitive, and so feminized, artistic rebel against both the respected patriarchs of literature and ordinary, conventional society. But she also must feel superior to him because she believes that the femininity, which is the best part of his work, would naturally be the essential part of her own. His rebellion opens ground that she, as a woman artist, is prepared to occupy.

Lawrence is the ideal precursor because Nin can feel that she is continuing and perfecting what he began, rather than that she is competing with him. In this way her artistic relationship to Lawrence is reminiscent of his to Emily Brontë. It differs in that she is fully conscious of and willing to acknowledge Lawrence's influence on her fiction, as she makes clear in *The Novel of the Future* by continually citing Lawrence as an authority for her own views and explaining how she has developed his techniques in her own work. Nin writes, "Defending and explaining Lawrence . . . gave me my own orientation."[88] Lawrence defends Brontë, but not in the same way. His understanding of life as dominated by conflict between the sexes and his early anxiety that his work would not be as respected as Brontë's made it impossible for him openly to discuss his work as a reassertion of Brontë's values. Nin's defense of Lawrence and admission of his influence can take the form of a triumph because she recognized his worth before the literary world could urge her to do so, and she published her own readings of his texts before any standard interpretations were developed. Lawrence certainly never had before and probably will never have again such an unambiguous relationship to women's literature as he does in Anaïs Nin's texts.

"*And as She Read She Asked Herself, What Has This Got To Do With Me?*": Lawrence's Female Successors

IN THE PRECEDING CHAPTERS, I have treated the existence of separable male and female literary traditions as a given, although by tracing various writers' forays and wanderings across the borders I have intended to call into question the idea that such borders are or ever have been absolutely fixed. My focus on the textual responses specific writers make to each other has reflected those writers' own consciousness of the ways gender difference affected their creative processes and determined their place within recognized traditions. As I move to writers whose careers significantly overlapped the feminist movement that began in the 1960s, however, I must also take into account the many challenges, which we might in the widest sense call postfeminist, to the idea that authorial gender marks written texts. Here, as before, it is in the intertext between Lawrence's and women's writings that a dialogue can be read about gender, tradition, and literature as a response to both.

A claim basic to most feminist criticism is that texts with feminine signatures are, or have been historically, received differently by professional readers than texts with masculine signatures. This claim is substantiated by studies that focus on cases in which the author is assumed to be of one sex and then, sometime after the first edition is reviewed, is revealed to be of the other.[1] The silly preoccupation of reviewers who should know better with expressing their own prejudices about gender continues to be a source of wry amusement in the periodicals room. The complementary claim that gender bias derives from the reader's own gender identification is harder to support.

It is often posed as a given in feminist criticism that the masculine identification of the male reader causes him to approach women's texts with certain prejudices that a female reader would not share. This would seem to be a logical enough explanation of the observable difference in reception of men's and women's literary products, since until very recently the majority of influential critics were male. Taking the gender of the critic into account, however, goes against the belief, current in some French feminist criticism, that women are unable to read or write *as* women because language itself is always already in service of patriarchy.[2] Despite the passionate disagreements between French feminisms, they have in common a tendency to describe women as particularly linguistically disinherited. For example, in Julia Kristeva's assertion of the present "women's desire . . . to nourish our societies with a more flexible and free discourse, one able to name what has thus far never been an object of circulation in the community: the enigmas of the body, the dreams, secret joys, shames, hatreds of the second sex," there seems to be a condemnation of the writings of women in the past as inadequate.[3] The quasi-utopian mood alone, in which such otherwise diverse critics as Kristeva, Luce Irigaray, Monique Wittig, and Hélène Cixous sometimes seem to look forward to a future more feminine mode of expression for women, however they each conceive of it, is highly suggestive of their dissatisfaction with women's literary products in previous generations.[4]

This historical perspective is at odds with the belief, more prevalent among American and British feminist critics, that women's literary traditions exist and constitute an empowering heritage.[5] Among recent critical texts, Patricia Yaeger's *Honey-Mad Women* makes a particularly strong case that "women have participated in the countertradition of emancipatory strategies" not only since the second wave of feminism in the 1960s, but as long as women have been writing.[6] Evidence that there are separable male and female critical traditions would suggest that woman's relation to language has been far more than that of a mute object, a half-incomprehensible hysteric, or a ventriloquist for patriarchal doctrine. It would suggest that even though women were unable authoritatively to challenge the aesthetics that have consistently devalued women's texts, an aesthetics based on female gender identification has coexisted with the dominant, masculinist discourse of literary criticism.

I have discussed Lawrence's expectation that men would read his work differently than women. My intention has been to show that he directed his writing to a female audience and tried to place it within a female tradition, so I have not addressed the question of whether Lawrence was correct in believing that men and women respond to texts differently. The history of critical response to Lawrence's texts shows, however, that at least in his own case he was. This history might offer hope to an unsuccessful male writer that he would eventually attain greatness in the eyes of future generations, especially if the gaze of those eyes continues to be directed by an elite of male academic writers. To a woman writer, Lawrence's critical fortunes reveal something else, something so different, in fact, that after a certain point, Lawrence's reputation with women diverged sharply from his reputation with men. It is often within women's fiction that the difference of their reading is revealed.

During his lifetime, Lawrence's reputation fell fairly steadily with both sexes from the height it had reached with the publication of *Sons and Lovers*. Shortly before his death, he seems to have had a nearly equal number of admirers among male and female writers. Immediately after his death, Lawrence was generally considered an interesting failure. With very few exceptions, his critics discussed his life in order to explain why he never fulfilled his early promise. Most of the books and articles published about him gave more attention to his personal idiosyncrasies than to his work. In the 1940s, interest in Lawrence both as a writer and as a man was at its lowest ebb. F. R. Leavis's and Harry T. Moore's serious and respectful attention to Lawrence's work started a Lawrence revival in the early fifties.[7] Since then Lawrence's prestige has steadily increased. Where the concept of a literary canon is considered valid, his work is included in it, and his status as a major modernist is rarely questioned now.

Feminist criticism of Lawrence's work has taken a different direction. From Virginia Woolf's comments until the 1960s, such responses have followed two patterns, briefly outlined by Hilary Simpson: identification with him as a womanlike man or pseudo-psychoanalytic portrayal of him as a gynophobe.[8] *The* feminist question about Lawrence was whether his work belonged to the dominant and misogynous literary tradition, which attempts to silence actual women in favor of a male-defined feminine, or whether Lawrence could be considered part of the ongoing revolt of the marginalized, through which women's voices intrude into the dominant discourse. The debate over Lawrence's relationship to women's literature remained lively and unresolved for almost two decades.

Then, between the publication of Simone de Beauvoir's *Second Sex* in 1949 and Kate Millett's *Sexual Politics* in 1970, a great change took place in the way most women read Lawrence. De Beauvoir's concern in discussing Lawrence is to demonstrate that despite his refusal to objectify woman, a careful examination of his work reveals that he does belong to the male tradition. Millett, far from seeing Lawrence as an apparent outsider to misogynous literary tradition, places him at the beginning of a modern antifemale movement and describes him as the inventor of "a religion, even a liturgy, of male supremacy." Yet even Millett's reading of Lawrence, with its attention to Lawrence's "curious absorption in the myth of the eternal feminine, the earth mother," his narrative reliance on the speech of female characters, and the "subtlety" of this strategy,[9] is almost friendly in comparison to the views expressed in most current feminist criticism, in which Lawrence is constructed as anything but subtle. At one time, women writers wondered about Lawrence's relationship to literary resistance to the dominant culture, a resistance they were trying to envision as a sustaining tradition. Now, to quote Lawrence's dismissal of G. I. Gurdjieff's philosophy, "One doesn't wonder about it *at all*. One Knows."[10] Lawrence has become the archetypal masculinist who defines by contrast what is female in literature. But how have we reached such certainty?

One must look closely at literary history, specifically the history of Lawrence criticism and of its reception, as it is articulated in women's texts, to begin to understand the female turn against Lawrence. From the mid-twenties until the early fifties, women writers could see Lawrence as a sort of literary brother attacked by the critical establishment in the same ways that women had always been. They could sympathize with him when he became the subject of gossipy and sensationalist memoirs that focused on his sexual behavior and when he was derided as irrational or hysterical. Their annoyance with his misogynous pronouncements could be mitigated by their knowledge that his ability to reason was despised by such famous intellectuals as Bertrand Russell and T. S. Eliot. When Lawrence's work was almost universally considered inferior to Mansfield's and Woolf's, it must have been fairly easy for women to view charitably his attempts to speak for them. But, in changing not only Lawrence's critical reputation but also the way his works were interpreted, Leavis and Moore also altered the ways women writers could respond to Lawrence's work.

Although he often criticizes Lawrence's assertions of male superiority, Leavis praises Lawrence's normative intentions and urges his readers to value Lawrence as a moralist. In his willingness to concede (and explain) Lawrence's sexism, Leavis overlooks some of Lawrence's subtlety and ambivalence. For example, he reads the conclusion of *The Fox* as an illustration of female submission that is called for by "the concrete specificity of the situation presented."[11] Yet, the story's ending expresses more doubt about male rule than affirmation of it, even in the particular case of March and Henry. One does not need to be as familiar with Egyptian religion as Lawrence was to catch the suggestion of death in Henry's reiterated desire "to go West" so that March will give up her individual consciousness.[12] March's struggle to stay conscious "as if sleep were death" is consistent with Lawrence's belief that unresolved conflict between man and woman is necessary to vital marriage (*Fox,* 178).

Leavis also does Lawrence a disservice by insisting that the "phase of the literary world which made, not only Virginia Woolf, but Katherine Mansfield into something substantial and even major" had to end before Lawrence could be seen as great. A large part of Leavis's discussion "Lawrence and Tradition" is devoted to explaining Lawrence's superiority to George Eliot, even in "his insight" into and depiction of young women like Maggie Tulliver. Without, I believe, meaning to suggest anything of the sort, Leavis often seems to be offering Lawrence as a replacement for the few women who had been accepted as major writers.[13] Leavis, then, tends to define Lawrence's genius by favorably contrasting him to famous woman writers. In *The Life and Works of D. H. Lawrence,* Moore emphasizes Lawrence's brilliance through extensive comparisons of Lawrence's fiction with that of the obscure women writers who participated directly in his work. One is left with the impression that if Lawrence's criticisms of their texts and appropriation of their material silenced these women it was for the best.

Like Leavis, Moore finds Lawrence morally praiseworthy for his creation of "a world of values."[14] There were many good reasons for Lawrence's defenders to urge that the moral teachings in his work be taken seriously. Above all, they needed to refute his reputation for immorality. He had been attacked as a pornographer since the publication of *The Rainbow,* and by the 1940s he was probably best known as the writer of *Lady Chatterley's Lover,* which was banned for another twenty years. Most of his acquaintances' published memoirs of him dwelled on his putative sexual problems and fascistic leanings. As Wayne Booth points out, a critical approach, like Leavis's, that conceived of itself as ethical could not ignore allegations that the author of texts it was engaged in saving was a perverted, demented fascist.[15] Women, however, were unlikely to accept happily an evaluation of Lawrence's work that seemed to endorse railing against women as moral teaching. Moore made matters worse by seeming to agree with Lawrence at his most sexist, as he does when he singles out the essay "Is England Still a Man's Country?" and "Matriarchy" as examples of Lawrence's authority and reasoning power. Moore closes his study with the assertion that Lawrence is an "important writer" because he shows us "what the world about us is really like"; such a writer "reveal[s] to us a chapter of the autobiography of the present world, which is our own autobiography too."[16] In the most general sense this is obviously true, but in the context of Moore's apparent agreement with Lawrence's masculinist doctrines it is an invitation to feminine dissent.

Whether the gender bias manifested in the Lawrence revival's reevaluation of Lawrence's work actually caused a reaction against him among women readers cannot be proven, because the reason readers read as they do are too complex to be exhaustively explained in terms of group circumstances or ideologies. It is even reductive to refer to *the* way that women read Lawrence since some women readers have continued up into the present to read Lawrence in ways very similar to those I have discussed in the previous chapter, and other women, Diana Trilling and Q. D. Leavis, for example, participated in the Lawrence revival by offering readings very similar to those of F. R. Leavis and Moore. If the Lawrence revival cannot be empirically proven to be a cause of gender-related differences in ways of reading Lawrence, however, it can be considered a node in critical tradition at which many women writers met a masculinist aesthetic and then swerved away from the mainstream into an oppositional metatextual relation to Lawrence.

Although we cannot be sure of the source of feminist reaction against Lawrence, we may observe that the reaction is a major part of many of the novels by women whose writing careers span the changes Leavis and

Moore brought about in Lawrence's reputation. At least three of these women—Doris Lessing, Elizabeth Bowen, and Christina Stead—were obviously very much inspired by Lawrence's fiction. Indeed, in a few works of each writer, allusions to Lawrence and his work so overdetermine structure and development that it is hard to imagine the texts being written except in response to him. In early texts, Lessing's, Bowen's, and Stead's revisionary responses to Lawrence often seem affectionate rather than challenging; they adapt his themes and images in ways a woman writer might those of a respected female precursor to fit them to another place and time. Hostility to Lawrence eventually imposes a new structure on their responses to him, however.

These two modes of response are not necessarily mutually exclusive. In describing the relationship between women modernists and their precursors, Gilbert and Gubar distinguish between influence and affiliation. The former, they say, "connotes an influx or pouring-in of external power [while] the concept of affiliation carries with it possibilities of both choice and continuity." Influence is associated with women's relationship to male precursors and affiliation with women's relationship to female precursors. They find evidence of women writers' self-empowerment in both their affiliation with a woman's tradition and their resistance of male influence, shown through their deconstruction of cultural and textual narratives of male primacy.[17] Resistance can be expressed even more subtly, however. It can, in fact, be framed in such a way that it is almost indistinguishable from acceptance, as Tania Modleski notes in her explication of Irigaray's ideas on feminine mimesis: "mimicry . . . is a time-honored tactic among oppressed groups, who often appear to acquiesce in the oppressor's ideas about it, thus producing a double meaning: the same language or act simultaneously confirms the oppressor's stereotypes of the oppressed and offers a dissenting and empowering view for those in the know."[18] Thus, within the most apparently daughterly texts of the women who accepted Lawrence's influence we, whom the passage of time has placed in the know, may read the almost-hidden beginnings of what will grow to be a strong reaction against him.

One of the most powerful rejections of Lawrence's fiction as our own autobiography comes from Lessing, who seemed originally closest to agreement with his vision. Several critics have discussed the strikingly Lawrencian qualities of Lessing's first novel, *The Grass Is Singing*. In particular, as Charles and Liebetraut Sarvan point out, the scene in which

Mary Turner, the white African farmer's wife, watches her black servant, Moses, washing himself outdoors closely parallels a scene in *Lady Chatterley's Lover*.[19] Lessing's association of women with socialized alienation and men with nature and authenticity is also reminiscent of Lawrence. For instance, her contrast of the Turners' attitudes toward their land evokes the opening of *The Rainbow*: "She was looking at the farm from the outside, as a machine for making money. . . . He . . . was part of it. He liked the slow movement of the seasons and the complicated rhythm of the 'little crops.' "[20] In *The Rainbow* the Brangwen men are caught up in the pulse of the earth, while the women look "beyond."[21]

The Grass Is Singing most resembles Lawrence's "The Princess" and "None of That." The plot summary is identical for all three: A white woman living in exotic but uncongenial surroundings and on the verge of a nervous crisis becomes fascinated with a man of a darker race. She assumes a mask of frigidity that keeps other men at a distance. The title phrase of "None of That," often repeated by Ethel Cane to dismiss the possibility of sexual desire, is echoed in the "not like that" which Mary Turner hears in reference to herself and repeats, after her breakdown, "like a gramophone that had got stuck at one point" (*GS*, 40, 221). But the dark man and the alienated woman are drawn together by a mystical connection which, in Lawrence's terms, makes them the same sort of "demon."[22] In each story, entering into secret communion with the more overtly "savage" male brings the woman to confront the violent and deathly drives within her. Because of its character, the connection between the woman and the man can only be destructive, but because the man is the figure for the repressed part of her, union is inescapable.

This inescapability is reified in terms of spatial boundaries. In "None of That," Lawrence uses a traditional Mexican linguistic courtesy to suggest that Ethel's doom is a sort of domestic entrapment. Cuesta, the bullfighter who fascinates her, repeatedly invites Ethel to meet him "at her—meaning his—humble house" ("None," 716, 720). When she does, she is "caught" and gang-raped ("None," 721). The Princess is also imprisoned and raped by her guide, Romero, in a "little hole of a cabin" ("Princess," 509). In Lessing's novel, the house in which Mary will be sexually and spiritually possessed by Moses is "tiny, tiny; and very low" (*GS*, 54). As Sandra Gilbert and Susan Gubar show, "concern with spatial restrictions" and consequently images of stifling enclosure "sometimes seem to dominate the literature of both nineteenth-century women and their twentieth-century descendents."[23] Since Lawrence is employing a traditionally female literary device, we might expect his use of it to reveal less empathy with the suffocating circumstances of women than Lessing has. Actually the reverse seems true.

Lessing shows what Michele Wender Zak calls an "essential lack of sympathy" for Mary.[24] Racist, sadistic, petty, and self-centered, Mary figures life-denying imperialism. Lessing's displacement of imperialism onto woman parallels her narrative disengagement from Mary as a feminine creature. Mary's feminine submissiveness is naturalized in the text. The failure of her marriage is explained in terms very like Lawrence's male supremacist dictates in *Fantasia of the Unconscious*: "She needed a man stronger than herself. . . . If he [Dick Turner] had genuinely, simply, because of greater strength of his purpose, taken the ascendency over her, she would have loved him" (*GS,* 145). Both Moses's name and his fatherly protectiveness of Mary imply that his domination of her offers her the possibility of redemption. If her world would allow her to live under his control, as "one of his own women," Lessing suggests, Mary could experience fulfillment (*GS,* 175–76). The voices speaking this apparently misogynistically pointed tale are generally disassociated from a female perspective. Scenes from Mary's point of view emphasize her lack of self-knowledge and are overbalanced by scenes in which male characters ponder Mary's opaque motivations. Lessing constructs herself as author in contrast to the feminine as represented by Mary, who seems the repository of whatever is excluded from the rebellious sensibility that allows the telling of an anticolonialist tale.

Lawrence clearly disapproves of both Ethel Cane and the Princess, Dollie Urquhart; however, he identifies them with the transcendent values that inform his critique of the "deathly" in other cultures. Their alienation is determined by the values that make Lawrence consider such cultures other. Ethel has a gorgeous, radiant vitality that is set against the ugliness of her world. And the Princess's defiant refusal to "have anybody's will put over" her is in accordance with Lawrence's own, frequently stated ethos ("Princess," 508). Her recoil from Romero's sexual violence does not result in a skittish, disgusting madness like Mary's but rather a cold, dignified acceptance of "a princeless world" ("Princess," 509). Lawrence's women are superior to their world, and their problematic, self-entrapping personalities are rooted in rebellion necessitated by that superiority; Mary, in contrast, agrees with and so epitomizes all that is wrong with her world.

All the similarities between *The Grass Is Singing* and Lawrence's fiction make it seem likely that Lessing wrote her first novel under his influence. That she identified with Mary Turner seems impossible, and it is equally unlikely that she meant this figure of weak evil to represent womankind. Rather, she seems to be revising Lawrence to emphasize her agreement with what she reads as his criticism of socially constructed femininity—from which she is anxious to disassociate herself. In doing so, she comes up against one of the problems that neo-Freudian feminist critics, like Juliet Mitchell, often face in their defense of Freud as descriptive of culture rather than nature. Because no natural language exists, Lessing cannot speak from a position outside of the culture in which, she has already agreed, women are constructed as feminine, evil, and weak.[25] Since Lessing must speak from within a culture that she is representing as inescapably male-dominated, seemingly the only strategy available to authorize her speech is alignment with the masculine perspective. Therefore, she castigates Mary for essential, gender-related flaws even while paradoxically reiterating that Mary is the victim of a femininity imposed from without. Judith Kegan Gardiner calls Lessing's strategy here "projective disidentification" and remarks that it "works toward domination rather than toward empathy with its object." While the novel's content does suggest "a covert feminist protest at the . . . violence used to keep women in place,"[26] Lessing's narratorial treatment of Mary functions to uphold the very attitudes, so often expressed by Lawrence's narrators, that legitimate violence against women.

The later Lessing is much less like a defensive daughter. Her attitude toward the dominant discourse's representations both of the feminine and of individual women seems more skeptical. By recognizing that other voices have always spoken woman differently, she finds a speaking position for herself that allows her more latitude to imagine her female protagonists as occasionally escaping male definition and often constructing their own personas in opposition to it. Meanwhile, Lessing's expressed respect for Lawrence as an artist remained strong through the writing of *Martha Quest* (published in 1952) and *The Golden Notebook* (published in 1962). In a 1963 interview, she refers to Lawrence as "a fine writer" and "a good critic."[27] Both of these later novels reveal a different understanding of Lawrence's ideas, however.

Like *The Grass Is Singing, Martha Quest* is filled with Lawrencian echoes.[28] The most prominent of these is the borrowing of two characters from *The Virgin and the Gipsy*. Lawrence's big, fair Charles Eastwood reappears as Lessing's Andrew Mathews, and the men's tiny Jewish mates, Stella and Mrs. Fawcett, are almost twins. While Yvette, the virgin of Lawrence's novella, becomes acquainted with the Eastwoods in the gypsy camp, virginal Martha gets to know the Mathewses among food stands that look "like a small gypsy camp."[29] In both stories, the newly formed couple helps the heroine become optimistic about marriage. But Lessing's depiction of the Mathewses' effect on Martha seems to comment adversely on Lawrence's vision of ideal female growth; their own sensualism and approval of sexual life misdirects Martha. Lawrence's ideology and consequently his depiction of female experience are called into question.

Martha Quest dramatizes a young woman's maturation as a battle between experience and a literary heritage that fails to describe it. As Dorothy Brewster shows, Martha Quest is "a Rhodesian white colonial Maggie Tulliver: rebellious, adventurous, romantic, chafing against the barriers of a narrow provincial society, and deeply influenced by books."[30] Martha's only standard for judging the books she reads is her own experience. She can only ask of each work, "What has this got to do with me?" (*MQ,* 200). Yet, again and again, we are shown that her perception of her own life is distorted because "she was seeing herself . . . in the only way she was equipped to do this—through literature"; "since she had been formed by literature, she could think in no other way"; "her mind was schooled . . . [by] literature" (*MQ,* 7, 166, 173). While passages like these might be read as suggesting that (Martha's) identity is conflicted because it is entirely textually constructed, in other places Lessing frames the confrontation between literature and experience in terms that imply that Martha's problems derive from the inadequacies of a particular body of literature, not the limitations of all literatures. A distinction is made between what has been represented in literature and what could or should be.

In an early aside, the narrator introduces the theme of the disjunction between literature and life by pointing out that Martha's access to a written theory of sexuality, which she finds alienating, parallels her exclusion from local women's experientially based discussions of sexuality, just as the orderly English farms in the fiction Martha reads displace, in her imagination, the sprawling, half-wild farm she inhabits. The stress Lessing puts on prestigious literature's failure to represent experience in a way that would help woman to realize herself makes the novel's evocations of Lawrence's fiction seem mocking. Phrases like "the literature that was her tradition," along with the narrator's emphasis on the absence of a recognizable/conventional pattern in Martha's world gives this opening scene a metafictional tone that underscores the novel's quest for realism outside both the tradition Leavis claims Lawrence continues and the pattern Lawrence imposed on all female experience (*MQ*, 2). As the Sarvans show, Lessing's sexualized landscape, with its "naked embrace of earth and sky," does evoke the English farm in *The Rainbow*.[31] The difference is that its sensual wholeness is placed absolutely beyond Martha's reach by the literary heritage that is always insinuating itself into her line of vision.

Martha has what seems to be her greatest victory when she persuades her fiancé, Douglas, to put aside the marriage manual, and they make love "without the aid of the book, in a way that please[s] them both" (*MQ*, 228–29). Martha discovers natural pleasure by overcoming her veneration for literature. Lawrence would approve of this valuation of spontaneous sexual expression over intellectually determined lovemaking, but to Lessing the triumph of natural sexuality has a different meaning than the one Lawrence gives it. In fact, her references to Lawrencian passions seem to parody rather than affirm his values. Martha and Douglas's moments of sexual rapport are isolated and ultimately unimportant. The books, presumably like Lawrence's, that taught Martha to believe that mutually satisfying sex could be the basis of connection to nature, future happiness, and even social change seem wrong. As all the horrors of their world, including Hitler's invasion of Bohemia and Moravia, leap back into the narrative at the end, Lessing shows us that Martha's sexual awakening and marriage are insignificant even to Martha herself. Unlike Birkin and Ursula who, at the "end-of-the-world" conclusion of *Women in Love,* rise passionately above their disintegrating culture, Martha and Douglas fall back into the decadence of "the capital city of a British colony in the great African continent" (*MQ*, 246).

In *The Golden Notebook* Lessing's rejection of Lawrence's valorization of sexuality and heterosexual union is even more pronounced. Once again apparent allusions to Lawrence's texts are pervasive. As Mark Spilka points out, the story by the novelist-heroine, Anna, of Paul and

Ella in the yellow notebook is frequently reminiscent of *Women in Love* and *Lady Chatterley's Lover,* and Anna's discussion of the superiority of "vaginal" to "clitoral" orgasm resembles Lawrence's moralizing about types of orgasm in *The Plumed Serpent* and *Lady Chatterley's Lover.*[32] But Lawrence's and Lessing's views of the function of love in the life of the individual are radically opposed. Unlike a Lawrencian heroine, Anna becomes successfully creative as she learns to suppress her desire to live with a man. Her love for Saul is perfected by desexualization and finally separation.

Because Lawrence makes the dialogue between oppositely gendered speakers the source of all valuable energy in his novels, he must insist that without heterosexual union his characters' lives would be meaningless, their efforts to change themselves and their world impossible. The sort of union that Lessing depicts as bringing wholeness is very like the nonsexual, mystic rapport caused, in part, by the breaking of connection between physical bodies, the end of erotic potential, at the conclusions of Mansfield's "Garden-Party" and Eliot's *Mill on the Floss.* And, as Catherine Stimpson indicates in her discussion of the *Children of Violence* series, this high valuation of separation and of a "willed indifference to sexual claims" increases in Lessing's later work.[33] Lessing opposes Lawrence's most fundamental belief by creating a fictional world in which separation is not a trial to be passed through, but a goal. In this sense, Lessing's revisions of Lawrencian stories can be considered sharp, if not completely conscious, parodic reversals.

Because *The Golden Notebook* is about writing, and specifically about the problems of women writers, Lessing's insistence on Anna's need to separate from men who are reminiscent of characters in Lawrence's fiction suggests her own sense that she must break away from his influence. And in her subsequent works, although she continues to allude to his fiction, the ideological distance between them seems to have increased dramatically. This is especially apparent in *The Fifth Child.*

Lessing's novel seems conceived in opposition to Lawrence's *Kangaroo*; the characters, themes, and values are all reversed. The central couple, Harriet and David Lovatt, have names that call Lawrence's protagonists, Harriet and Richard Lovat Somers, to mind, but these determinedly old-fashioned, virtual addicts of domesticity are the antitheses of Lawrence's restless, bohemian pair. The Lovatt's emotionally dead, nihilistic child Ben is the mirror image of the sentimental, fatherly, reactionary Ben (Kangaroo) Cooley. Lawrence's novel ends by leaning (with his disenchanted protagonist) away from all social structuring toward anarchy. Lessing wittily literalizes the idea that the overvalued family gives birth to the atavistic force that will destroy it, but her descriptions privilege the very middle-class home life that she presents as selfish and doomed. The loving husband and wife conceiving their first golden baby by "the old lilac [which] showed its vigorous buds, soon to burst into flower," the Easter garden full of "magical eggs," and the continual production of aromatic bread and jam are, indeed, "happiness, in the old style."[34] In *Kangaroo* only the antisocial, represented by the Somerses, has a human face. While Lawrence's text is in rebellion against all authority, Lessing's novel's revolt seems to be directed primarily against Lawrence.

In rejecting Lawrence, Lessing has strengthened rather than broken the intertextual connection between them. Traces of her responses to his texts deeply mark some of Lessing's characteristic authorial practices. For instance, the ironic tone with which Lessing distances herself from woman as she might be written by Lawrence's didactic narrators also distances her from the autobiographical Martha Quest and even more so from Anna in love. We could attribute the growth of this distance to the development of Lessing's feminism. Similar development in Lawrence's contemporaries, notably Woolf, Mansfield, and H. D., had an opposite effect. The more interested they became in articulating female experience and the more exception they took to Lawrence's descriptions of that experience, the closer they seem to have drawn to their female protagonists. This is particularly evident in *Orlando,* "At the Bay," and *Bid Me to Live,* where an inverse relationship exists between the narrative attitude toward the heroine and the narrative attitude toward a concept of woman identified with Lawrence's texts.

What is essentialist about Woolf's, Mansfield's, and H. D.'s vision is fundamentally untroubled by confrontation with Lawrence's rival view of woman's nature. For them, feminist revision of Lawrence is largely a matter of replacing annoyingly false representations of female experience with ones that are presumed to be more accurate. They seem to conceive of their battle with Lawrence as situated within a predominantly female tradition, and to conceive of what is at stake as an authoritative definition of female experience. They seem reasonably confident of their power to contradict Lawrence. For Lessing, the battleground often seems to lie within her female characters themselves. As soon as she identifies Lawrence's texts with the dominant discourse, she begins to create female protagonists that fight against Lawrence's definition of woman as if it were a sort of demonic possession. And she, unable to cast Lawrence out because of his prior authority, can only disassociate herself from his definition of woman by the dual strategies of distancing herself from her own female characters and reconstructing him as a representative of masculinist tradition. It is only in texts produced by women whose growth in consciousness of sexual politics parallels the changes in Lawrence criticism that we see Lawrence written out of female tradition and transformed from fraternal rival to threatening patriarch.

Elizabeth Bowen, who is more inclined toward the comic, expresses disenchantment with Lawrence more obviously than Lessing does, but also more playfully. In some ways Bowen's literary relationship to Lawrence is analogous to that of Mansfield, who was one of Bowen's favorite writers.[35] Because their situations as writers were similar to his, both women had reason to consider themselves in competition with Lawrence. Born in 1899, Bowen was just fourteen years younger than Lawrence and had published three collections of short stories and two novels before Lawrence's death. Not only their careers, but also their social worlds overlapped somewhat when Bowen was befriended by Ottoline Morrell in 1931.[36] Bowen cannot be considered Lawrence's contemporary, however, since she outlived him by forty-three years and did not gain recognition until well after his death. Moreover, Bowen, unlike H. D., Anaïs Nin, and Mansfield, has never attained the degree of respect that has been bestowed on Lawrence. She had ample time to see him change from a rival to a predecessor, from a literary sensation to "The Great Unread," as Moore called him in a 1940 essay, and then to one of the most popular and respected of modernists. Bowen's parodies of Lawrence reflect increasing anxiety about her literary relationship to him.

Bowen's direct comments on Lawrence make it easy to predict her literary turn against him. At first her description of his work was ostensibly admiring, although it also used the language of pathology: "his vision not only fuses with but permanently affects the vision of his reader."[37] In the late 1940s, like the male critics who had just begun defending Lawrence, Bowen discussed him as an unappreciated prophet of social disintegration, but unlike those Lawrence advocates, she completely rejected his doctrine of personal and social regeneration through sexual fulfillment. Twelve years later, when Lawrence no longer needed defense, Bowen expressed more extensive disapproval of his ideas, especially about women, but said "his self-parodies" redeemed his fiction.[38] Her fiction shows a growing awareness that others do not read Lawrence as she does and a corresponding concern that her depictions of female experience will not gain the authority of his.

Bowen's most sustained response to Lawrence is her 1932 novel *To the North,* which repeatedly alludes to *Women in Love*'s characters, plot, and symbology. The story follows the experiences in love of two sisters-in-law, Cecilia and Emmeline Summers, and ends when Cecilia has settled into domesticity and Emmeline has destroyed her lover and herself. Emmeline, a widow when the story begins, shares Gudrun's dreamy alienation from ordinary people and their standards, "knowing no wrong, only what is repugnant."[39] Emmeline's lover, Markie, is similar to Gerald in his physicality and his utilitarian approach to life. Lawrence uses the doomed lovers as foils for Birkin and Ursula, whose story dominates the narrative. Bowen focuses on Markie and Emmeline to explore the ways male plots doom woman.

Gudrun longs for "a comrade-in-arms," as does Emmeline, who when Markie fails to understand her sexual and emotional needs and to equal her passion kills them both on the Great North Road.[40] Bowen could be seen as defending Mansfield/Gudrun against Lawrence's criticisms. But Bowen is not going against Lawrence's doctrine in concluding that woman's power turns destructive if her man cannot read her.[41] The difference is that Bowen imagines male failure not primarily in terms of inadequate interpretation of woman, but as a gender-bound tendency to create deathly fictions.

Bowen's texts are full of allusions to their own fictional nature. Through frequent references to writers and writing, she reinscribes gender difference in literary production and reception, always associating both privilege and deathliness with men's fictions. Bowen's women generally find it difficult to express themselves in writing, especially to men. Cecilia fills her desk with long letters that she can only hope will be posted after her death. Emmeline finds it impossible to give Markie the letter she has written him because "[n]ot to speak was her instinct" and "his black-and-white bulk . . . made what she had written meaningless" (*TN,* 108–9). He is black and white because of his evening clothes, but he is so symbolically as well because he is strongly self-written, self-defined. In contrast, Emmeline is the page across which he is "writing himself" (*TN,* 71). After they become lovers, she feels that "[h]is being was written all over her; if he was not, she was not" (*TN,* 188). The deadly, cold whiteness of the snowfield where Gerald dies becomes, in Bowen's novel, the white page of Emmeline's mind after she has erased Markie from it. To Bowen, women are made into white goddesses of destruction because men insist on writing over and obliterating all that is worthwhile in their lives. In this depiction of woman as blank pages helpless to avoid being written upon, Bowen reveals her fear of feminine powerlessness in relation to misogynous discourse. Unlike Lawrence's heroines, who successfully fight to revise what man and culture have written upon them, Bowen's women can neither remove nor alter the male script. Susan Gubar, writing about ways in which the trope of the blank page has been used by women writers, remarks that deliberate blankness, the refusal to write what is expected or to allow oneself "to be written on" is "the condition of new sorts of writing for women."[42] This act of defiance is unavailable to Bowen's women.

Women do create fictions in Bowen's work. These fictions are beneficial, however, because they lack the defining power of those created by men. Bowen calls the domestic life in which Cecilia encloses Emmeline a fiction, but as Edwin Kenney observes, it is "an acceptable fiction, something to hold on to against the flux."[43] A few of Bowen's women are more powerful plotters than Cecilia and Emmeline. In *The House in Paris,* written in 1935, Bowen draws heavily on Lawrence's language in her depiction of Mme. Fisher, a manipulative witch-figure. For example, Mme. Fisher's protégé Max says, "her sex is all in her head."[44] Like Lawrence's most powerful witch-mother, Gertrude Morel, she undermines the son-figure she loves, but while Lawrence protagonists, like Paul Morel in *Sons and Lovers,* Lou Carrington in *St. Mawr,* Virginia Bodoin in "Mother and Daughter," and Yvette Saywell in *The Virgin and the Gipsy,* break free of domineering mothers into fuller life, Max can imagine no escape except suicide. In Lawrence's fiction such smothering mothers impose sterility, but although Mme. Fisher's motives are selfish, if not evil, her plot, like that of Nature herself, is generative. Without her plot, the child Leopold would not have been born. And, as the story of the origins of the cool, detached, motherless Leopold, *The House in Paris* is also a savagely ironic answer to Lawrence's insistence that children must be freed from maternal control. If Max is a character seeking a life outside the fiction-making mother-mind, the more male-determined world he opens for the others cannot sustain a complete human.

The antipathy between male fiction making and fulfilling existence is again asserted in Bowen's 1941 story, "The Disinherited," in which a young woman, Davina, must decide whether to inhabit a man's or a woman's fiction. Davina's aunt, Mrs. Archworth, offers the myth of a gracious traditional England in which everyone has a place and knows it, to their benefit. She is somewhat reminiscent of Lady Beveridge, the "old-fashioned little aristocrat," called "the soul of England," in *The Ladybird*.[45] Davina resists this fiction because it leaves little scope for her passion for her friend, Marianne, who—"big-limbed, wide-browed . . . like a diffident goddess"—recalls both Daphne, in *The Ladybird,* and Lady Chatterley.[46] In seeking to create an alternative story in which she could be Marianne's dashing savior, Davina becomes entangled in the strange plotting of her aunt's chauffeur, Prothero. It is as if female creativity can only move backward, into the lady-novelist tradition, to escape engulfment by masculinist vision.

Because his writings make up a discrete section of the story, Prothero's voice rivals the narrator's. Victoria Glendinning calls his tale "a sub-Lawrentian fantasy," probably because it is a variation on the theme of *Lady Chatterley's Lover*.[47] Like Mellors, Prothero has a secret love affair with a woman who ranks far above him, but he kills her when she refuses to take his interpretation of their affair seriously. After the murder, he becomes literally the author of his own story, rewriting it nightly. Like Lawrence, Prothero is preoccupied with producing textual definitions of his masculinity that explain his relationship with one woman, but unlike Lawrence, he can only feel connection to a dead woman. Prothero's obsessive writings seem meant to parody Lawrence's frequent use of the story of Persephone as a parable for the male fantasy of a marital fulfillment derived from the wife's dying away from her own consciousness and will. We may be reminded of *The Fox,* the technique of which Bowen greatly admired, in which the male protagonist is a "Lord of Death" who demands a sleeping/dead bride. By consenting to deal with Prothero on his own terms, Davina allows herself to be written into his fiction and so risks "going West" into the Hell of his imagination.

Mrs. Archworth's world, although made to complement the fictions of men with much more worldly power than Prothero, seems the only one which can offer Davina shelter. Nevertheless, Bowen seems to incline more toward Prothero and his rebellious, Lawrencian fiction. To a certain extent, Prothero's writing and rewriting of woman seems part of a struggle with the cultural construction of gender identity. One can read as resistance to the patriarchal powers that have disinherited Davina his decision that death is better than a life like his mistress's as "the great business man's daughter . . . the great big business man's wife" ("The Disinherited," 394). Bowen's depiction of the ironic grace with which Prothero bears his suffering betrays her attraction to Lawrencian heroic defiance, even as she exposes its complicity with the misogyny of the dominant discourse that both Lawrence and she seek to subvert.

There is no hint of such attraction in Bowen's 1968 novel, *Eva Trout*. Continuing the metafictional trend in Bowen's work, Eva's adventures often seem to represent a woman writer's futile attempts to express herself in forms determined by male perceptions. Here the relationship to Lawrence is different, in part, because the issue is not what has been withheld, the disinheritance of the modern writer/heroine, but the poisonous patrimony that has been passed on. Emphasis has been moved from the (dangerous) alliance between the marginalized sisters and brothers to the war between the fathers and daughters. At the beginning of the story, Bowen uses the epithet "the heiress" interchangeably with the protagonist's name.[48] Eva inherits more than money; Bowen implies that Eva's inheritance includes the dominant constructs of Western literary tradition.

Willy Trout deprives his daughter of her rightful property, his love and her mother's, because of his passion for Constantine Ormeau, and he builds up around Eva a mythic world of male eroticism that deprives her of meaning. She learns early that females are only objects of exchange within Willy and Constantine's classically determined world. The two men's struggle over "Kenneth of the Parthenon torso" results in Eva being packed off to a ghastly experimental school and then removed from it just as she falls in love with Elsinore, another student (*ET,* 41). In *Eva Trout* gender determines inheritance. That Eva is "not Prince Hamlet" is not a handicap that unites her with Prufrockian male outcasts; it is part of the condition of being a woman within a male "Great Tradition." She can never be even a pretender to Elsinore. Years after school, Eva finds Elsinore still ruled by a figure out of patriarchal myth. She stands "in a chained way, a doll-size Andromeda" before "Herk's Dad," a "horrible old Greek," the "patriarch" of Elsinore's new family, who ignores the women's unhappiness and sympathizes with Eva's father (*ET*, 135–37). Still later, on a country excursion with Henry, the young man she loves, Eva tries to appear, herself, as a mythical object of desire, but she seems to him less like "a nymph in flight" than "Abraham's ram" (*ET*, 240). With no role at all granted her in Greek myth or the ongoing struggles of rebellious sons that continue it, Eva is given, in the Christian cosmos, only this dismal place.

Her role within her Christian heritage is always sacrificial. Bowen compares Eva, at the time that she is sent away to Kenneth's school, to Jephtha's daughter, who consented to be given as a burnt offering to fulfill her father's pledge to Jehovah (*ET*, 42; Judg. 11:36). At school, Eva is compared to Joan of Arc; "Elle fut carbonisée" (*ET*, 44). Right after giving up Elsinore forever in order to make the appointment to receive her adoptive son, Eva opens a Gideon Bible and reads, "This is the law of the burnt offering . . ." (*ET*, 143). As her name suggests, Eva is also a sort of Eve, but not the defiant, ebullient Frieda-like Eva of Lawrence's "New Eve and Old Adam" and similar stories. Instead, Bowen implies that Eve is a restrictive role imposed on women by men. Caught in shady doings, Henry excuses himself by saying about Eva, " 'The woman tempted me' " (*ET*, 114). Professor Holman, who meets Eva over an apple, thinks hopefully that she might take his sins upon herself.

Holman also thinks that her "gaze gives size to what is contained within it" (*ET*, 123). Bowen seems to be alluding to Virginia Woolf's remark that "women have served all these centuries as looking-glasses possessing the magic and delicious power of reflecting the figure of man at twice its natural size."[49] As Woolf does, Bowen suggests that the status and moral authority men give women is a fiction created to enhance the self-confidence of men. The professor's name is a pun (Portman C. Holman/Part man see whole man) that elucidates Bowen's argument with Lawrence. Whereas Lawrence sees the ideal Eve, the essential woman, as the foundation of male heroic action, Bowen sees such a woman as a fiction-maker in service of male illusions, and thus a scapegoat.

Although Woolf is not the only woman writer Bowen uses as an authority for her own vision, each allusion to a female precursor paradoxically strengthens the impression of Eva's entrapment in male-determined fictions. The first line of the chapter in which we are introduced to Henry's moralistic father, Mr. Dancey, is, "The vicarage had witnessed various scenes of clerical life" (*ET,* 20). This allusion to George Eliot serves two purposes. First, it is a reminder of the bleakness of Eliot's early depictions of the relations between the sexes. Like Amos Barton, in *Scences of Clerical Life,* Mr. Dancey uses his wife and daughters unmercifully. Second, by making us think of Eliot, Bowen stresses the theme of women's forced acceptance of masculine definition. The women writers of Eliot's generation took male names because the public paid more attention to and gave more respect to the words of men. The subtitle of the novel, *Changing Scenes,* seems ironic because, beginning with the scenes of clerical life, little seems changed. Certainly, in Bowen's opinion, the injustice that caused Eliot to call herself George (and Charlotte and Emily Brontë to call themselves Currer and Ellis) is unaltered. Bowen opposes Lawrence's vision of a feminized and matriarchal England with her re-evocation of Eliot's patriarchal vicarage, where religious law always demands that man name woman as the sacrificial Other.

Eva wishes to define herself as something other than a scapegoat, but in her world women are silent. The only creative woman in the novel, Applethwaite, says, "Words do not connect, for me" (*ET,* 201). Elsinore begins by attempting to put her own sense of life's injustice into words, writing over and over "the same long letter" (*ET,* 46). Finally "lost" to a husband, three sons, and the Greek patriarch, Elsinore can force no sound through her desperately moving "frosted lips" when she needs to ask Eva for rescue (*ET,* 141–42). Eva expresses herself "like a displaced person," is "unable to speak—talk, be understood, converse" (*ET,* 10, 57). Nor can she pray (*ET,* 188). But above all, she cannot write clearly (*ET,* 56). Kenney observes, "Eva literally can find no language in which to speak on her own terms, and she does not resign herself to being translated imperfectly."[50] Consequently, she is much more socially isolated than her father is by his homosexuality. For him separation from the heterosexual norm is also connection to a male system of meanings; for his daughter separation from the male norm is disconnection, meaninglessness. As in Mansfield's texts, and the theories of *l'écriture féminine,* the only place woman can find her speaking voice is outside of symbolic language.

The one woman who seems able to break through the obscure pre-Hellenic silence that enwombs all other females is Eva's teacher, temporary guardian, sometime friend, and finally deadly enemy, Iseult. Her occupations demonstrate her mastery of language; she is an English teacher and a translator. She first appears to Eva as a sort of Apollonian priestess; her teaching is like "a pythic mystery" (*ET,* 88, 52). Marble temple fragments weigh down the books on her desk, implicitly connecting her to *Jane Eyre's* Miss Temple, whose "marble" brow is duplicated as Iseult's most prominent feature.[51] Like Miss Temple, Iseult criticizes and undermines the man who pays her (Constantine). Both are the sort of women who prosper under even the most repressive patriarchal regime because of their talent for restraining their emotions and giving a show of deference. Moreover, their minds are temples for male ideas. Thus, the doubleness implied in Iseult's name seems more of a threat to her female pupil than to her male patron. Hers is always what Mitchell calls the hysteric's voice, which "both refuses and is totally trapped within femininity," that is, male definition.[52] But as a teacher or model, she can only pass on madness. Her lesson, like that of the Victorian women writers, as seen through Bowen's texts, is that we must find ourselves within male fictions and allow them to structure even our complaints.

To Iseult both the most attractive and the most confining structures have been provided by Lawrence. Although she reveres several male writers—even thinking of Dickens as a sort of literary Christ—the fiction she inhabits and allows to inhabit her is shaped by her reading of Lawrence. Bowen says explicitly that Iseult's reading of Lawrence inspires her ridiculously impractical plans to live her married life surrounded by plum orchards. Iseult's disenchantment with her husband, Eric, when he shows himself to be a "born" mechanic is also consonant with Lawrence's values (*ET,* 16). At her best, Iseult, whom Bowen frequently associates with sunlight, is the sun-woman Lawrence praises in his poem "Sun-women" and his short story "Sun." Lawrence's sun-woman turns "like a marigold to sun" in a man's face.[53] Similarly Iseult's radiance comes from her submission to male authority. Her intellect, symbolized by "her high white forehead," can only be revealed when she is male directed. But like all the priestesses of male power in Lawrence's works, Iseult poses a threat to the less socialized woman. Even as a medium for sunlight, Iseult suggests Winifred Inger in *The Rainbow* whose potentially corrupting presence affected Ursula like "the rays of some enriching sun, whose intoxicating heat poured straight into her veins" (*RB,* 335).

Lawrence's Winifred is what later feminists might call a male-identified woman, not because she accepts male definition but because her values are those traditionally associated with masculinity. According to Lawrence's essentialist belief in gender difference, Winifred is warped in a way that predicts her eventual alliance with a soullessly modern mine owner. "His real mistress was the machine, and the real mistress of Winifred was the machine. She too, Winifred, worshipped the impure abstraction, the mechanisms of matter" (*RB,* 349). She is the foil to Ursula, whose more female (at least in Lawrence's terms) love of organic life and oppositional value system cause her to reject the available, conventional, machine-worshipping men as her inferiors. Bowen, however, suggests not only that women are all trapped beyond hope of escape, but that Lawrence, as a literary father, has helped write the entrapping fiction.

Iseult cannot write herself into independent being. When she rebels against her husband and patron and tries to write her own novel, Iseult succeeds only in becoming a Lawrencian antiheroine. Like Ethel Cane, she wears her hair "in a bull fringe coming down low." Like Dollie Urquhart, she is slightly maddened by the knowledge that she can "never again" be "intact" (*ET,* 91). Like Gudrun, she has a "willed" sensuality (*ET,* 219). But without a man, she is unable to attain successful creativity; her novel is "born dead" (*ET,* 284). As if in obedience to Lawrence's railing against female emotionalism, Iseult gives herself "an emotional hysterectomy," also renounces her intellectual life, and resubmits to her husband's direction (*ET,* 231). At her last appearance, with Eric's "retaining hand" on her, she has "removed the hair from her forehead" and reflects his Lawrencian "coppery manly glowingness" (*ET,* 267).

Eva's responses to Iseult parallel Bowen's responses to Lawrence's texts. At first she tries to follow the same pattern in the same spirit, studying as Iseult dictates. But later, seeing that Iseult has "cast away everything," Eva tries instead to use the forms she has been taught while rejecting their content (*ET,* 188). Her strategy becomes subversive rather than imitative. She forces her way into Christian lore by staging a virgin birth in December. She tries to eliminate the patriarch by becoming "Jeremy's father as well as mother" (*ET,* 228). As female deity, she installs them in "an Eden" (*ET,* 117). Together they reclaim and alter mythology: "Jeremy capering naked on Eva's bed like Cupid cavorting over the couch of Venus" (*ET,* 192). But Jeremy is mute, and Iseult intervenes to make sure he receives language (via a special school). She also gives him a gun, which he uses to kill his mother, Eva.

Thus, early acceptance of the Lawrencian woman, in Bowen's view, seems to have fatal consequences. Eva's hopeless struggles to imitate Iseult, as well as Iseult's own failure to achieve a sense of self-worth, suggest that Lawrence's vision of woman is both highly seductive and impossible to live up to for a woman who has any existence outside his mind. Bowen implies that because both Lawrence and his critics have given his heroines religious and mythic significance, the imagination of a woman trying to write a woman-centered myth is likely to be invaded by Lawrencian values. Religion and myth have been co-opted by Lawrence's world and cannot be reclaimed.

To Bowen, Victorian sentimental literature, not without its own pitfalls, has also been displaced by Lawrence's vision. Eva tries to locate her love for Henry in what Bowen implies is Eva's feminization of the Dickensian world. When Eva sees a portrait of the young Dickens, she thinks of Henry, who is trying to rewrite her life. But Eva, with her usual disregard of sex roles, counters by treating Henry as if he were one of Dickens's heroines. Bowen, however, connects him thematically and imagistically to Henry in *The Fox.* Eva's submission to Henry echoes the death references in Lawrence's description of March and Henry's love affair. Contemplating her future as his wife, Eva says, "I am frightened, as though I were to die" (*ET,* 230). And, in fact, their wedding journey takes her to her death.

Although, from the beginning, Bowen rejects Lawrence's prescriptions for living, in her earlier work she is clearly attracted by his vision of redemption through transgressive sexual passion. While agreeing with George Eliot about the necessity for renunciation to preserve social decorum, Bowen does not depict renunciation as a type of consummation. Lovers, like Emmeline and Prothero, who destroy themselves in their attempts to break through the social world into some new and more passionate mode of being receive her sympathy. Their lack of self-control is shown as perversely beautiful, even romantically heroic, and their destruction as tragic. To the extent that these are Lawrencian characters, they are ennobled. Bowen continually suggests that if Lawrence could write over the world that is, life would be worthy of our essential, most authentic selves. In these early works, the Lawrencian vision is not identical to the male vision; rather a character like Emmeline can embody it in her opposition to conventional male fictions. With Emmeline, Bowen celebrates Lawrence's witch characters, as Anaïs Nin does, despite her knowledge that Lawrence, at least overtly, disapproves of them.

Lawrence is constructed intertextually as a wounded brother who has fought his way further than a woman writer can but is moving toward the same goal. Bowen's attitude toward him seems analogous to Woolf's, as it was expressed in a speech in which Woolf held Lawrence up as an example to her personified Imagination to show what constrictions and distortions afflicted the imaginations of those who dared to "run[ ] against convention." Woolf voices "doubt that a writer can be a hero," and cautions her Imagination to "wait another fifty years" before bringing her information "about women's bodies . . . their passion—and so on"; her Imagination sulkily pronounces it "a pity."[54]

In *Eva Trout,* Bowen's last novel, however, Lawrence is depicted as the definitive male writer. He is no longer the artistic rebel; instead he exemplifies patriarchal tradition. All of the competing fictions that have influenced life and thought are subsumed into his. His vision has written over everything else in the collective unconscious. He no longer provides material for feminist revision; the meanings of his works are fixed inalterably. Admiration for his women is no longer possible because their existence undermines female creativity. Because he possesses language, the (literary) mother dies. *Eva Trout* shows us a creative imagination so taken over by Lawrence that the only possible retreat from him is silence. It is a powerful, although playfully exaggerated, response both to Lawrence's new status as a great artistic moralist and to Bowen's own recognition that she has found his influence irresistible. The cutting edge of her humor turns in upon herself for becoming the "monstrous heiress" of a precursor who would disconnect her from women's tradition and take over her words (*ET,* 57).

Lessing shows a confidence in her authorial power that Bowen lacks. Lessing admits Lawrence's ideas into her world and then shows that they are inadequate to describe it. Like Martha in bed with Douglas, many of her protagonists forcefully put aside the book and act out their own compelling drama of female passion. Like Anna they write their own stories, in which Lawrence's values are tried and found insufficient. To the extent that they remained locked in conflict with his prior vision, Lessing seems to disown them, finding her narrative position in contrast to their compromised femininity. Bowen, however, like her female characters, remains trapped within Lawrence's fictions. Yet both women's development as writers involves Lawrence in ways too complex to call reaction. For each of them, finding her voice seems deeply connected to locating her work in relation not only to Lawrence's writing, but also to the world's reception of it. Christina Stead's fiction is also strongly marked by her struggles with Lawrence's influence and changing reputation. In that she seems to model major characters, at least partially, on Lawrence, as well as rewriting and revising scenes from his texts, her involvement with the Lawrence constructed by criticism seems the most intense.

In some ways, of the three writers, Stead would seem to have been the least connected to Lawrence. Only slightly younger than Bowen, Stead did not begin her life as a writer until after Lawrence's death, with the publication of *The Salzburg Tales* in 1934. Although, like Lawrence, Stead spent much of her life traveling, she does not seem to have had any significant contact with the Lawrence circle. She first read Lawrence's work during her stay in Paris (1929 to 1935), when her companion, William Blake, brought her Lawrence's poems. She went on to read Lawrence's fiction, most of which she seems to have enjoyed. But unlike Lessing and Bowen, she did not seem interested in commenting overtly in writing on his texts. When asked about him, by Joan Lidoff in a 1973 interview, Stead described him as "a marvelous man" and a genius but added that she did not "worship D. H. Lawrence. He has mortal sins." Lidoff's suggestion that Lawrence might have been a model for parts of Stead's 1944 novel, *For Love Alone,* met with Stead's vehement denial: "I never imitated him *at all*."[55]

Yet Lidoff was not the first critic to find *For Love Alone* reminiscent of *Women in Love*. Diana Trilling called her contemporary review of Stead's novel "Women in Love." Although Trilling does not mention Lawrence by name, she begins her review with the claim that men write better "novels about female love" than women do. Trilling praises two attributes of Stead's novel—sexual frankness and "a salutory carelessness"—which suggest she is using Lawrence as a standard. Trilling's main point, however, is that *For Love Alone* typifies modern women's novels about love which ironically "expose, all unconsciously, women's fatal inability to love."[56] Stead had every right to be annoyed that her novel was treated as a failed modernization of *Women in Love,* since it is filled with critical allusions to Lawrence's ideas as they are expressed in that novel and a great number of his other texts. While her familiarity with Lawrence's fiction, essays, and poetry is strikingly evident, *For Love Alone* is more of an answer to *Women in Love* than an imitation.

A few similarities between *Women in Love* and *For Love Alone* are readily apparent. Like *Women in Love,* Stead's novel begins with a wedding which is discussed by young women to show "the hypocrisy and limitations of social conventions."[57] *For Love Alone* also uses the Alps to symbolize the barrenness of a love affair. Shared "dreams of the cold, cold snow" bring Teresa and Jonathan into their first emotional rapport, and "a photograph from the Tyrol" is both the only picture Teresa has of Jonathan and the emblem of her goal.[58] Both novels are set on the eve of world wars. And as Lidoff observes, "[i]n style and vision, Chapter 33, 'The Deserted Sawmill,' is reminiscent of the scenes of sheer male-female antagonism in D. H. Lawrence's *Women in Love.*"[59] Even the setting, because it is a mill, recalls Birkin's rooms at the mill in *Women in Love.* But the storm-threatened mill is more powerfully evocative of the climactic scenes of *The Mill on the Floss,* and there are strong intertextual connections between Stead's novel, Eliot's, and the Lawrence novel it inspired, *The White Peacock.* Stead responds to several writers in *For Love Alone* but concentrates on Lawrence and Eliot, bringing various novels of theirs into dialogue with each other. The way she contextualizes this dialogue reveals both her arguments with some aspects of Lawrence's vision and the overall closeness of her ideology to his. Conversely, her profound opposition to Eliot's most fundamental ideas is also exposed.

The plot of *For Love Alone* recalls *The Mill on the Floss* because in each the heroine is passionate but repressed, and has two lovers, one of whom offers escape from an oppressive home but at the expense of fleshly pleasure, and another who offers sexual satisfaction and social status at the expense of honor. Like Maggie Tulliver, Teresa Hawkins is driven by physical desire to give up her idea of herself as an unshakably honorable, loyal lover. Nevertheless the novels do not present parallel problems. Teresa's first love, Jonathan Crow, has none of Philip Wakem's loving kindness or other virtues. Following Eliot's lead, Lawrence is relatively uncritical of the inadequate lover (Leslie), yet emphasizes the destructiveness of the woman (Lettie) who gives up fulfillment for his sake. But Stead depicts Jonathan as a parasitic monster. She neatly reverses Lawrence's image of the sensuality-renouncing woman as white peacock by making Jonathan, the man for whom Teresa would renounce the world, a carrion crow, not only in name but in dark, beak-nosed, black-clothed appearance. To choose Jonathan would be to choose absolute martyrdom. In the storm scene, the rain and rising "grinding and groaning" waters seem to Teresa not evidence of divine intervention—as they are to Maggie—but of "how unhuman" the world is. In the water-threatened mill, she sees the meaninglessness of her love and self-sacrifice. But the scene also parodies the fatalistic climax of Eliot's novel. Seemingly trapped and endangered, Jonathan and Teresa are actually both safe and free to leave, as he demonstrates when he impulsively announces "I'm hopping it," and runs to catch the eleven o'clock train (*FLA,* 400–401). As in *The White Peacock,* renunciation of sexual pleasure is shown to be pointless and foolish, not ennobling.

Stead's revisionary responses to *Middlemarch* are even more prominent than her allusions to *The Mill on the Floss* and even more sharply delineate the areas of disagreement with Eliot that Stead shares with Lawrence. As in Stead's revision of Maggie's climactic renunciation, she subjects the most conventionally moralistic elements of Eliot's vision of female heroism to a mocking skepticism that is often articulated in Lawrencian terms.

As Lidoff notes, Stead's heroine's name and writing project ("The Seven Houses of Love") recall the discussions of Saint Teresa that frame Eliot's novel. Like Eliot's "modern Theresa," Dorothea, Teresa Hawkins wants and expects to do great works. Both disdain ordinary marriage and domestic life, and both risk wasting themselves through their devotion to dry, selfish, and uninspired scholars. Eliot suggests that without a "coherent social faith" to guide them, young women direct toward men the intense emotions once spent in acts of "heroic piety."[60] Stead's Teresa is drawn toward this error. Her worship of Jonathan grotesquely parodies Dorothea's admiration of Casaubon, emphasizing its function as a substitute for religious ecstasy. In her "quaint" medieval style, she makes "a panel in seven sections" showing stages of Jonathan's life (*FLA,* 233–34). She plans to embroider a cloth with an image of Jonathan "as a priest of learning in a chasuble, green, gold, and white" (*FLA,* 275). When she realizes that her love for Jonathan is hopeless, Teresa dreams of "martyrdom" (*FLA*, 413). The comically horrible excesses of Teresa's passion explain her resistance, at the end of the novel, to peaceful domesticity with a man she loves. Stead contradicts Eliot's vision of idealistic questing as a stage through which heroic young women pass on their way to marriage by showing that the woman who yearns to serve a god will never be contented with ordinary marriage to a man.[61]

Stead rejects all the alternatives Eliot offers her modern St. Teresa, along with the inclination toward the displacement of female desire from sexuality to beneficial works that is implicit in Eliot's valorization of "a coherent social faith" as an absent but longed for site of redemption for the passionate heroine. Stead envisions her heroine's quest enacted within the Lawrencian cosmos in which sexuality is a transcendent value and the most worthy women are those who seek a man with whom they can achieve a deifying sexual communion. Teresa's thoughts, as she waits for the appearance of such a man, reveal Stead's concern with Lawrence's writings about sun-people:

> It was the hot, intolerable hour . . . when . . . the sun begins to embrace the earth and crush it with his weight. . . . At this time, there is no more love, conscience, remorse, or sin. In that room, in the furnace, she understood herself and knew what was wrong with the world of men. She felt like a giantess . . . somehow growing like an incommensurable flower from a root in the earth, pouring upwards into the brazen sky, "the woman clothed with the sun." At this hour each day, the sun, reckless, mad with ardour, created her newly. This was the hour when she lived as a heart lives inside a beast, she was the blood and the convulsion; outside was a living envelope, the world. (*FLA*, 98)

The first, organic simile used to describe Teresa is probably the most frequently recurring image in Lawrence's texts. More than half of his major characters are compared to flowers at one time or another, and the importance of roots "in the earth" is repeatedly stressed. In *Apocalypse*, Lawrence devotes a chapter to discussion of the meaning of "the woman clothed with the sun." The quotation is from the Bible (Rev. 12:1), but its context and interpretation are clearly from Lawrence. His observations are directly relevant to Teresa's life. He sees this sun-woman as a beneficent aspect of the Magna Mater necessary to "the religions of power" and antithetical to "the religions of renunciation, which are womanless." According to Lawrence, the fall of the pagan world drove her into the desert and "[s]ince she fled, we have had nothing but virgins and harlots, half-women."[62] When Teresa represses her pagan impulses and embraces renunciation for Jonathan's sake, she turns from a "large, robust" young woman to a frail, virginal half-woman, "Death and the Maiden in one person" (*FLA*, 285, 280). Eliot heroines like Maggie Tulliver and Dorothea continue to bloom and even ripen into luxuriant womanhood while practicing religions of renunciation; Teresa, like Lawrence's heroines, is only fully a woman while enjoying her power. Her existence in this passage as the powerful yet motionless center of a physically dynamic world connects her to the Teresa who exemplifies quiet female power in Lawrence's *Plumed Serpent*.

The *Plumed Serpent, Middlemarch,* and *For Love Alone* touch in the names of their protagonists and the women who serve as their foils: Eliot's modern Teresa and her sister who is nicknamed Kitty, Stead's sisters Teresa and Kitty, and Lawrence's quasi-sisters-in-law Teresa and Kate. Stead's pair suggests a reversal, like her transformation of the white peacock into the dark crow, that calls into question Lawrence's representation of human essences, and perhaps Eliot's, too. Like Kate, Stead's Teresa is a big, blond, aggressive woman who often expresses her refusal to defer to men and criticizes the other woman for her deference. Her early sense of the sexual power in her echoes that of Kate, who knows "what it is to rise grander and grander, till she fill[s] the universe with her womanhood."[63] Little dark Kitty resembles Lawrence's Teresa not only physically but in her position as the victim of brutish, bullying brothers. Stead, like Mansfield in her reenvisioning of Gudrun and Ursula, shows that the differences between the sisters are an illusion. By the middle of the novel they have exchanged roles, Teresa shrunken into Jonathan's neglected devotee and Kitty expanded by reciprocal love into a powerful "new woman" (*FLA*, 268). What seemed to have been their essences are suddenly revealed as their roles. In *The Plumed Serpent*, Kate and Teresa are offered fulfillment, without loss of the characteristics that differentiate them, as the exalted mates of men through whom the divine forces of nature flow. Stead considers the possibility of such salvation for her Teresa.

It is in Stead's working out of this alternative, through sections of her novel that echo Lawrence's short story "Sun," that her disagreement with one of Lawrence's prescriptions for women emerges. Like Juliet in "Sun," Teresa comes to understand, through her mystical connection with the sun, "what was wrong with the world of men."[64] Stead stresses various similarities between Teresa's and Juliet's situations. She compares "the blue and burning sky of Greece," which heals and sexually awakens Juliet, to that of Teresa's "own country as hot, as naive, as open" (*FLA,* 100). Both women free themselves of their inhibitions by going naked, and both, when experiencing communion with the sun, question their societies' sexual mores. Juliet wants a brief sexual encounter, for "as long as the desire lasts, and no more," with a sensual peasant whom she sees as a kind of sun-god. Teresa desires, and achieves, a brief affair with a man, who resembles the peasant, even to having a "dark-faced," jealous mate whose love is a kind of hatred ("Sun," 542). Although Teresa and her lover are in England, she makes the sun the figure of her passion (*FLA,* 458, 460).

The lover's name, Girton, suggests that she receives her education through him.[65] Certainly in this he resembles Ladislaw, who radiantly bestows a sensual education on Dorothea instead of the intellectual schooling she had sought. But while Stead seems to agree with Lawrence that such a substitution is no tragedy, she goes further away from gender mores than he does with her dramatization of free play with desire, rather than union with any one man, as the heroine's proper goal. Like Kate, in *The Plumed Serpent,* Teresa cannot rest, even with the man who puts her in contact with the "living god" in "an inner room of herself" (*FLA,* 479). She is driven on by the "voluptuous sense of power" Lawrence condemns in Kate. Teresa, like Kate, wants to travel "unlimited" out into endless discovery of the world (*PS,* 480–82).

Stead's reading of Lawrence, as expressed in her own text, recalls Nin's. She disregards Lawrence's apparent disapproval of women who refuse monogamy, and she finds the true heroine in the female characters whose energy he seems to have meant us to consider misdirected. Stead takes from Lawrence a style in which to describe the pleasure Teresa finds with Girton, but she also shows us that Lawrence's prescriptions for women are inadequate for Teresa. Diana Brydon convincingly argues that Stead's refusal to see any contradiction between her heroine's desire to love freely and her artistic creativity not only goes against "traditional male assumption[s]," but also places Stead's fiction in a peripheral relation to most recognized literary traditions.[66]

Like Lessing's Martha Quest, Teresa has "ravaged libraries" since girlhood searching for books that can both describe and guide her experience. She soon discovers that "her world existed and was recog-

nized by men [but] not by women" (*FLA*, 73–74). Like Woolf's personified Imagination, Teresa sets out eagerly in Lawrence's tracks. But this
early discovery of the path blazed by literary brothers is modified by her
later experiences of the barriers they have (re)placed in the way of
women. Stead shows us that Lawrence's prescriptions for women only
replace one type of repression with another. As in *The Golden Notebook,*
woman must pass beyond sexual involvement to achieve freedom. If
Lawrence's vision can take Teresa farther toward happiness than Eliot's,
it still fails to provide her with an adequate guide to life.

Since a subtext of this semiautobiographical novel is that we find or
create fictions by which we live, this failure has metatextual significance.
All of the major characters in *For Love Alone* are storytellers. The first
chapter opens with Andrew Hawkins, Teresa's father, telling his daughters self-aggrandizing stories and urging them to say they believe him.
Because Teresa refuses to credit his stories, Andrew creates the further
fiction that she is "frozen," "too cold" to be loved (*FLA*, 5, 10). She
remains entrapped by this description throughout the first section of the
novel, as if her father had written rather than begotten her and she must
live out his story. The two men who most powerfully define her, after
her father, also do so in Lawrencian terms. And through their development as characters, Stead reveals her sense of her own relationship(s) to
Lawrence, as his texts created him.

Jonathan's characterization brings Lawrence to mind in several ways.
His experiences recall those of Lawrence's fictionalized self, Paul Morel,
and most accounts of Lawrence's early life. He is a poor boy who rises
above his circumstances. "His mother [is] a sturdy, brave woman who
[keeps] the family together and his father a weak kind of fellow" (*FLA*,
125). His manner with this "fair caution" who "keeps her men" "under
her wing until pretty late in the day" is flirtatious (*FLA*, 425). He attracts
a retinue of women, "a group of admirers of himself, sedulously collected, carefully selected," whose "Female Psychology" he coolly studies (*FLA*, 182). He sends "amazingly fluent," "ardent, innocent letters"
(*FLA*, 318, 198). But in person he is "passive"; "the restless tumultuous
breed of women always did the work of passion for him" (*FLA*, 190).
Much in his insistent and brutal categorization of Teresa as a born
spinster seems to parody Paul's treatment of Miriam (or Lawrence's of
Jessie Chambers). As if to stress the similarity between Paul and Jonathan, Stead shows the end of Jonathan's affair with a married woman

named Clara (like Paul's married lover), whom he sends back to her husband, as Paul does. In this episode, however, and in every other in which we see him, his behavior is exaggeratedly sadistic. He is more a satire on than an imitation of Lawrence.

Jonathan's ideas, too, parody Lawrence's least appealing pronouncements. Lawrence argues, notably in *Fantasia of the Unconscious* and *Education of the People,* against teaching children liberal-humanist ideals and in favor of encouraging them to be bold and physically brave; Jonathan tells Teresa, "A real educational system would take them and knock them around . . . turn them into real tough guys" (*FLA,* 125). Some of his assertions sound exactly like Lawrence's: "It isn't analysis that gets you anywhere in these human beings, but touch"; "we can do without the St. Teresas as well as the legendary libertine"; and "women must not imitate men's civilization which had only a bread-winning purpose" (*FLA,* 286, 409, 181). His intentions are grotesquely self-serving, however, and he is not talented enough to succeed at anything more demanding than "writing forewords to great works" and deceiving naïve women (*FLA,* 422). Teresa is deceived for a while, but, just as she grows beyond her father's control, she develops beyond Jonathan's. As a figure for the misogynistically doctrinal Lawrence, Jonathan is not powerful or attractive enough permanently to write over or limit an intelligent woman. Stead, like Lawrence's female contemporaries, is sure enough of her own creative authority to stand against the Lawrence that demanded the right to cast woman in a subordinate role.

The prophetic Lawrence, who called himself the priest of love and so often seemed the priest of woman, exerted a more seductive force. This Lawrence appears in James Quick's attempts to create a fiction that can both contain Teresa and bind her to him. Quick is based on Stead's lover, William Blake, a great admirer of Lawrence's work. Quick's speeches often reveal Lawrence's influence on his concept of love. His ritualistic kissing of Teresa echoes Lawrence's poem "Seven Seals," and her description of this action as "chaining her to him" is particularly evocative of the poem, in which Lawrence refers to the kisses twice as a chain (*FLA,* 438). Quick's belief that "a woman satisfied, slept, became languid, lazy and fat," may come from "hundreds of queer stories, part of the legend of the male," but it is also a crucial part of Lawrence's philosophy of love (*FLA,* 468).

Stead's ambivalence about Lawrence's definitions of woman seems to structure the love story. Although Quick brings Teresa lifesaving warmth and is, in Lawrence's diction, "quick" rather than "deathly," he still presents a threat to her. His words make "a world for" her (*FLA*, 416). He wants to "make her over entirely" (*FLA*, 444). And, as Lidoff notes, when Teresa gives herself to Quick, "[t]he sun imagery of their courtship clouds into storm imagery."[67] Quick goes "cold" when Teresa tries to tell him her own version of their love (*FLA*, 449). He urges her to accept his "storm of words" and allow herself to be carried off by the "high tide" of his emotions that flood over all she knows, but she shrinks from it like the miscast Maggie Tulliver she is (*FLA*, 444, 485).

Inextinguishably sunny, silent Girton seems to promise a reversal of Teresa's situation. He is the hero of fictions, "extraordinary tales," not their author ("It was not Girton but others who told the story of his home life"); the object not the creator of representations ("like a pictured Englishman he was") (*FLA*, 462, 456). But instead of allowing her the artist's shaping role, Girton travels alone into countries and situations that will determine his life in a way that Teresa's imagination cannot. He moves beyond the range of her fiction making.

Like Bowen, Stead believes that life is composed of fictions, which one either writes or is written into. Teresa's great realization at the end of *For Love Alone* is that she and Jonathan were locked in a struggle for narrative control (which is represented in the shifting narrative perspective). Her thought upon seeing, but not recognizing, him is, "I'd like to write a story on that incomprehensible type." When Quick questions her interpretation of her and Jonathan's perceptions of each other, at the moment of mutual recognition, Teresa is left with a "bitter" sense that "it will go on being repeated for ever": love necessitating inaccurate and limiting definition of the beloved and the truth nowhere (*FLA*, 490–91). But, like a poem about the impossibility of writing a poem, or like a feminist text about women's absolute lack of access to language, *For Love Alone* contradicts its own conclusion. The silence that she believes must be eternal about both "the steps which had led her from Jonathan to Quick" and her affair with Girton, is broken by the novel (*FLA*, 450).

Teresa dreams of somehow "weaving" her lovers into her life in such a way that she is free while they are "prisoners" (*FLA*, 483). Stead finds this power as the writer of all their stories, and, as H. D. did, she resolves her problems with Lawrence by incorporating him, too, into her fiction. It does not seem accidental that Teresa's most compelling lover, Girton, is compared explicitly to Lawrence. Girton is prefigured by her father, the first to define her, whom he resembles even to the "somewhat bloodshot eyes" and "pale yellowish flesh"; and by Quick, who shares Girton's sun and storm imagery, foreshadows his effect on Teresa, and acts as Teresa's male half. So much like her they seem to be "brother and sister," Girton stands for the male presence without whom Teresa's creed of passionate love would be meaningless (*FLA,* 456, 461, 477). For a woman writer like Stead, who finds other women's fictions inadequate because they deny her own experience, revisionary use of Lawrence's works has a special attractiveness.

In *For Love Alone,* Stead deals with Lawrence confidently, using whatever she finds empowering in his texts while easily rejecting his negative judgments of independent women and unsparingly satirizing the flaws in his vision. But in the 1966 novel *Cotter's England,* her confidence in her equal authority seems shaken and her attitude toward Lawrence is correspondingly dark, even despairing. Lawrence's place in the novel is slight, yet the few references to his ideas are chilling. The protagonist, Nellie (Cotter) Cook, is an obsessive storyteller whose stories are meant to enslave and destroy her listeners. The exact opposite of Teresa, who is the woman clothed with the sun, Nellie is the terrible moon-goddess Birkin fears. Her final and successful ploy in urging her friend Caroline to commit suicide is to force her to watch a moonlit, Lesbian orgy. Nellie demands the suicide as a "beautiful sacrifice" to her "power."[68] As Susan Sheridan observes, Nellie's speeches resemble those of Stead's other female protagonists in their disruption of patriarchal systems of meaning. But rather than inverting "the conventional hierarchy of signification" and so revealing "a capacity to see the centre afresh from the margins," as the "woman-centered" prose of *For Love Alone* does, Nellie's dishonest, contradictory discourse undermines all interpretive positions, including that of the feminist-outsider.[69] She is woman the enemy of woman, as Lawrence imagines her in such characters as Hermione in *Women in Love* and Mrs. Bolton in *Lady Chatterley's Lover.*

Nonetheless, Nellie's evil comes not from going against Lawrence's ideas, but from her agreement with them. Like Lawrence, Nellie is fond of the word *submission* and browbeats poor Caroline with "constant advice about submitting" (*CE,* 293). Her demand that Caroline " 'Sink the turbulent selfish soul' " recalls Lawrence's frequent recommendations to his friends and the characters in his fictions to give up "self," and it is especially reminiscent of his discussion of Kate's need to "sink some of [her] individuality" and "make [her] submission" (*CE*, 294; *PS*, 481–82). Lawrence is again evoked when Caroline speculates that Nellie is obsessed with submission because of her repressed knowledge that she is dying of lung disease.

The terms in which Nellie discusses her marriage are also Lawrence's. She speaks of herself and her husband, George, knowing "each other as man and woman in perfection" (*CE*, 16). The reality, however, recalls Lawrence and Frieda at their worst. We see them in bed together substituting fighting for sex, shouting until "the whole house [is] stirred up, wakened, kept awake" (*CE*, 305) Nellie's brother, Tom, enacts with his own big, blond lover, Frida, another unpleasant part of the Lawrence legend. A motherly woman, Frida is moved by Tom's declaration that he "must be warmed." He explains to her that he is "two men," one strong and passionate, the other frail and cold (*CE*, 243). But the strong, passionate Tom is an illusion. Like Jonathan Crow, he attracts female admirers whom he cannot satisfy.

The brother and sister who are connected by an emotional intensity that supersedes all other bonds recall both *The Mill on the Floss* and *Wuthering Heights*. Like Eliot and Emily Brontë, Stead depicts a relationship in which the brother represents a part of his sister's essential self that she can neither repress nor assimilate into her chosen persona. Their preoccupation with each other is inevitable but unnatural, as is illustrated by its destructive impact on them and those who love them. Like Lessing and Bowen, however, Stead reaches Brontë and Eliot through Lawrence. The "fatal brother and sister" are like the impotent, infantile Lawrence of his enemies' memoirs and a nightmare of the woman storyteller who would use his preachings to destroy others. Their sterile yet sex-obsessed world brings to mind Bowen's comment on contemporary sexual behavior: "The pattern [Lawrence] projected is being approximated now—how lifelessly, sometimes, only Lawrence could know!"[70]

The unions in death of Tom and Maggie and Cathy and Heathcliff are presented by their authors as partial triumphs, wholeness snatched back from socially compelled division. But Bowen, Lessing, and Stead insist, as Lawrence does, on the importance of sexuality to the connection between the woman and her brother-figure. Consequently, all four modern authors show that the union must be achieved in life and the flesh. But for all the women writers, except Brontë, the coming together of the divided woman with her male half is a real death, the end of the possibility of female wholeness, the state of being utterly written over by the male. Bowen's Davina, Lessing's Anna, and Stead's Teresa can survive only by recognizing the male double as a part of themselves and then separating from him. That the writers themselves seem to see Lawrence as a sort of brother-self who is always on the verge of becoming a devouring father (or an overwriting, patriarchally empowered precursor) necessitates both their recognition of his influence and their efforts to distance themselves from it by manipulating it.

Stead's use of Lawrence in *Cotter's England* comments on the modern woman author's sense of her inability to contain and control Lawrence's influence. For her female storyteller, Lawrence's ideas have not stood the test of time. Nellie, like Eva Trout and Mary Turner, inhabits a morally empty world. She can no more truly understand Lawrence's values than she can interpret the references to honor in Caroline's last letter. While Lessing seems to believe, at least in *The Golden Notebook,* that the creative woman can fight through to a paradoxically loving freedom from the Lawrencian male twin, for Stead, like Bowen, the postwar world seems to have become too corrupt, too devoid of values to make constructive use of Lawrence's work. For the creative-imaginative woman of this period, he can be no more than another corrupting influence. And to the extent that criticism has invested him with the moral authority to define woman, he is a demon lover to the woman writer, seducing her and then eating up her inner self.

Lawrence seems to have a great deal to do with the fiction of our female contemporaries. Engagement with Lawrence's ideas is one of the most striking common elements in Lessing's politically conscious novels about cultural subgroups, Bowen's mandarin stories of manners, and Stead's black comedies. Lessing, Bowen, and Stead seem, in their earlier works, to take Lawrence's texts as models in their depiction of female experience, just as if he were another woman writer. All three implicitly compare him with George Eliot. Stead apparently, like Leavis, finds his descriptions of female inner life superior to Eliot's. Until after the rise of Lawrence's critical reputation in the fifties, Lessing remains in at least surface agreement with his doctrine, while, during the same period, Bowen and Stead seem to read Lawrence as Nin did, treating his rebellious creative women as positive figures. In these treatments of Lawrence, we can see a freemasonry of the marginalized such as Woolf hoped for: literary tradition leaping beyond the lines culture draws around sex.

But even before the Lawrence revival, his female admirers had to confront Lawrence's sexist pronouncements. Under this pressure, Lessing splits herself into narrators at cross-purposes and parodically dramatizes what she overtly confirms. In a sense, both Bowen and Stead could be considered to have responded by dividing him into a helpful and a destructive Lawrence, one of whom facilitates the female self-expression that the other forbids. In Bowen's pre-1950s work, he appears in versions of both his female characters (whom she shows creating generative, open fictions) and his male characters (whom she shows restrictively writing over them). In Stead, the deathly, misogynous Lawrence threatens the female ineffectually while the "quick" Lawrence opens the door to creativity for the developing woman writer.

A large part of Lessing's, Bowen's, and Stead's fiction is devoted to metafictional references to the special problems they must surmount as women writers. This may account for their strenuous rejection of Lawrence's ideas after he was elevated to the position of a literary master and moral teacher. When Lawrence suddenly surpassed them, and his rise was justified through praise of his misogyny and at the expense of his female contemporaries' literary achievements, it must have been a powerful reminder of the privileging of men's texts. Their fears that Lawrence would invade, cancel, or corrupt their work might otherwise seem inappropriate to such talented and important writers. The ways all three writers find to express these fears in their fiction tell us almost as much about the negative effects that the hegemony of masculinist aesthetics in some of the most influential ethical criticism of the 1950s had on the imaginations of many talented women as they do about the growth of antagonism in the relationship between Lawrence's and women's fictions. But it seems to be specifically the criticism, which changed Lawrence's place in literature, that intruded upon the previously fruitful interplay between his texts and women's and restructured it. Although this intrusion has utterly altered the direction of feminist criticism of Lawrence, it does not seem to have affected all women's fictive responses to Lawrence. Eudora Welty remains an instructive exception to the general trend; her many revisionary responses to Lawrence's work seem to defy historicization, at least of this sort.

"The Flowing of Two Rivers Side by Side"

Floods of Female Desire in D. H. Lawrence and Eudora Welty

IN RECENT YEARS THOSE of us who are interested in literary history have become divided over questions about the appropriate relationship of feminist criticism to the literary canon. By definition the study of women's literature has most often excluded consideration of men's works. The focus of most feminist criticism on women's texts has done much to correct the traditional underestimation of the role played by female experience and modes of expression in shaping literary forms and determining the themes favored by literature. The beneficial influence of women's writings on men's texts is now established. We recognize the magnitude, for example, of Dorothy Wordsworth's influence on her brother, William, and of George Eliot's influence on Lawrence. But perhaps in reaction to the past, male writers' positive participation in female literary tradition receives little attention.

Many feminist critics follow Elaine Showalter's recommendation that we "stop trying to fit women between the lines of the male tradition, and focus instead on the newly visible world of female culture."[1] While this approach is attractive because it eliminates the problem of how to compare traditions without conferring an implicit primacy on one, it is also troubling because it ignores the dialogue between male and female authors that contributes to female literary traditions. Critics like Adrienne Munich argue for the feminist study of male-authored texts because "the literary canon contains . . . a valuable record of a conflict between sex, gender and common humanity."[2] For Munich this conflict takes place within texts, while for Sandra Gilbert and Susan Gubar, in *The War of the Words,* it takes place between texts. What both of these approaches have in common is their assumption that hostility and conflict determined by gender identity play a major role in shaping literary traditions. But in a literary relationship where we might expect to see intense conflict and hostility, the one between women's writings and Lawrence's, we can frequently see something quite different: an impulse toward revisionary response that is often apparently friendly to the precursor and almost always enabling for the respondent. If female literary tradition is in some sense fluid, it does not seem to flow away from or against Lawrence's work.

Much modern feminist literary criticism starts with the idea that women flow, and it uses water or liquid as a metaphor for femaleness.[3] With great regularity and less connection to the methodology of the critic than might be expected, male thought is characterized as rigid, static, fixed while the female imagination is fluid. These metaphors have a logical relationship to the social structure, and in particular to the structure of the academic and literary worlds in that both have been dominated by men. From the female viewpoint, men's ideas created the structures that limit female expression. What is female in literature, whether seen as an individual woman's creative product or a force disruptive of masculine discourse, is whatever escapes exterior definition and control, what flows free. While this idea is most prominent in French feminist criticism, which questions processes of signification, Anglo-American feminist criticism, which begins with the assumption that female experience can be expressed in language and concerns itself (primarily) with women's texts and traditions, also claims rebellion against and escape from literary and linguistic conventions as particularly female attributes. Gilbert and Gubar's reading of *Wuthering Heights* exemplifies this attitude.[4]

Because of the seductiveness of this way of thinking, it is especially important to remember that it is metaphoric. Since our ideas about what distinguishes women's literature from men's, *écriture féminine* from patriarchal discourse, or simply the female voice from the male are informed by the metaphor of fluidity, a close look at its place in literary tradition can help us reach a deeper understanding of what a feminist approach to literature includes and also how such an approach has been included in literary tradition, as women writers make revisionary responses to male precursors. It may also yield a way to understand the interplay between Lawrence's and Eudora Welty's fiction that does justice to both authors' opposition to fixed concepts of gender without ignoring their participation in specific traditions.

Lawrence's and Welty's texts often seem to be following the same traditions. In the high-modernist mode exemplified by Joyce and Yeats, both writers appropriate myth to create a sense of profundity beneath the romantic exploits of unthinking characters. Welty's many references and allusions to Yeats show her deliberate affiliation with him. To many critics, however, she also seems to be Lawrence's inheritor. Characters in her fiction are often described as Lawrencian. And she has written in praise of the greatness and the poetic beauty of Lawrence's fiction.[5] The specific myths she chooses to rework and her fondness for sun imagery are strongly reminiscent of Lawrence's texts. Lawrence's and Welty's visions come closest to converging, however, in their reliance on traditional associations of woman and water to provide a foundation for their representations of female desire.

In order to raise some necessary questions about why and how we imagine women as flowing, I will look at Lawrence's and Welty's treatments of the metaphoric connection between women and water and how these treatments fit into a greater context of thought about women and desire. The most logical starting point in each writer's work is the text that takes the awakening of a girl's desire and a flood as its dual subjects.

D. H. Lawrence's short novel *The Virgin and the Gipsy* is about a climactic flood and the events that lead up to it. The life of the young female protagonist, Yvette, is restricted by both the memory of an absent, rebellious mother and the presence of a dictatorial, ultraconservative grandmother, called the Mater. Yvette's surname, Saywell, symbolizes the family's preoccupation with presenting a proper front to society. But Yvette herself seems oblivious to decorum. She moves through the story like a somnambulist, utterly absorbed in the formation and development of her own sexual feelings. She becomes fascinated by a gypsy. A flood comes, literally sweeping her into the gypsy's arms and destroying the Mater. The gypsy saves Yvette's life and awakens her sexually. Afterwards she falls into inertia, "moaning," "prostrate" with desire for the gypsy, who has gone away.[6] The story leaves her waiting for his return.

Eudora Welty's short story "At the Landing" is about a climactic flood and its aftermath. Jenny, the girlish protagonist, is completely dominated by the memory of her dead mother, who had "died of" her longing for escape, and the domineering grandfather who forbad that escape. Even though Jenny's family name, Lockhart, comes from her father, it well describes the attitude of the grandfather, who shuts himself and his female descendants into a narrow world of old-fashioned propriety. Jenny drifts through the story seemingly motivated only by her attraction to Billy Floyd (a near rhyme for flood), whom one of the town's Greek chorus of old ladies calls "Gipsy."[7] A flood that coincides with the grandfather's death (as was predicted in his last dream) brings Jenny and Floyd together briefly when he saves and then "violates" her ("Landing," 251). She pursues him in a sort of dream that deepens into what seems to be a trance after she is gang-raped. Her almost catatonic condition is described as "waiting for Billy Floyd" ("Landing," 258).

The thematic similarities between the two stories, their publication dates (*The Virgin and the Gipsy,* 1930; "At the Landing," 1943), the interest Welty has shown in Lawrence's work, the pervasiveness of Lawrencian imagery in her work, and especially the nearly identical use of water to represent female desire in these two texts could easily lead us to consider this a straightforward case of influence. This idea must be much modified, however, if we look at the two texts with almost any other that brings together female sexuality and water, for instance, the following lines from "Khubla Khan":

> But oh! that deep romantic chasm which slanted
> Down the green hill athwart a cedarn cover!
> A savage place! as holy and enchanted
> As e'er beneath a waning moon was haunted
> By woman wailing for her demon-lover!
> And from this chasm, with ceaseless turmoil seething,
> As if this earth in fast thick pants were breathing,
> A mighty fountain momently was forced: (12–19)

The relationship between the texts immediately seems more complex. And if we try to understand the relationship in feminist terms, it becomes more difficult still. Are we looking at a female response to a traditionally male way of representing woman—an appropriation and reenvisioning—or at an instance of male-identification and transmission of male myths in Welty's work? Or at the breaking through of the feminine to assert a truth of the female body in all three texts? Familiarity with the language of feminist criticism only adds another dimension to the problem.

The use of flowing liquid (fountains, rivers, floods) to represent sexual passion is obviously determined by physical reality. As the lines from Coleridge suggest, the seeming simplicity of this imagery is disturbed by its feminization of desire and sexual response. The fountain, which we might expect to be phallic, issues from the female cleft in the body of earth and is associated with the sexual longing of the "woman wailing." In depicting spurting, flooding desire as exclusively feminine, Coleridge is adhering to an ancient tradition. Marina Warner traces back to Tuccia the Roman Vestal Virgin and Horace's ode on the Danaides the figuration of woman as a full vessel that would spring leaks at her expression of any sexual desire—even one to preserve an unlawful virginity.[8] What we see in this trope is a place at which the two major symbolic functions of woman in Western culture touch.

On the one hand, woman is flux, the tides and floods man cannot control. On the other she stands for abstract virtues. If she is the land man conquers and the waterway he claims, she is also the figure of Liberty, Justice, or Courage on his flag. According to Warner, a hard, shell-like structure—whether it is armor enclosing the woman's body or an impermeable vessel enclosing a body of water signifying her essence—reverses the inscription of uncontrol, chaos, and makes the female body, instead, a "fitting container of high and virtuous meanings." Fluids that are miraculously prevented from flowing (the brimming sieve of Tuccia, proof of her chastity; the sealed fountain that symbolizes the Virgin Mary) seem to represent purity in this imagistic system.[9] But when woman asserts her (desiring) self against such external definition and (implicitly masculine) control, she is imagined as the source of a flood of variously exciting and repellent fluids. As Gail Kern Paster shows, the "leaky vessel" concept of woman is used to justify the patriarchal order; when a culture conflates all that comes out of woman, from speech to urine, into a sign of female uncontrol, it seems best to seal off female self-expressiveness with a second container, a hard social body that completely encloses woman's leaky natural body.[10] Then her floods can be released at (man's) will and so made useful, that is, subordinated to man's purposes.

Stephen Heath reads Lawrence as belonging to this patriarchal tradition, in contrast to the modern women writers who celebrate the female body and text as unrestrained fluidity. But the very fact that Lawrence, too, sees woman as fluid, in Heath's view, makes "problems quickly emerge" with the concept of flowing femaleness that he finds in Hélène Cixous, Michèle Montrelay, Luce Irigaray, Virginia Woolf, Dorothy Richardson, and Gillian Beer. It seems to me, however, that what Heath refers to as "the existing system" of correspondences between concepts of gender difference and concepts of flow/fixity is more complex than what he describes, and there seems to be room, within the system, for more differences than the two he sees: men's use of the fluidity trope to categorize woman as "in every sense a sex object" and women's rebellious use of it to assert a positive female identity.[11] The trope frequently marks a point within texts where many different attitudes toward gender, sexuality, and socialization converge. The broader the historical context in which we place the text, the more voices become audible within the representation of woman-as-water—and the less easily we can place Lawrence and Welty in relation to each other.

Clearly it was convenient for the Greeks, who held rigid self-control to be the most masculine of virtues, to imagine sexual abandonment as a fluid rush and boiling over that was natural and beneficial only to woman and only when she was directed by man,[12] and for medieval churchmen, who believed celibacy was the most fundamental of their virtues, to describe woman as an "improperly stoppered container" of vile liquids.[13] Moreover, as Paster points out, in eras when childbirth was frequent and gynecology primitive, the commonness of vaginal injury resulting in urinary incontinence supported the view of woman as "leaky vessel."[14] And, of course, even healthy women may lack bladder control during pregnancy, and at other times noticeably leak menstrual blood and breast milk. Consequently, while the vision of woman as the source of a flow she cannot fully control is a necessary part of patriarchal ideology, it is also derived from physical reality. Thus flowing woman signifies the material world against which man defines his controlling, structuring, idealizing self. Because her flux is a reminder of mortality, she also represents the inner life of the body, the revelation of which is always disturbing.

What flows from the image of woman is not limited to physical secretions. As much as she produces tangible (if also symbolic) liquids, she produces that fluid substance desire. Klaus Theweleit hardly seems to be overstating the situation when he claims that "in all European literature (and all literature influenced by it), desire . . . always flows in relation to the image of woman." Consequently fluid represents her, and she excites the same fears as unchanneled water and unruly bodily fluid, historically blamed for both passion and madness. But as the numerous examples Theweleit provides in *Male Fantasies* amply demonstrate, not all male writers associate female fluidity with threatening dissolution; some celebrate it as "a new transcendence that finally abolishes lack."[15] When the discovery of boundaries to the self is perceived as a loss and diminishment and brings a terrifying sense of mortality, deifying female fluidity can restore a primal feeling of infinite connectedness. Some male authors' images of woman-as-water recall Wilhelm Reich's description of orgasm as "a 'streaming' " and Romain Rolland's characterization of the spiritual sense of limitlessness as "oceanic." In the flood of (imagined) female desire, male writers may find their own, but unfortunately in the process female desire is confused with and finally subsumed into the desire the thought of it releases in the male author. The subjectivity in which the female desire originates is dissolved in the flood that makes woman the object of man's desiring. Such oceanic women appear as usually nameless, always depersonalized pleasure sources.[16]

Although Lawrence has some affinities with both the writers who fear watery women and those who idolize her, his works defy such categorization because of the primacy he gives female experience. Those of his texts that connect women and water seem to belong to a slightly different trend of thought than that which leads from archaic sealed fountains and leaky vessels to modern oceanic goddesses and fiends in flood. While Lawrence's watery women are not utterly different from those whom men have traditionally imagined, because of their stubborn retention of subjectivity they are best understood in relation to women's fictions on the same topic.

In the Victorian period, the renaissance of women's fiction making, George Eliot notably altered the use of water as a figure for woman. But the triumphal rise of feminized waves in *The Mill on the Floss, Romola,* and *Daniel Deronda* are not without precedent. As Elaine Showalter points out, *Jane Eyre,* as well as *The Mill on the Floss,* makes water emblematic of *wrongly* repressed female passion and uses flood imagery to signify its release, although what is explicit in Eliot's novel is only suggested in Brontë's.[17] When Jane tries to deny her love for Rochester, she "hear[s] a flood loosened in remote mountains," and, because she cannot sincerely pray to resist, "the torrent pour[s] over" her.[18] The threat that Jane will be destroyed through union with the unloving minister, Rivers, links the image of the flooding river to the danger posed to the passionate soul by a narrow and conventional Christianity. In contrast to earlier texts, *Jane Eyre* condemns the containment of female passions and consequently hints at a redefinition of flood as (female) nature's revenge. So, in its own way, does *The Mill on the Floss*. But in Maggie's case, the sudden release, the rush of "water flowing under her," is literally the answer to her prayer to be spared the "trials" a repressive, patriarchal society imposes.[19] In the moment of flood, both heroines find and enter their own essences. As Mary Jacobus says, "It is at this moment of inundation, in fact, that the thematics of female desire surface most clearly."[20] The impact on Lawrence's imagination of Eliot's, and perhaps Brontë's, use of flood imagery seems particularly strong.

Like Eliot and Brontë, Lawrence quite naturally associates rising waters with female sexual arousal. Lawrence refers, in *The Ladybird,* to Daphne's desire for Psanek as a "full river," seemingly in allusion to flood imagery in *Jane Eyre* and *The Mill on the Floss*. But this bringing together of female desire and water is by no means limited to two of Lawrence's texts. In *The Trespasser,* a "small, inaccessible sea cave" becomes the objective correlative for the body of the girl whose desire lures the hero, Siegmund, to his destruction.[21] But Lawrence usually gives flood a more positive valuation. In *Kangaroo,* inrushing sea water represents revitalizing contact with female sexuality to Richard Lovat Somers. Paul and Clara, in *Sons and Lovers,* experience a soul-renewing sexual communion on the red bank of the Trent swollen with "flood water."[22] The flood in *The Rainbow* immediately follows Anna and Will's discovery of "a sensuality violent and extreme as death."[23] Cornelia Nixon convincingly argues that fluidity in both this novel and *Sons and Lovers* stands for a female power that allows the characters who feel it to "leap beyond social convention into sexual fulfillment."[24] Alvina, in *The Lost Girl,* "swoons" with sexual desire "as if the flood–gates of her depths opened."[25] All of these floods are beneficial not only because they stand for the expression of valuable, natural feelings but because they symbolically sweep away the outdated (usually conventionally Christian) belief systems that had perverted, apparently by channeling, streams of passionate darkness. As in *The Plumed Serpent,* the "dark twilight" of the miraculous new age follows "the massive rain" and the consummation "far down under the tides."[26]

Both Brontë and Eliot treat the social world and its rules as unalterable; consequently their floods are ambiguous, capable of drowning as well as freeing their female sources. Jane's and Maggie's passions can flow wildly, even healingly, within or over the patriarchal structure, but can go entirely out of it only into death. Lawrence goes further than Brontë and Eliot in assigning female floods power and positive value. In his novels, they become apocalyptic forces opening space for an era of fulfillment and wholeness. And nowhere in his work is this theme more prominent than in *The Virgin and the Gipsy.*

That Lawrence was thinking about *The Mill on the Floss* when he wrote *The Virgin and the Gipsy* is suggested not only by their shared symbolic use of water but by similarities in their depiction of gypsies. Maggie and Yvette both identify with gypsy alienation only to discover that beneath the surface strangeness of the gypsies are ordinary Englishmen. (These experiences are prefigured by Rochester's fortunetelling masquerade in *Jane Eyre.*) We might go so far as to speculate that Lawrence's novel was meant in part as a revisionary response to Eliot's because of the number of thematic correspondences: a young girl grows up in an atmosphere in which any display of strong feelings is considered indicative of a fatal personality flaw, her father is obsessed with his social position, she defines herself against a domineering matriarch (Mrs. Glegg/the Mater), she is drawn to an outcast, her innocence leads to social compromise, and finally her irrepressible desire seems to call up a flood. In retelling this story, Lawrence does away with all the fatalistic acquiescence to the world that determines the possibilities Eliot allows Maggie. Most of Eliot's work dramatizes the pain of passionate women who can only hope that the raging rivers of their "full nature[s]" will be broken by marriage and maternity and so "spent . . . in channels which [have] no . . . name on . . . earth"—rather than building to drowning force.[27] Nature is a weak sister to Maggie; it can only resolve her struggle with herself. But Lawrence's heroine rises triumphantly above the wave of her desire, invulnerable as long as she defies social rules to express it, because nature takes her part against man's world. In flooding with desire, the Lawrencian woman is invoking a powerful goddess.

"At the Landing" is both the most Lawrencian of Welty's stories, in its readily apparent echoes of *The Virgin and the Gipsy,* and the least in accord with his values. Welty and Lawrence often seem to draw on mythological traditions for similar reasons. She has praised Lawrence's honesty, which, to her, is manifested in his concentration on the "poetic world" that underlies "the everyday world."[28] Both writers see the hidden world, the reality behind the veil of appearance, as one in which myth still retains its potent meaning because nature exercises its own will. As William Jones has shown, beginning with "Death of a Traveling Salesman," her first published story, Welty frequently uses the same mythic imagery that Lawrence does to depict the magical power of "the organic world."[29] Here images of rising waters and floating are connected to desire and "delirium."[30] In another early story, "Clytie," her use of sun imagery recalls Lawrence's story "Sun," as Jones points out,[31] but her use of water forecasts her later much more extensive development of the central themes of *The Virgin and the Gipsy.*

Clytie is one of a number of Welty's women who sink beneath the flood of their passion. The story is based loosely on the myth of Clytie and Apollo as told in Ovid's *Metamorphoses,* but some of Clytie Farr's behavior resembles that of Lawrence's heroines. Like Juliet in "Sun," Clytie turns away from self-regard and society, which fosters it, and gives her full attention to the sun god.[32] But her loss of self does not bring her closer to the sun. Instead, she goes deeper and deeper into sunless, watery realms: first her dark madness which makes her stand out in the rain and then death at the bottom of the rain barrel. Ovid says of the desolate Clytie, "she hated her sisters."[33] Welty's Clytie also hates her sister, for the same reasons Lawrence's women often do. Octavia is a domineering would-be matriarch who shuts away from the natural world everything and everyone in the house; "Rain and sun signified ruin, in Octavia's mind."[34] In this she resembles the Mater, who fights to keep the windows of the rectory tightly closed in *The Virgin and the Gipsy.* The "diamond cornucopia she always wore" hints at Octavia's sterility; like the Mater, she is a false mother, an artificial Ceres. Clytie, who opens herself and the house to sun and rain and who reaches out to touch the stranger's face, is akin to Yvette, who cannot conform to the rules made by a life-denying woman. But when Clytie breaks free of Octavia's control, she falls into the waters of death.

On the surface, "Clytie" seems perfectly consonant with Lawrence's values. Nothing in the story or the manner in which it is told contradicts

Clytie's sense that her own outlook on life is superior to Octavia's. Yet Clytie's resistance to Octavia's control ends in death. Lawrence's didactic intentions keep him from ending stories this way. Instead, he generally imposes poetic justice, punishing those who oppose nature and rewarding those who subordinate the socially determined self to it. Welty maintains a far greater distance from her characters than Lawrence does. Thus in her stories, as in life, nature is allowed to be as dangerous as it is powerful, and, to the degree that it is in league with a woman's desires, it threatens her.

Delta Wedding is also reminiscent of much in Lawrence, while very different in tone. The bride, Dabney, resembles many of Lawrence's heroines in being naturally aristocratic, antimaterialistic, sensual yet innocent, and proudly aware of the "burning" "core" within her that is beyond identity.[35] Her love affair with Troy, her social inferior—who is "sprung all over with red-gold hairs" (*DW*, 122), and who is identified by one critic as a "field god" and avatar of "the male mystery"—is decidedly Lawrencian.[36] The novel also makes allusions to the myth of Persephone and Hades similar to those in Lawrence's *Ladybird,* "Bavarian Gentians," and "Purple Anemones." Welty emphasizes the fiery aspect of the ruler of the underworld,[37] the sexual vitality of the man who will take Dabney away "to sleep under" "Delectable Mountains" (*DW*, 113). However, while in Lawrence's work this male energy revitalizes the woman despite her initial resistance to it, in Welty's it is partially destructive because of the waters that rise to meet it.

Noel Polk has pointed out the central importance of water imagery to *Delta Wedding*'s antisentimental portrait of marriage in the extended family.[38] As Michael Kreyling shows, Welty explores her theme through the consciousness of several female characters, to a large extent by using the Yazoo River as the locus of their meetings with "the world of menace and disorder" that she always associates with sexual desire and experience.[39] As an image for female sexual experience, the Yazoo is similar to the Floss. We are told that Yazoo means "River of Death" (*DW*, 194). Like Maggie, who cannot choose when to leave the river but is reclaimed by it when she tries to retreat, Welty's women are given to the river forever by their loving vulnerability to men. Laura's adored cousin, Roy, throws her into it because he thinks girls "float," but they do not (*DW*, 179).

Whereas Lawrence leaves Yvette shortly after her immersion in sexual knowledge via the river, Welty follows her female characters to show the consequences of such initiation into womanliness. It is beside the Yazoo that the beautiful "lost girl" meets George, the family hero, who has sex with her (*DW*, 79). She apparently throws herself under a train afterwards. George's wife, Robbie, plays "at drowning" with him in the early days of their marriage, but at the end goes under to her role as a Fairchild woman (*DW*, 25). Pregnant, beside the river, she listens submissively to George's plans for a life she expects to "hate" (*DW*, 243–44). Before her own wedding, Dabney goes to the river's whirlpool, parts the vines, "thick as legs," and feels "vertigo" drawing her down (*DW*, 123). After her honeymoon, she lies in Troy's arms "like a drowned girl" (*DW*, 244–45). Although the Fairchild women do not actually die in the river's waters, as Maggie does in the Floss, the river is aligned with the forces that consume their lives and deny their individuality. By its banks, at the novel's conclusion, the major female characters seem to blend into one weak, motherly, submissive presence. Like Dorothea, they are broken, channeled, and like Maggie, they have been paradoxically destroyed by the very source of their strength, their full, passionate and fluidly desirous natures. Critics have found the tone of *Delta Wedding* elusive, partly it seems, because the central image, water, is so overdetermined, signifying fertility and death, passion and passivity, female power and female defeat. The earlier, and in some ways prototypical, appearance of this symbol in "At the Landing" is, if anything, more complicated, more resistant to interpretation.

In contrast *The Virgin and the Gipsy* has a reassuring simplicity. As John Vickery shows, the water imagery is consistently used to allude to the mythology of purification and renewal.[40] The Mater is removed by the flood as if nature would not tolerate a pretender to the title of Great Mother who is an enemy of sexuality, marriage, and fertility. Yvette finds true goddesses of natural life in the "big, swarthy, wolf-like gipsy-woman" who encourages Yvette's interest in her husband and would "strangle Granny with one hand," and the old gypsy woman whose prophetic dream guides Yvette to safety (*VG*, 62–63). Here Lawrence's text moves very close to feminism. Bonnie Kime Scott has described how Joyce's work parallels the woman-centered modernism of Woolf, Djuna Barnes, and H. D., as well as current feminist theory, in its revision of the " 'mythic method' " to include myths both of the Mother, who is associated with water, and of the female wanderer who pursues no goal but "delights in flow, as life itself."[41] In *The Virgin and the Gipsy,* Lawrence effects a similar recovery of matriarchal mythos with the difference from Joyce being that the female wanderer is Lawrence's protagonist and her quest for the Mother/life-source is his main theme.

Consequently the narrative of romantic love promised by the title seems underplayed. The physical consummation Yvette experiences with the gypsy man is not sexual intercourse but a literal sharing of vital warmth. The open-endedness of the story is optimistic. As Keith Cushman shows, the flood equalizes Yvette and the gypsy by letting her see the vulnerable man "beneath the fantasy figure."[42] The waters strip them both, and he is revealed as an individual (Joe Boswell) with an identity beyond his symbolic meaning, a gentle devotion to Yvette, and a romantic desire to see her again. The happy union of Eastwood and Mrs. Fawcett and the continued "flourishing" of the delinquent mother with her "despicable young man" (clearly standing for Lawrence and Frieda) show that it would be possible for Yvette's unlawful love for the gypsy to lead to a satisfying union.

"At the Landing" takes place in a world of different possibilities. Some of its complexity comes from the text's fatalism about love and desire. That the flood follows Jenny's domineering grandfather's death suggests that she is released from the constraints of social traditions and abandoned to the dangers of the natural world at the same time. The identity that society (through the patriarch) has constructed for Jenny, like that of the feminized virtues, is both container and armor. Its removal releases a flux that seems destructive of the body in which it figuratively originates. The flood "attacks" Jenny not her grandparent. Like Lawrence's gypsy, Floyd saves the girl from the flood, but he also takes her into it in order to use her sexually, without love, with "the same thoughtlessness of motion" with which he "spear[s] a side of wild meat from an animal he had killed and had ready." The gypsy responds to Yvette's interest gallantly. Moreover, her affection is answered by his, but Floyd is emotionally untouchable; Jenny can "make him neither sorry nor proud" ("Landing," 251–52). Not only is the flood (Floyd) outside Jenny's control, it is outside her understanding. Jenny wants her experience to lead to action, but she cannot chart a course by which she can move on or with the waters of her desire as Floyd does on the Mississippi. Neither Floyd himself nor anyone around them can offer Jenny any guidance. The three old wise women of The Landing only want "to celebrate her ruin" ("Landing," 254). And yet, Jenny's life is "a following after"; she is incapable of finding "any way alone" ("Landing," 256).

The conclusion of the story is particularly troubling. While Lawrence moves his story, at the end, from mystic strangeness to a promising everyday reality, Welty takes us from a lyrical dream world to an unfolding of grotesque horror at a river bank encampment where "all things" are "the color of day when vision and despair are the same thing" ("Landing," 257). The fishermen take turns first throwing knives at a tree and then raping Jenny. As the "younger boys" begin imitating the men's actions, Jenny lies silent and immobile. " 'Is she asleep? Is she in a spell? Or is she dead?' " ("Landing," 258). Given up to instinctual love, sexuality, and the cycles of nature (as represented by the appearances and disappearances of Floyd and flood), Jenny has become a thing, like the tree that receives the knives, without language, will, or power. As in "Clytie" and *Delta Wedding,* love of the flaming one brings a drowning rush of desire. The men remain, radiating an untouched power and energy which the woman, at best, reflects distantly; "the original smile" returns and lingers on her face "no matter what [is] done to her, like a bit of color that kindles in the sky after the light has gone" ("Landing," 258).

Still Welty hints that Jenny's experience contains something of value. Jenny goes down to the river to "gain the last wisdom" ("Landing," 256). The interest in her situation taken by the wise old woman links the girl's ordeal to tribal initiation ritual, but into what is she being initiated? The older women are clearly unfulfilled and even resent the possibility that Jenny might have enjoyed brief pleasure. Longing, waiting, spitefulness, and a bitter wisdom expressing itself in cynical predictions seem to be the lot of the women who live within the river's reach, whose lives are determined by its ebbs and flows.

The differences in the way Welty and Lawrence imagine their protagonists' futures center in differences in the ways they understand female sexual openness as fact and metaphor. Lawrence's story is shaped by contrastive definitions of the terms openness and enclosure. Lawrence repeatedly asserts that to live in a traditional family is to be enclosed. The Mater insists that the Saywells present "to the outer world, a stubborn fence of unison" (*VG,* 12). Yvette is raised "inside the pale" (*VG,* 143). Making the figurative concrete, the Mater demands that the openings in the house be kept closed. This enclosure is never pictured as beneficial or protective; it is stinking, "stifling," and poisonous (*VG*, 14), while the gypsy camp, open to the elements, is fresh, green, and clean (*VG*, 21). All this suggests that if Yvette's sexual opening, taking place throughout the story, is repressed by social forces into closure, what is fresh and delightful will rot. For Yvette the symbol of sexual repression is plumbing. She believes that because people who live in houses, unlike the gypsies, have bathrooms, theirs is a "stagnant, sewerage sort of life" (*VG*, 61–62). Condemnation of the containment of water in pipes is also hinted at in Mrs. Fawcett's repudiation of her name and notoriously dishonest husband for the rather ingenuous, out-doorsy Eastwood. As Theweleit shows, this revulsion against plumbing, quirky as it seems, might have some validity in connecting "the repression of human desire in bourgeois societies" to the modern equation of washing and purification, reflected in this era's obsession with cleaning the genitals after sex, the popularity of " 'bathing therapy' " for mental and physical ailments, and the fetishization of sparkling whiteness in the home.[43]

Lawrence, however, resists seeing culturally determined enclosure as entrapment. If desire is denied its flow because the women are locked away, "the keys of their lives [are] in their own hands," though "there they dangled inert" (*VG*, 31). To dramatize this, throughout chapter 4, Lawrence connects Yvette to Tennyson's Lady of Shalott. Yvette and her sister Lucille clash with the Mater and her repressive "second in command," Cissie, over misuse of the "Widow Fund" (mostly raised by "the farce called *Mary in the Mirror*") and the near breaking of a mirror (*VG*, 53). The chapter ends with Yvette's habitual watching of the river road in expectation, "like the Lady of Shalott," that someone will come along and free her (*VG*, 74).

The novel works out its attitude toward female passivity through water imagery. As usual, Lawrence opposes the exercise of will, especially female will. Because the gypsy is stronger than Yvette, "the surface of her body seem[s] to turn to water" (*VG*, 47–48). His "dark, complete power" flows over her, "washing her at last purely will-less" (*VG*, 102). But this power is clearly derived from the gypsy's connection to the female principle and nature-based matriarchy. Yvette acknowledges his dominance, to the extent she does, because she sees in his defiant, outcast posturing and even the free swing of his hips "her own kind of strength, her own kind of understanding" (*VG*, 48). That he goes against society is important, but that he does so in ways society describes as effeminate is even more so. His camp is presided over by the old wise woman whose prophetic dreams guide his life. His wife offers him to Yvette in a sort of trafficking in men that bonds the two of them. In being freed by him, Yvette is freed by and into the female essence. What she must see in the magical mirror, to break the spell, is not the masculine knight she expects, but a reflection of the power that is most profoundly her self.

Her contact with the gypsy woman allows Yvette to understand the contradictions in the matriarchy that governs her life. The Mater's power comes from being "a faithful wife and a faithful mother," without love or passion but rigidly loyal to the forms of patriarchal order (*VG*, 135). In other words, she dams the flow of female energy. Her only daughter, Cissie, is a sterile virgin whose "life and sex" were "sacrificed" to the Mater (*VG*, 10–11). To free herself, Yvette must give her self up to another sort of matriarchy, that of the gypsy woman, which is informed by the "great sardonic female contempt" for "domesticated" men and which comes from a sex that is "unyielding," antisocial, and unrestrained. This is the femaleness that is not drowned in its own fluid release; "Nothing would ever get that woman down" (*VG*, 62–63). It is also a femaleness suited to Yvette's "slightly ambiguous" gender identity, which, as Cushman points out, calls into question conventional femininity.[44] In opening herself and allowing her desire free flow, Yvette empowers both herself and a beneficial and protective female principle. This female principle seems primary because the value of individual characters is determined in relation to it.

In Lawrence's explanation of the cause of the flood that breaks Yvette free of the house and its false matriarchy, one might even see a fore-shadowing of Freud's analogy in *Civilization and Its Discontents* between the first settlements on the site of Rome and the pre-Oedipal state, which is defined by its oceanic feeling of boundlessness.[45] Lawrence's explanation also anticipates some feminist critics' interpretations of Kristeva's theory of the semiotic to assert the presence of woman-identified consciousness underlying the (masculine) symbolic order.[46] The "ancient, perhaps even . . . Roman mine tunnel," a vaginal opening, "unsuspected, undreamed of" "undermines" the reservoir dam, causing the water that would have been safely channeled into pipes to charge the house "like a wall of lions" (*VG*, 155). Since Yvette's mother, whom the girl's admiration for the powerful gypsy woman and former Mrs. Fawcett causes her to resemble, is compared to a lion (*VG*, 9), the flood seems to symbolize the vengeful return of the Mother to remove the male-defined Mater who mythologized her into "the pure white snow-flower," "She-who-was-Cynthia" and denied her true existence (*VG*, 7).

The mother's name, Cynthia, hints her connection to the goddess of female chastity as self-possession, the moon goddess, ruler of tides. In her restored presence, culture-bound gender difference dissolves as the gypsy nurtures Yvette, gives her his warmth, respects the integrity of her body, and achieves an unconscious merging with her in sleep. Instead of bodies connecting because (genital) difference makes linkage possible, we see multiple selves flowing together outside the boundaries maintained by the conscious state. Masculine and feminine disappear in the sea of desire that flows free when the house of the social breaks.

Nothing could be further from the meanings Welty gives openness and closure. If the enclosure of the house restricts, it also protects. Jenny's house is a magic circle "full of prisms" with their Divine rainbow promise of no more floods. The charm of this enclosure is deeply rooted in literature. As an emotionally sleeping beauty, Jenny is closed into the pavilion by "an ancient circling thorny rose, like the initial letter in a poetry book." The house provides a refuge for "books that had been . . . through fire and water" ("Landing," 241–42). The water's opening of the house means that the free space for imagination at the center of the enclosure is invaded. The "books without titles," formerly weathered into indeterminacy, seem "to have been opened and written on again by muddy fingers" ("Landing," 253). In the flood, the profane and earthy writes over the ethereal and imaginary. Jenny is changed from magical virgin to degraded whore, without "a place to hide in," exposed to insult and rape ("Landing," 253). Yet openness, too, is ambiguous. Jenny's attraction to the wanderer, Floyd, arises first from her hope to be "free to come and go." She feels her initial opening to sexual desire, as she watches him at the spring in the ravine, as a loss of "innocence" ("Landing," 243–44). But much pleasure is mixed in with this loss, just as the mysterious way her cry of protest "could easily have been heard as rejoicing," and her subsequent enigmatic smile will later somewhat mitigate the tragic force of her prostrate immobility after the gang-rape.

The waters that surround and permeate the Mississippi Delta town of The Landing sometimes seem to erode the boundaries between the very meanings of the words open and closed. The Lockhart house seems held together by its encircling "black high-water mark" ("Landing," 245). The safe (an armored enclosure) at the store must be left open to the flood lest it "rust shut" ("Landing," 248). Openness makes (beneficial) enclosure possible in these instances, as it does when Jenny, walking with Floyd by "the little river," tells him everything with her eyes and so remains isolated in silence ("Landing," 249–50). The domesticated water at the bottom of the well looks to her like the gateway into "some strange other country" where her desperate desire for freedom could be realized ("Landing," 246). But, as we know, such escape is death, the ultimate closure. Similarly the openness brought by the flood of desire proves illusory. Jenny is most profoundly possessed and controlled when she opens herself to Floyd. The opening in her body made possible by the outrush of desire is claimed by men as their common property.

What makes Welty's depiction of the consequences of the free flow of female desire so dismal? The most obvious answer is that, to a large extent, her story reflects social reality. As literature, as well as ordinary observation, tells us, both men and women often seem to interpret a woman's violation of sexual mores as indicative of a willingness to be used sexually by whomever wants her. Language reflects this assumption in that the word "whore" is used to describe the prostitute, the woman who has had many sexual partners (even if they are discriminatingly chosen), the woman whose sexual behavior seems indiscriminate, and the woman who has illicit (against patriarchal law) sexual relations, even if only with one partner. The confusion in signification that surrounds female sexual transgression places the female transgressor not only dangerously outside the protection of the laws made by the fathers, but outside language, the Law of the Father. According to this understanding of female sexuality, to break the father's Law is to lose coherence, to break the body open so that it can never again be closed from within. The story's tone, as Welty has said of Lawrence's work, "protests the world."[47] The whole movement of the story, from "a river of golden haze" to "dark night" ("Landing," 241, 258), implies tragedy. Nonetheless, Jenny's entire experience is depicted as inevitable. The story says that The Landing will be engulfed at intervals by filthy, destructive waters, its inhabitants will not move away, as one explains, "because we live here," and sensitive young virgins will love, open in desire, and so fall to the depths of victimization. The reader is shown not a lively play of choice but a doomed girl who is, as Luce Irigaray puts it, "left with the impossible alternative between a defensive virginity, fiercely turned in upon itself, and a body open to penetration that no longer knows, in this 'hole' that constitutes its sex, the pleasure of its own touch."[48]

In contrast, Welty's Victorian precursors are complicitous, in their use of irony, with their society's most prescriptive myths about female desire. In both *Jane Eyre* and *The Mill on the Floss,* the narrator makes her climactic ironic swing out against society's values from the fixed point of her understanding that the heroine could have chosen pleasure (sexual openness) but chose virtue (virginity) instead. The suspicions about Jane's character shown by many of those who encounter her after her flight from Thornfield are bitterly ironic, because, as the reader is made well aware, Jane is a martyr to her high morals. Likewise Maggie Tulliver's rejection by her brother on the grounds that she "must have behaved as no modest girl would have done," the insulting gallantries offered to her by the gentlemen at the billiard-rooms, and the general social ostracism she suffers are ironic because we know they are the result of her resistance of sexual temptation (*MF,* 613). That these ironies come as final blows emphasizing the antagonism between true virtue and society's values paradoxically implies Brontë's and Eliot's reluctance to contradict (in writing) the most essential social law concerning women, that the flow of their sexuality must be diverted by men either into the channels of virtue or the pool open to every man's thirst. Welty is far more overtly critical of the system she describes. If there is any irony in Welty's treatment of the fishermen's brutal enforcement of patriarchal law, it reveals itself in the possibility that, as Louise Westling claims, Jenny finds even in the sexual violence done to her an emotional "fulfillment she lacked while living with her genteel grandfather."[49] This conclusion hints that female desire can, despite everything done to it, trickle away into its own subterranean meanings, that woman defined is not woman contained. The significance of Jenny's experience remains closed to the world that has forced her open. The story's antagonistic resistance to interpretation based on patriarchal understandings of female desire is strongest in these ironies.

At the height of the second wave of feminism, women writers aggressively reclaimed the image of woman-as-water. Examples of this that come immediately to mind are Adrienne Rich's "Diving into the

Wreck," Lois Gould's *A Sea Change,* Margaret Atwood's *Surfacing,* Toni Morrison's *Sula,* Bertha Harris's *Lover,* and Iris Murdoch's *The Sea, the Sea.* Interestingly, in *No Man's Land,* to illustrate how women's texts currently revise and question the values expressed by female precursors, Gilbert and Gubar chose to discuss two texts, Margaret Drabble's *The Waterfall* and Jean Rhys's *Wide Sargasso Sea.*[50] In addition to rewriting respectively *The Mill on the Floss* and *Jane Eyre,* these novels take as a major concern, as the titles indicate, fluid female desires. An earlier work worth noting both for its response to Lawrence's *The Rainbow* and its celebration of woman-as-water is Anaïs Nin's "Houseboat." In *Les Guérillères,* Monique Wittig begins her narrative of the struggle of women to overthrow the patriarchy with an account of a rain so powerful that it seems to be coming from both above and below; "it is as if springs hollow out the pebbles at the places where it reaches the ground." One woman gives in to her identification with this release. Others "form a circle around her to watch the labia expel the urine."[51] A woman-centered mystery pours out with it. The process by which "les femmes" will discover, release, and possess their own desires has begun.

And Wittig has placed her work in a tradition that comes down to us through Charlotte Brontë and George Eliot, D. H. Lawrence and Eudora Welty, of imagining the waters of unlimited desire as beginning in and returning to woman, of the fluidity trope finding its primary signifying power not in relation to man's desires but in relation to woman's. The female flood becomes not the sign of the (feminized) shameful and destructive, that-which-must-be-repressed, or the solvent of all women's identities and claims to individual desires, in which (individual) men can voluptuously bathe, but a force for the liberation of each woman according to her ever-emerging desires.

Some feminist critics, like Hilary Simpson and Cornelia Nixon, see in Lawrence's work a progressive hostility toward feminism and even toward conventional, male-identified women. Certainly Lawrence's work contains a full measure of misogyny, yet to me it seems too fluid, changeable, and even self-contradictory to fit this developmental pattern, especially when one considers that *The Virgin and the Gipsy,* written in 1926, has in common with intentionally feminist texts like *The Mill on the Floss* a concern with combating the negative connotation traditionally given to female flow. *Jane Eyre, The Mill on the Floss, The Virgin and the Gipsy,* and "At the Landing," despite their differing pretensions to realism, all contain fantasies about female desire as flood. Each text establishes, always in the context of a narrative of one particular woman's specific desires, the intrinsic importance of female desire and the value of giving it free flow. Surely this is an essentially feminist endeavor, and the large number of women writers (including literary critics) who have engaged in it allows us to call it a women's literary tradition, yet there is Lawrence in the midst of it. One might say that Lawrence intrudes upon this tradition, but still his work seems to contribute to the female tradition's reinscription of flood. One might say Welty rebuffs his intrusion with "At the Landing," by reminding us that nature is not a fairy-godmother (or latent Great Mother) waiting to free us from a culture that problematizes women's desire. Yet in this way the two texts stand in somewhat the same relation to each other as *Jane Eyre* and *The Mill on the Floss*. I am not arguing that Lawrence should be considered a feminist writer. But to deny his participation in the formation of this crucially important women's literary tradition is to ignore one of the keys to women's history and culture, experience and self-expression that still dangles in our hands.

"We Need One Another"

In the last twenty years, as feminist criticism has gradually changed from the province of the alienated but powerless woman English major whom Judith Fetterley called "the resisting reader" to a field so respected that prominent male literary theoreticians have shown interest in entering it, Lawrence's critical fortunes have once again begun to alter. Generally women no longer seem to like Lawrence's work. Feminist critics who found the first confirmation of the appropriateness of their ideas in studies like Kate Millett's *Sexual Politics* may have difficulty reading Lawrence's books as anything but guides to the oppression of women. Since there are so many modern authors whose work either inclines toward feminism or is openly feminist, feminists concentrating on the modern period may not want to read Lawrence at all.

When women critics do read and write about Lawrence it often seems to be with the intention of exposing the ways in which what is seen as an insane degree of misogyny developed. As in the years immediately after his death, Lawrence is often treated as a fascistic, sexually perverse madman. To read Lawrence in this way distances him from women's literature and so makes his claims to understand and speak for women less threatening. If his work is regarded as exemplary of the worst impulses of an oppressive dominant group, women can justify their disapproval of Lawrence, can even forget about him except when they need to refer to a writer whose themes, style, and attitudes, we all agree, represent the exclusively and obsessively masculine voice.

Whether or not feminists want it, however, Lawrence's work belongs to women's literature. His place in discussions of women's literary traditions is as undeniable, although not as immediately obvious, as that of the multitude of women writing for a mass market who eroticize and approve men's domination of women. As feminist critics and readers, we may sometimes wish we could sweep the library and bookstore shelves clean of such disconcerting books, but we cannot. Nor can we edit misogynous elements out of the great novels written by women. *The Mill on the Floss* will forever tell us that "not the world, but the world's wife" denies Maggie the mercy which might have saved her (*MF*, 619). We will always find in *Martha Quest* and *Jane Eyre* an association of pronounced female secondary sexual characteristics with stupidity and inferiority. Nor can those who oppose all representations of gender difference erase them from the record of our attainment of authorial voice. We may wish to move beyond what Teresa de Lauretis calls "the maze of sexual difference" into the space where the term *woman* ceases to be useful, but we must keep in mind that even theorists like Wittig who are now exploring this territory began with attention to feminist essentialism because it privileges woman's experience.[52] Both as an influence and as a receiver of influence, Lawrence is firmly entrenched in our study of women's literature.

Lawrence's work belongs to women's literary traditions because they provide the context in which we can best understand it. By responding to Victorian women writers in so many of his texts, Lawrence has made it necessary for us to think about these precursors when we consider his intentions. His view of sexual relationships as battles over connectedness to nature, his fascination with the dark, natural male and the Magna Mater, his belief in a female essence and his vehement rejection of the social practices and cultural ideals that prescribe its containment, his high valuation of unrestricted female anger and desire, even his fear of women and somewhat contradictory insistence that heterosexual union is best, become more comprehensible when we consider them in the context of his interest in *Wuthering Heights, The Mill on the Floss, Jane Eyre,* and *The Story of an African Farm.* Since Lawrence's writing developed in reaction to his reading of Victorian women authors, familiarity with them and with the central tenets of Victorian feminism must inform our analyses of his fiction's themes and language.

This approach to Lawrence opens up his work in a new way. It allows us to understand aspects of his fiction that other theories cannot account for. His need to reinterpret women's texts, rather than an inclination toward fascism, can be seen to be the general structuring force behind his fiction. Thus developmental theories are no longer undermined by Lawrence's attitudinal shifts and inconsistencies. Lawrence's repudiation of male leadership in *Kangaroo* and his seeming celebration of it in *The Plumed Serpent* can be seen as subsidiary themes in novels whose main concern is how man can break woman and himself free from society and enter a communion with wild nature. The contradictions in Lawrence's work can be understood as involving what he saw as relatively minor issues if we keep in mind his lifelong struggle to find a solution to the problem Emily Brontë presents. Powerful, intellectual female characters and elemental yet dependent male characters who seem inexplicable in terms of Lawrence's doctrinal pronouncements about the sexes make sense as versions of Eliot's and the Brontës' characters. The triumph of the dissenting female voice in his fiction can be seen not as evidence of artistic failure caused by mental problems but as the natural outcome of a conscious choice to follow women's traditions.

Our understanding of these traditions can be enhanced if we consider the ways in which Lawrence participates in them. His participation in women's literary traditions is not limited to his own writings but, instead, is confirmed and expanded in women writers' responses to him. Where writers like Virginia Woolf and Anaïs Nin point out connections between Lawrence's and women's fiction, they reveal the characteristics they associate with women's literary work, what besides a female name after the title makes them see a particular text as female. Thus they clarify the sources of their own identities as women writers. The surprising similarities between the feminine qualities they find in Lawrence's work and the qualities attributed in feminist criticism to the female/feminine voice suggest that this voice is not produced solely by women's irresistible or unconscious responses to cultural conditions. Implicit in women writers' descriptions of Lawrence's encroachment on female literary territory is the idea that this territory has been mapped out by previous generations and remains, despite changes in women's status, the ground on which they choose to construct their fictions.

In the reactions of writers like Katherine Mansfield and Doris Lessing against Lawrence's attempts to appropriate the female voice, we can see one of the impulses behind women's affirmations of their female precursors' visions. Changes in these writers' uses of Lawrence, as they find his misogyny increasingly alienating, parallel changes in their attitudes toward earlier women writers like Eliot. The need for a description of female experience that can include female creativity (and its precondition of some independence from male definition) pushes them away from Lawrence, despite their sympathy with his anti-Victorian focus on women's sexual needs and anger. It also pushes them toward familiar Victorian women novelists. Their rejection of Lawrence brings them into accord with his female models; one might say that they are better able to transcend the cultural differences between their own values and those of Victorian women because they first tried and failed to align their work with Lawrence's.

Women writers like H. D., Elizabeth Bowen, and Christina Stead do not seem seriously inclined to cast off Lawrence's influence. On the contrary, their attraction to his fiction, ideas, and even personality shapes several of their works. Like his female followers, they seem to have come to terms with their own position as creative women through identification with him. Just as he seems compelled to give voices in his writing to women whom he sees as his ideological opposition, these writers, the more they reject his vision, make him the dominant masculine voice in their fiction. And, at the same time that they locate themselves in opposition to Lawrence the man, they find themselves as writers through both his heroines and his heroes. By claiming the power he attributes to women and also the right to the definitive overview of life (which he believes belongs only to men) they gain the authority to create fictional worlds that rival his.

What all the women writers who respond to Lawrence seem to have in common is that, in one way or another, they find his influence enabling rather than disabling. Even when, like Bowen, they implicitly complain that he has reduced them to silence, he has not. Rather, like the voices of his fictional heroines, their protesting and contradicting voices continue, even prevail. Moreover, just as we cannot understand exactly what

Lawrence is struggling with in his fiction—or how he succeeds—unless we pay attention to his literary relationship to his female precursors, we cannot fully appreciate many modern women's writings unless we recognize their engagement with Lawrence's work. One of the reasons that the brilliant writing of Bowen, Stead, and Welty is so underrated seems to be that their responses to Lawrence are mostly unnoticed. Subtle, rich rethinkings of Lawrence's stories, like Welty's "At the Landing" or Bowen's *To the North,* are too often dismissed as cryptic because their responses to prior texts are unrecognized.

Feminist critics do think of Lawrence when they think of women's literature. He is one of the most frequently mentioned male authors in feminist criticism. But the way in which he is often thought of, as the author who defines the male voice and attitude and against whom the literary feminine can be defined, does not help us understand the work of his female contemporaries or our own. We might, instead, consider Lawrence as a middle term, a writer who deliberately stands between and so links modern and Victorian writers, a writer whose presence, because of the reactions it elicits from women, fosters a sense of female identity in women writers and so strengthens the bonds, which we call traditions, between them and their female precursors.

Myra Jehlen once recommended that feminist critics compare closely related men's and women's works with the hope that the "border" between "two literary worlds created . . . out of one thematic clay" might provide us with a locus from which to examine and begin to comprehend both "the dominant male traditions" and women's traditions.[53] This sound advice becomes even more helpful if we note that the border is not always, as she calls it, a "no-man's-land," because the identification of the marginalized with each other can cut across gender lines, making boundaries indefinite. Lawrence provides a better image for the relationship of his work to women's literature in his essay "We Need One Another": "the relation of man to woman is the flowing of two rivers side by side, sometimes even mingling, then separating again, and travelling on."[54] Lawrence needed women so much that he caused his works to flow beside theirs, from the same sources. Now, in order to understand our own literary heritage, we need him, because it is at the points where borders slip and women's and men's visions meet, mingle, and then flow apart that we can see women's literary traditions taking form.

Notes
Bibliography
Index

Notes

Introduction

1 Miller identifies this as one of her primary goals in "Arachnologies: The Woman, the Text, and the Critic," in *The Poetics of Gender,* ed. Nancy K. Miller (New York: Columbia University Press, 1986), p. 288.

2 Mary Jacobus, *Reading Woman: Essays in Feminist Criticism* (New York: Columbia University Press, 1986), p. 4. Jacobus aligns herself with Felman in this introduction to the essays.

3 Nina Baym, "The Madwoman and Her Languages: Why I Don't Do Feminist Literary Theory," in *Feminist Issues in Literary Scholarship,* ed. Shari Benstock (Bloomington: Indiana University Press, 1987), p. 46.

4 Linda Alcoff, "Cultural Feminism Versus Poststructuralism: The Identity Crisis in Feminist Theory," *Signs* 13 (1988): 415, 420.

5 Toril Moi, *Sexual/Textual Politics: Feminist Literary Theory* (New York: Methuen, 1985), p. 82.

6 Alcoff, "Cultural Feminism," p. 419.

7 Alice A. Jardine, *Gynesis: Configurations of Woman and Modernity* (Ithaca, N.Y.: Cornell University Press, 1985), p. 37.

8 Naomi Schor, "Dreaming Dissymmetry: Barthes, Foucault, and Sexual Difference," in *Men in Feminism,* ed. Alice Jardine and Paul Smith (New York: Methuen, 1987), p. 109.

9 In *Another Mother Tongue: Gay Words, Gay Worlds,* Judy Grahn discusses cross-dressing and "genderfuck" posturing as assertions of gay male or lesbian sexual identity (Boston: Beacon Press, 1984). She says repeatedly that gay men and lesbians who cross-dress expect others to recognize their gender and are annoyed if they do not. In Holly Devor's study of women habitually taken for

men, *Gender Blending: Confronting the Limits of Duality,* many of the "gender blenders" describe such incidents as threatening to their identity and self-esteem, although they have chosen to wear masculine-appearing clothing and to have their hair cut short ([Bloomington: Indiana University Press, 1989], p. 121).

10 Eve Kosofsky Sedgwick, "Epistemology of the Closet (I)," *Raritan* 7, no. 4 (1988): 58.

11 Susan Suleiman, "(Re)writing the Body: The Politics and Poetics of Female Eroticism," in *The Female Body in Western Culture: Contemporary Perspectives,* ed. Susan Suleiman (Cambridge: Harvard University Press, 1986), pp. 16–24; Frances L. Restuccia, "'A Cave of My Own': E. M. Forster and Sexual Politics," *Raritan* 9, no. 2 (1989): 112.

12 Schor, "Dreaming Dissymmetry," pp. 109–10.

13 Simone de Beauvoir, *The Second Sex,* trans. and ed. H. M. Parshley (1953; rpt., New York: Bantam, 1961), p. 209.

14 Annis Pratt, "Woman and Nature in Modern Fiction," *Contemporary Literature* 13 (1972): 481–83.

15 Sandra M. Gilbert and Susan Gubar, *The Madwoman in the Attic: The Woman Writer and the Nineteenth-Century Literary Imagination* (New Haven: Yale University Press, 1979), pp. 14, 356.

16 Jacobus, *Reading Woman,* p. 30.

17 Eve Kosofsky Sedgwick, *Between Men: English Literature and Male Homosocial Desire* (New York: Columbia University Press, 1985), pp. 215–17.

18 D. H. Lawrence, "Study of Thomas Hardy," in *Phoenix: The Posthumous Papers of D. H. Lawrence,* ed. Edward D. McDonald (1936; rpt., Harmondsworth: Penguin, 1978), p. 479. All further references to this work, designated "Study," are incorporated in the text.

19 D. H. Lawrence, *The Symbolic Meaning: The Uncollected Versions of Studies in Classic American Literature,* ed. Armin Arnold (New York: Viking, 1964), p. 18.

20 D. H. Lawrence, *Studies in Classic American Literature* (1923; rpt., New York: Viking, 1964), p. 2.

21 Frank Kermode, *D. H. Lawrence* (New York: Viking, 1973), pp. 15, 63.

22 Wayne C. Booth, *The Company We Keep: An Ethics of Fiction* (Berkeley and Los Angeles: University of California Press, 1988), p. 446. Booth is more skeptical than I am about whether any of these voices actually represents the author.

23 Ibid., pp. 445–47; Dale Bauer, *Feminist Dialogics: A Theory of Failed Community* (Albany: State University of New York Press, 1988), p. xiii.

24 D. H. Lawrence, *Women in Love* (1920; rpt., New York: Viking, 1960), p. 473. All further references to this work, abbreviated *WL,* are incorporated in the text.

25 E. M. Forster, *Aspects of the Novel* (1927; rpt., New York: Harcourt, Brace, 1954), p. 141.

26 Hilary Simpson, *D. H. Lawrence and Feminism* (DeKalb: Northern Illinois University Press, 1982), p. 160.

27 Kermode, *D. H. Lawrence,* p. 117.

28 F. R. Leavis, *D. H. Lawrence: Novelist* (New York: Knopf, 1956), pp. 30–31, 50, 41.

29 Booth, *Company,* p. 446.

30 Julian Moynahan, *The Deed of Life: The Novels and Tales of D. H. Lawrence* (Princeton: Princeton University Press, 1963), pp. 69, 101.

31 Graham Hough, *The Dark Sun: A Study of D. H. Lawrence* (1956; rpt., New York, Putnam's Sons, 1959), p. 123.

32 Cornelia Nixon, *Lawrence's Leadership Politics and the Turn Against Women* (Berkeley and Los Angeles: University of California Press, 1986), p. 199. See Hilary Simpson's *D. H. Lawrence and Feminism* for a feminist attempt to place Lawrence's thought historically.

33 Philip Callow, *Son and Lover: The Young D. H. Lawrence* (New York: Stein and Day, 1975), p. 261.

34 D. H. Lawrence, *John Thomas and Lady Jane* (1954; rpt., Harmondsworth: Penguin, 1973), p. 374. All further references to this work, abbreviated *JTLJ,* are incorporated in the text.

35 D. H. Lawrence, *Fantasia of the Unconscious* (1923; rpt., London: Heinemann, 1933), pp. 88, 131.

36 "To Sallie Hopkin," 23 December 1912, letter 529, *The Letters of D. H. Lawrence,* ed. James T. Boulton et al. (Cambridge: Cambridge University Press, 1979), 1:490. All further references to this work, abbreviated LL, are included in the text and accompanied by volume number.

37 D. H. Lawrence, *Sons and Lovers: Text, Background, and Criticism,* ed. Julian Moynahan (New York: Viking, 1968), pp. 278, 297.

38 Callow, *Son and Lover,* p. 222.

39 D. H. Lawrence, "Foreword to *Sons and Lovers,*" in *The Letters of D. H. Lawrence,* ed. Aldous Huxley (London: Heinemann, 1932), p. 102. All further references to this work, abbreviated "FSL," are incorporated in the text.

40 Beauvoir, *Second Sex,* p. 209.

41 Kingsley Widmer, "Lawrence and the Fall of Modern Woman," *Modern Fiction Studies* 5 (1959): 48; Catherine Carswell, *The Savage Pilgrimage: A Narrative of D. H. Lawrence* (1932; rpt., Cambridge: Cambridge University Press, 1981), p. 82.

42 Gayatri Chakravorty Spivak, "Displacement and the Discourse of Women," in *Displacement: Derrida and After,* ed. Mark Krupnick (Bloomington: Indiana University Press, 1983), p. 169.

43 Ibid., p. 174.

44 Ibid., p. 186.

45 Diana J. Fuss, "'Essentially Speaking': Luce Irigaray's Language of Essence," *Hypatia* 3 (1989): 77, 76.

46 D. H. Lawrence, *Kangaroo* (1923; rpt., New York: Viking, 1960), p. 178.

47 In *Kangaroo*, Lawrence gives this title to the man who imagines himself "lord and master" of the wife to whom he offers "perfect love" (p. 172).

48 Rosi Braidotti, "The Politics of Ontological Difference," in *Between Feminism and Psychoanalysis*, ed. Teresa Brennan (New York: Routledge, 1989), pp. 100–102.

49 Simpson, *Lawrence and Feminism*, p. 152, quoting Delavenay, *D. H. Lawrence: L'Homme et la Genese de son Oeuvre* (Paris: Librarie C. Klinckieck, 1969), 2:709; Frieda Lawrence, *Memoirs and Correspondence*, ed. E. W. Tedlock, Jr. (New York: Heinemann, 1965), p. 190.

50 Simpson, *Lawrence and Feminism*, pp. 146, 160. Simpson compares Lawrence to Samuel Richardson and Scott Fitzgerald in this regard. She might also have compared his use of women's writings to Joyce's, since both men use women's voices to disrupt male speech.

51 Alcoff, "Cultural Feminism," p. 413.

52 Jonathan Dollimore, "Different Desires: Subjectivity and Transgression in Wilde and Gide," *Genders* 2 (1988): 36.

53 Daniel J. Schneider, *D. H. Lawrence: The Artist as Psychologist* (Lawrence: University of Kansas Press, 1984), p. 109.

54 Emile Delavenay, *D. H. Lawrence: The Man and His Work: The Formative Years, 1885–1919*, trans. Katherine M. Delavenay (Carbondale: Southern Illinois University Press, 1972), p. 383.

55 D. H. Lawrence, *The Rainbow* (1915; rpt., New York: Viking, 1961), pp. 373, 377, 404. All further references to this work, abbreviated *RB*, are incorporated in the text.

56 Bonnie Kime Scott, *Joyce and Feminism* (Bloomington: Indiana University Press, 1984), p. 236n.

57 D. H. Lawrence, *The Plumed Serpent* (1926; rpt., New York: Vintage, 1959), pp. 465, 478, 486.

58 Laurence Lerner, *The Truthtellers: Jane Austen, George Eliot, D. H. Lawrence* (New York: Schocken, 1967), p. 114.

59 Moynahan, *Deed of Life*, p. 144.

60 Fuss, "'Essentially Speaking,'" p. 68.

61 Suleiman, "(Re)writing the Body," p. 18.

Chapter One: Voices Heard from the Periphery

1 Wayne C. Booth, *The Company We Keep: An Ethics of Fiction* (Berkeley and Los Angeles: University of California Press, 1988), p. 150.

2 Emily Hahn, *Lorenzo: D. H. Lawrence and the Women Who Loved Him* (New York: Lippincott, 1975), pp. 93–94, 133.

3 Mabel Dodge Luhan, *Lorenzo in Taos* (New York: Knopf, 1932), p. 70; emphasis Luhan's.

4 Harry T. Moore seems to find Luhan particularly distasteful because of her two divorces and her interracial third marriage (to an "Indian-buck"). See Moore's *The Priest of Love: A Life of D. H. Lawrence* (1974; rpt., Harmondsworth: Penguin, 1980), pp. 436, 452.

5 Luhan, *Lorenzo,* pp. 95–97; emphasis Luhan's.

6 Luhan refers to "Plum" as "a parody" (Ibid., p. 244) but does not say what it is meant to parody. The poem's subject and title and its general structure of short lines frequently beginning with the same word are reminiscent of Lawrence's "Peach" in the collection *Birds, Beasts, and Flowers,* on which he worked in Taos. Thus, it seems likely that Luhan meant to adopt Lawrence's style, but since Luhan sent the poem to Lawrence as a peace offering, she must have considered the parodic elements of the poem mild and affectionate. There is no suggestion in anything she says about the poem that she considered it less than a skillfully wrought and honest representation of Lawrence.

7 Ibid., p. 244.

8 Meanwhile, actual women like George Eliot and fictional women like Virginia Woolf's Orlando alternated gender in response to the demands of the public and of their own creativity.

9 Luhan, *Lorenzo,* p. 69.

10 Carroll Smith-Rosenberg, *Disorderly Conduct: Visions of Gender in Victorian America* (New York: Knopf, 1985), p. 90.

11 Ibid., pp. 101–2.

12 Lillian S. Robinson, *Sex, Class, and Culture* (New York: Methuen, 1986), p. 6.

13 Rita Felski, *Beyond Feminist Aesthetics: Feminist Literature and Social Change* (Cambridge: Harvard University Press, 1989), p. 70.

14 Robinson, *Sex,* pp. 231–32.

15 Jessie Chambers, *D. H. Lawrence: A Personal Record,* ed. A. J. Bramley (1935; rpt., New York: Barnes and Noble, 1965), pp. 30–31.

16 Ibid., pp. 28–30.

17 Cynthia Asquith, *Remember and Be Glad* (New York: Scribner's, 1952), p. 147.

18 Frieda Lawrence, *Not I, But the Wind . . .* (New York: Viking, 1934), pp. 4–5.

19 Barbara Weekley Barr, "Memoir of D. H. Lawrence," in *D. H. Lawrence: Novelist, Poet, Prophet,* ed. Stephen Spender (London: Weidenfield and Nicholson, 1973), pp. 26–27.

20 Frieda Lawrence, *Not I,* p. 168.

21 Catherine Carswell, *The Savage Pilgrimage: A Narrative of D. H. Lawrence* (1932; rpt., Cambridge: Cambridge University Press, 1981), p. 67.

22 Ibid., pp. 74, 210–11.

23 Dorothy Brett, *Lawrence and Brett: A Friendship* (1933; rpt., Santa Fe, N. Mex.: Sunstone, 1974), pp. 170–71, 154, 112.

24 Ibid., pp. 64–65.

25 Ibid., pp. 58, 171.

26 Luhan, *Lorenzo*, p. 170.

27 H. M. Daleski, *The Forked Flame: A Study of D. H. Lawrence* (Evanston, Ill.: Northwestern University Press, 1965), pp. 34, 33, 35.

28 May Chambers Holbrook in Edward Nehls, *D. H. Lawrence: A Composite Biography* (Madison: University of Wisconsin Press, 1959), 3:571; emphasis mine; 3:580.

29 A. J. Bramley, "D. H. Lawrence and 'Miriam,' " in Chambers's *D. H. Lawrence: A Personal Record*, pp. xxxii–xxxiii.

30 Emile Delavenay, *D. H. Lawrence: The Man and His Work: The Formative Years, 1885–1919*, trans. Katherine M. Delavenay (Carbondale: Southern Illinois University Press, 1972), pp. 66–67.

31 Chambers, *D. H. Lawrence*, pp. 153, 139.

32 Harry T. Moore, *The Life and Works of D. H. Lawrence* (New York: Twayne, 1951), p. 31.

33 Hahn, *Lorenzo*, p. 36.

34 Chambers, *D. H. Lawrence*, p. 67.

35 Robinson, *Sex*, pp. 101–2.

36 Chambers, *D. H. Lawrence*, pp. 58, 126, 133.

37 J. D. Chambers in Nehls, *A Composite Biography* 3:356–57.

38 Helen Corke, *D. H. Lawrence: The Croydon Years* (Austin: University of Texas Press, 1965), p. 44.

39 D. H. Lawrence, *Sons and Lovers: Text, Background, and Criticism*, ed. Julian Moynahan (New York: Viking, 1968), p. 10.

40 Corke, *D. H. Lawrence*, p. 44.

41 Alicia Ostriker, "The Thieves of Language: Women Poets and Revisionist Mythmaking," in *The New Feminist Criticism: Essays on Women, Literature, and Theory*, ed. Elaine Showalter (New York: Pantheon, 1985), p. 320.

42 Chambers, *D. H. Lawrence*, p. 116.

43 Hilary Simpson, *D. H. Lawrence and Feminism* (De Kalb: Northern Illinois University Press, 1982), p. 152.

44 Chambers, *D. H. Lawrence*, pp. 117, 197, 201, 210–12.

45 "To Louisa Burrows" [c. 29 October 1906], letter 27, *The Letters of D. H. Lawrence*, ed. James T. Boulton et al. (Cambridge: Cambridge University Press, 1979): 1:32. All further references to this work, abbreviated LL, are incorporated in the text and accompanied by volume number.

46 Letter to Harry T. Moore, February 1951, quoted in Moore's *Priest of Love*, p. 129.

47 Helen Corke, "The Writing of *The Trespasser*," *The D. H. Lawrence Review* 7 (1974): 232; emphasis mine.

48 Luhan, *Lorenzo*, p. 268.

49 Frieda Lawrence, *Not I*, pp. 115, 56, 57.

50 Brett, *Lawrence*, pp. 128–29.

51 Anne Smith, "A New Adam and a New Eve: A Biographical Overview," in *Lawrence and Women*, ed. Anne Smith (New York: Barnes and Noble, 1978), pp. 45, 10, 11, 14, 18.

52 Hahn, *Lorenzo*, p. 49.

53 R. W. Connell, *Gender and Power: Society, the Person and Sexual Politics* (Stanford: Stanford University Press, 1987), pp. 109–11.

54 Carswell, *Savage Pilgrimage*, p. 6.

55 Brett, *Lawrence*, pp. 63–64.

56 D. H. Lawrence, *Kangaroo* (1923; rpt., New York: Viking, 1960), p. 8. All further references to this work are incorporated in the text.

57 D. H. Lawrence, *Mr. Noon*, ed. Lindeth Vasey (Cambridge: Cambridge University Press, 1984), pp. 204–5. All further references to this work are incorporated in the text.

58 Barbara Johnson, *A World of Difference* (Baltimore: Johns Hopkins University Press, 1987), pp. 180–82.

59 Sandra Gilbert and Susan Gubar, *The Madwoman in the Attic: The Woman Writer and the Nineteenth-Century Literary Imagination* (New Haven: Yale University Press, 1979), p. 50; see Smith, "A New Adam" (p. 20), for a good discussion of his distrust of male readers, and Lawrence's collections of poems and aphorisms, *Nettles* and *Pansies*, for numerous expressions of his belief that all his censorship woes were caused by vicious male readers.

60 Patricia Meyer Spacks, *The Female Imagination* (New York: Knopf, 1975), p. 7.

61 Angeline Goreau, "Aphra Behn: A Scandal to Modesty," in *Feminist Theories: Three Centuries of Key Women Thinkers*, ed. Dale Spender (New York: Pantheon, 1983), pp. 17–20.

62 Moore, *Priest of Love*, p. 284.

63 "A View From the Pit," in *Sons and Lovers: Text, Background and Criticism*, p. 452.

64 Elaine Showalter, "Critical Cross-Dressing: Male Feminists and the Woman of the Year," *Raritan* 3 (1983): 138, 147.

65 Spacks, *Female Imagination*, p. 160.

66 Gilbert and Gubar, *Madwoman*, p. 50; LL, 1:510.

67 Gilbert and Gubar, *Madwoman*, p. 50.

68 Myra Jehlen, "Archimedes and the Paradox of Feminist Criticism," *Signs* 6 (1981): 582, 594.

69 Gilbert and Gubar, *Madwoman,* p. 50.

70 Sandra Gilbert and Susan Gubar, *The War of the Words,* vol. 1 of *No Man's Land: The Place of the Woman Writer in the Twentieth Century* (New Haven: Yale University Press, 1988), p. 170.

Chapter Two: Lawrence's Responses
to His Female Precursors

1 Harold Bloom, *The Anxiety of Influence: A Theory of Poetry* (New York: Oxford University Press, 1973), p. 71.

2 Jonathan Culler, *The Pursuit of Signs: Semiotics, Literature, Deconstruction* (Ithaca, N.Y.: Cornell University Press, 1981), p. 103.

3 Nancy K. Miller, "Changing the Subject: Authorship, Writing, and the Reader," in *Feminist Studies/Critical Studies,* ed. Teresa de Lauretis (Bloomington: Indiana University Press, 1986), p. 106.

4 Judith Fetterley, *The Resisting Reader: A Feminist Approach to American Fiction* (Bloomington: Indiana University Press, 1978), p. xxiii.

5 See Thaïs E. Morgan's "Is There an Intertext in This Text?" for a good discussion of ways that, in the period before the New Criticism gained ascendency, the rival theories of influence and inspiration worked to stigmatize one text's references to another (*American Journal of Semiotics* 3, no. 4 [1985]: 2–5).

6 Elaine Showalter, *A Literature of Their Own: British Women Novelists from Brontë to Lessing* (Princeton: Princeton University Press, 1977), p. 13.

7 M. M. Bakhtin, "Discourse in the Novel," in *The Dialogic Imagination,* trans. Carl Emerson and Michael Holquist, ed. Michael Holquist (Austin: University of Texas Press, 1981), pp. 342, 344.

8 Lawrence's practice here seems comparable to that of many feminist psychoanalytic theorists. Juliet Mitchell's work on Freud and Jane Gallop's on Lacan come to mind.

9 See F. R. Leavis, *D. H. Lawrence: Novelist* (New York: Knopf, 1956); H. M. Daleski, *Unities: Studies in the English Novel* (Athens: University of Georgia Press, 1985); Keith Sagar, "The Originality of *Wuthering Heights,*" in *The Art of Emily Brontë,* ed. Anne Smith (London: Vision, 1976); Daniel J. Schneider, *D. H. Lawrence: The Artist as Psychologist* (Lawrence: University of Kansas Press, 1984); Harold Bloom, Introduction to *The Brontës,* ed. Harold Bloom, Modern Critical Views (New York: Chelsea, 1987).

10 D. H. Lawrence, *Phoenix: The Posthumous Papers of D. H. Lawrence,* ed. Edward D. McDonald (1936; rpt., Harmondsworth: Penguin, 1978), p. 265. All further references to this work are incorporated in the text.

11 D. H. Lawrence, "Blessed Are the Powerful," in *Reflections on the Death of a*

Porcupine and Other Essays (1925; rpt., Bloomington: Indiana University Press, 1963), p. 148.

12 D. H. Lawrence, *John Thomas and Lady Jane* (Harmondsworth: Penguin, 1973), p. 342. All further references to this work, abbreviated *JTLJ*, are incorporated in the text.

13 Emily Brontë, *Wuthering Heights,* ed. William M. Sale, Jr. (1847; rpt., New York: Norton, 1972), p. 74. All further references to this work, abbreviated *WH,* are incorporated in the text.

14 D. H. Lawrence, *The White Peacock* (1911; rpt., Harmondsworth: Penguin, 1950), p. 177. All further references to this work, abbreviated *WP,* are incorporated in the text.

15 See chapter 1, "Representation, Reproduction, and Woman's Place in Language," of Margaret Homans's *Bearing the Word: Language and Female Experience and Nineteenth-Century Women's Writing* (Chicago: University of Chicago Press, 1986). I find Homans's thesis generally persuasive, but see Lawrence, as he so often is, as an exceptional case.

16 Susan Griffin, *Woman and Nature: The Roaring inside Her* (New York: Harper, 1978).

17 See Sandra Gilbert and Susan Gubar's *The Madwoman in the Attic* for a persuasive discussion of Edgar as a figure for patriarchal law ([New Haven: Yale University Press, 1979], pp. 280–82).

18 Françoise Basch, *Relative Creatures: Victorian Women in Society and the Novel* (New York: Schocken, 1974), p. 92.

19 As is so often the case with Lawrence, his honesty is at the expense of his artistry. Keith Sagar attributes the failure of Lawrence's first novel to his imitation of and identification with Brontë's narrator. *D. H. Lawrence: Life into Art* (New York: Viking, 1985), p. 17.

20 Jessie Chambers, *D. H. Lawrence: A Personal Record,* ed. A. J. Bramley (1935; rpt., New York: Barnes and Noble, 1965), p. 130.

21 Charlotte Brontë, "Biographical Notice," in *WH,* p. 8.

22 Rose Marie Burwell, "A Catalogue of D. H. Lawrence's Reading from Early Childhood," *D. H. Lawrence Review* 3 (1970): 208, 211.

23 Elizabeth Gaskell, *The Life of Charlotte Brontë,* ed. Alan Shelston (Harmondsworth: Penguin, 1975), p. 268.

24 Bette London, "*Wuthering Heights* and the Text between the Lines," *Papers on Language and Literature* (Winter 1988): 49–50.

25 Sagar, *Life into Art,* p. 17.

26 D. H. Lawrence, *The Lost Girl* (1920; rpt., Harmondsworth: Penguin, 1977), p. 60.

27 Julia Kristeva, "Within the Microcosm of 'The Talking Cure,'" trans. Thomas Gora and Margaret Walker, in *Interpreting Lacan,* vol. 6 of Psychiatry

and the Humanities, ed. Joseph H. Smith and William Kerrigan (New Haven: Yale University Press, 1983), p. 33.

28 Jane Gallop, *Reading Lacan* (Ithaca, N.Y.: Cornell University Press, 1985), p. 27.

29 Bakhtin, "Discourse," p. 344.

30 Sandra Gilbert, "Potent Griselda: 'The Ladybird' and the Great Mother," in *D. H. Lawrence: A Centenary Consideration,* ed. Peter Balbert and Philip L. Marcus (Ithaca, N.Y.: Cornell University Press, 1985), p. 151.

31 D. H. Lawrence, *The Ladybird,* in *Four Short Novels* (1923; rpt., New York: Viking, 1965), p. 65. All further references to this work, abbreviated *LB,* will be incorporated in the text.

32 Gilbert, "Potent Griselda," pp. 146–49.

33 Gilbert and Gubar, *Madwoman,* p. 264.

34 See Showalter, *Literature of Their Own* (pp. 199–201), and Sandra Gilbert and Susan Gubar, *Sexchanges* (vol. 2 of *No Man's Land: The Place of the Woman Writer in the Twentieth Century* [New Haven: Yale University Press, 1989], pp. 56–57), for fine discussions of the similarities.

35 Joanne Feit Diehl, *Dickinson and the Romantic Imagination* (Princeton: Princeton University Press, 1981), pp. 15–16, 77, 83.

36 Christopher Heywood, "Olive Schreiner's *The Story of an African Farm*: Prototype of Lawrence's Early Novels," *English Language Notes* 14 (1976); and Christopher Heywood, "Olive Schreiner's Influence on George Moore and D. H. Lawrence," in *Aspects of South African Literature,* ed. Christopher Heywood (London: Heinemann, 1976).

37 Olive Schreiner, *The Story of an African Farm* (1883; rpt., Chicago: Academy, 1977), p. 235. All further references to this work, abbreviated *SAF,* are incorporated in the text.

38 "To Jessie Chambers," [c. June 1910], letter 158, *The Letters of D. H. Lawrence* (Cambridge: Cambridge University Press, 1979), 1:161.

39 Heywood, "Prototype," p. 50; *WL,* p. 437.

40 Gilbert and Gubar, *Sexchanges,* pp. 53–57.

41 U. C. Knoepflmacher, "The Rival Ladies: Mrs. Ward's *Lady Connie* and Lawrence's *Lady Chatterley's Lover,*" *Victorian Studies* 4 (1960): 154.

42 Chambers, *D. H. Lawrence,* p. 103.

43 H. M. Daleski, *Unities,* p. 85.

44 See Sagar, *Life into Art,* p. 132, for a succinct and well-informed statement of this developmental theory of Lawrence's fiction.

45 George Eliot, *The Mill on the Floss* (1860; rpt., Harmondsworth: Penguin, 1979), pp. 89, 66. All further references to this work, abbreviated *MF,* are incorporated in the text.

46 Gilbert and Gubar, *Madwoman,* p. 492.

47 Daleski, *Unities,* p. 95.

48 D. H. Lawrence, "Daughters of the Vicar," in *The Complete Stories* (Harmondsworth: Penguin, 1976), 1:143. All further references to this work, abbreviated "DV," are incorporated in the text.

49 Sandra M. Gilbert, "Life's Empty Pack: Notes toward a Literary Daughteronomy," *Critical Inquiry* 11 (1985): 364.

50 D. H. Lawrence, *Sons and Lovers: Text, Background, and Criticism,* ed. Julian Moynahan (New York: Viking, 1968), p. 7. All further references to this work, abbreviated *SL,* are incorporated in the text.

51 Gilbert, "Life's Empty Pack," p. 364.

52 Homans's theory, in *Bearing the Word* (pp. 8–14), interestingly applies Nancy Chodorow's ideas on the role of the figure of the mother in psychological development to the question of gender difference in language use.

53 Gilbert, "Life's Empty Pack," p. 378.

54 Daleski, *Unities,* pp. 84–85.

55 D. H. Lawrence, *St. Mawr,* in *St. Mawr and the Man Who Died* (1925; rpt., New York: Bantam, 1953), p. 139.

56 George Eliot, *Daniel Deronda* (1876; rpt., Harmondsworth: Penguin, 1967), p. 803.

57 Showalter, *Literature of Their Own,* p. 117.

58 Charlotte Brontë, *Jane Eyre,* ed. Richard J. Dunn (New York: Norton, 1971), p. 279. All further references to this work, abbreviated *JE,* appear in the text.

59 David Leon Higdon comments interestingly, although briefly, on this topic in his "Bertha Coutts and Bertha Mason," *D. H. Lawrence Review* 11 (1978): 294–96.

60 Lawrence, "Pornography and Obscenity," in *Phoenix,* pp. 176–77. All further references to this work, designated "Pornography," are incorporated in the text.

61 Harry T. Moore, *The Priest of Love: A Life of D. H. Lawrence* (1974; rpt., Harmondsworth: Penguin, 1980), p. 186.

62 George Eliot, *Adam Bede* (1859; rpt., New York: Signet Classics–New American Library, 1961), p. 501.

63 Eve Kosofsky Sedgwick, *Between Men: English Literature and Male Homosocial Desire* (New York: Columbia University Press, 1985), pp. 142–43.

64 Patricia Meyer Spacks, *The Female Imagination* (New York: Knopf, 1975), p. 64.

65 Eliot uses similar methods in *Middlemarch* and *Daniel Deronda* where she punishes Casaubon and Grandcourt on behalf of Dorothea and Gwendoline, who can, thus, remain unsullied by any displays of unfeminine anger.

66 *JE,* p. 32; Gilbert and Gubar, *Madwoman,* pp. 344–47.

67 D. H. Lawrence, "Mother and Daughter," *Complete Short Stories* 3:816.

68 D. H. Lawrence, "The Woman Who Rode Away," *Complete Short Stories* 2:546, 579.

69 Higdon, "Bertha Coutts," pp. 294–96.

Chapter Three: Responses to Lawrence from Some Shapers of Modern Women's Literature

1 Kate Millett, *Sexual Politics* (New York: Avon, 1971), p. 317.

2 Alice A. Jardine, *Gynesis: Configurations of Woman and Modernity* (Ithaca, N.Y.: Cornell University Press, 1985), p. 217.

3 See Jardine, *Gynesis,* for a good discussion of the relationships between male perceptions of female knowledge, male paranoia, and "becoming woman" (pp. 97–99).

4 Harry T. Moore, *The Priest of Love: A Life of D. H. Lawrence* (1974; rpt., Harmondsworth: Penguin, 1980), pp. 293–94, 313–14.

5 Virginia Woolf, 20 June 1921, *The Letters of Virginia Woolf,* ed. Nigel Nicolson (London: Hogarth, 1979), 2:474. All further references to the letters of Virginia Woolf, abbreviated LW, are incorporated in the text.

6 She comments in her diary for 28 May 1931 on having read the first two.

7 Virginia Woolf, Sunday, 2 October 1932, *The Diary of Virginia Woolf,* ed. Anne Olivier Bell (London: Hogarth, 1982), 4:126. All further references to Woolf's diary, abbreviated DW, are incorporated in the text.

8 Robert Keily, *Beyond Egotism: The Fiction of James Joyce, Virginia Woolf, and D. H. Lawrence* (Cambridge: Harvard University Press, 1980), pp. 4, 11.

9 Rachel Blau DuPlessis, "For the Etruscans," in *The New Feminist Criticism: Essays on Women, Literature, and Theory,* ed. Elaine Showalter (New York: Pantheon, 1985), p. 286.

10 Bonnie Kime Scott, "The Strange Necessity of Rebecca West," in *Women Reading Women's Writing,* ed. Sue Roe (New York: St. Martin's, 1987), p. 276.

11 Virginia Woolf, "Notes on D. H. Lawrence," in *The Moment and Other Essays* (London: Hogarth, 1947), p. 95.

12 Virginia Woolf, "The Leaning Tower," in *Folios of New Writing,* ed. John Lehmann (London: Hogarth, Autumn 1940), p. 18.

13 Woolf explains at some length in both *A Room of One's Own* and *Three Guineas* that the gravest problem facing women of all classes who wish to work and think independently is their common financial dependency. Hence, according to Woolf's inclusive system, Lawrence, as a miner's son, shared the economic situation of women generally considered to be in the class above his own.

14 Virginia Woolf, *A Room of One's Own* (1929; rpt., New York: Harcourt

Brace Jovanovich, 1957), p. 73. All further references to this work, designated *Room,* are incorporated in the text.

15 Virginia Woolf, "*Jane Eyre* and *Wuthering Heights,*" in *The Common Reader: First Series* (1925; rpt., New York: Harcourt Brace Jovanovich, 1953), pp. 162–63.

16 Carolyn Heilbrun, "Virginia Woolf in Her Fifties," in *Virginia Woolf: A Feminist Slant,* ed. Jane Marcus (Lincoln: University of Nebraska Press, 1983), pp. 240–45.

17 Woolf, "Leaning Tower," pp. 31–33.

18 See Suzanne Henig's "D. H. Lawrence and Virginia Woolf," (*D. H. Lawrence Review* 2 [1969]: 265–71) for a discussion, based on this assumption, of Woolf's recognition of Lawrence's literary marginality.

19 Virginia Woolf, review of *The Lost Girl,* by D. H. Lawrence, *TLS,* 2 December 1920, in *D. H. Lawrence: The Critical Heritage,* ed. R. P. Draper (New York: Barnes and Noble, 1970), p. 142.

20 Woolf, "Notes," p. 96.

21 Virginia Woolf, *The Voyage Out* (1915; rpt., New York: Harcourt Brace Jovanovich, 1948), p. 96. All further references to this work are included in the text designated *Voyage.*

22 Virginia Woolf, *Jacob's Room* (1922; rpt., London: Granada, 1977), p. 43; Alex Zwerdling, *Virginia Woolf and the Real World* (Berkeley and Los Angeles: University of California Press, 1986), pp. 71–76.

23 Jane Marcus, "The Niece of a Nun: Virginia Woolf, Caroline Stephens, and the Cloistered Imagination," in *Virginia Woolf: A Feminist Slant,* ed. Marcus, p. 25.

24 Bonnie Kime Scott, " 'The World Split Its Husk': Woolf's Double Vision of Modernist Language," *Modern Fiction Studies* 34 (1988): 371–85 passim.

25 Virginia Woolf, *Three Guineas* (1938; rpt., New York: Harcourt Brace Jovanovich, 1966), p. 4. All further references to this work are included in the text designated *Guineas.*

26 Cornelia Nixon, *Lawrence's Leadership Politics and the Turn against Women* (Berkeley and Los Angeles: University of California Press, 1986), pp. 190–91.

27 Woolf, "Notes," p. 93.

28 Virginia Woolf, *Orlando,* (1928; rpt., New York: Harcourt Brace Jovanovich, 1956), pp. 268–69. All further references to this work, designated *Orlando,* are incorporated in the text. Mark Schorer has pointed out that since the first copies of *Lady Chatterley's Lover* reached England in July of 1928 and *Orlando* was published in October, Woolf seems to have put her response to Lawrence into her last revisions (*D. H. Lawrence* [New York: Dell, 1968], p. 98).

29 Gérard Genette, *Palimpsestes: La Littérature au second degré* (Paris: Editions du Seuil, 1982), p. 10.

30 Woolf was given the task of reviewing the novel for *TLS* when Mansfield became too ill to finish her review.

31 Woolf, review of *Lost Girl,* p. 142.

32 Katherine Mansfield, *The Scrapbook of Katherine Mansfield,* ed. John Middleton Murry (London: Constable, 1939), pp. 182–84. According to Murry, he received these notes in December 1920. All further references to this work, designated *Scrapbook,* are incorporated in the text.

33 Antony Alpers, *The Life of Katherine Mansfield* (New York: Viking, 1980), p. 308.

34 Katherine Mansfield, *Journal of Katherine Mansfield,* ed. John Middleton Murry (New York: Knopf, 1931), p. 167.

35 Ibid., p. 167; "To Richard Murry," February 1920, *The Letters of Katherine Mansfield,* ed. John Middleton Murry (New York: Knopf, 1929), 2:299.

36 D. H. Lawrence, *The Man Who Died,* in *St. Mawr and The Man Who Died* (1929; rpt., New York: Random, 1953), pp. 204–7. All further references to this book, abbreviated *MWD,* are incorporated in the text.

37 See Jeffrey Meyers's *Katherine Mansfield: A Biography* (1978; rpt., New York: New Directions, 1980), especially pp. 36, 69, and 182, for a harrowing description of the miseries of Mansfield's own sex life and her gradual movement toward resignation about her sufferings.

38 Katherine Mansfield, "The Little Governess," *The Short Stories of Katherine Mansfield* (1937; rpt., New York: Knopf, 1950), p. 201.

39 Keith Cushman, "D. H. Lawrence at Work: 'The Shadow in the Rose Garden,'" *D. H. Lawrence Review* 8 (1975): 35.

40 D. H. Lawrence, "The Shadow in the Rose Garden," *Complete Short Stories* (Harmondsworth: Penguin, 1976), 1:233.

41 Murry destroyed the letter after Mansfield's death, but a full account of its history and witnesses is given in Alpers's *Life of Katherine Mansfield,* pp. 310, 311–12n.

42 [10 February 1920], *Katherine Mansfield's Letters to John Middleton Murry 1913–1922,* ed. John Middleton Murry (New York: Knopf, 1951), p. 473.

43 D. H. Lawrence, *The Lost Girl* (1920; rpt., Harmondsworth: Penguin, 1950), p. 326. All further references to this work, abbreviated *LG,* are incorporated in the text.

44 Katherine Mansfield, "The Daughters of the Late Colonel," *Short Stories of Katherine Mansfield,* p. 466. All further references to this work, designated "Daughters," are incorporated in the text.

45 Dale Bauer, *Feminist Dialogics: A Theory of Failed Community* (Albany: State University of New York Press, 1988), p. 160.

46 Calvin Bedient, *Architects of the Self: George Eliot, D. H. Lawrence, and E. M. Forster* (Berkeley and Los Angeles: University of California Press, 1972), p. 8.

47 Nancy K. Miller, "Emphasis Added: Plots and Plausibilities in Women's Fiction," in *The New Feminist Criticism,* ed. Elaine Showalter (New York: Pantheon, 1985), p. 357.

48 D. H. Lawrence, "Odour of Chrysanthemums," *Complete Short Stories,* 2:283–87, 289.

49 Katherine Mansfield, "The Garden-Party," in *Short Stories of Katherine Mansfield,* pp. 536, 537, 543. All further references to this work, designated "Garden-Party," are incorporated in the text.

50 Sandra Gilbert and Susan Gubar, *The War of the Words,* vol. 1 of *No Man's Land: The Place of the Woman Writer in the Twentieth Century* (New Haven: Yale University Press, 1988), 95.

51 Naomi Scheman, "Missing Mothers/Desiring Daughters: Framing the Sight of Women," *Critical Inquiry* 15 (1988): 64.

52 D. H. Lawrence, *Women in Love* (1920; rpt., New York: Viking, 1960), pp. 87, 421. All further references to this work, abbreviated *WL,* are incorporated in the text.

53 Jardine, *Gynesis,* p. 147.

54 See Toril Moi's *Sexual/Textual Politics: Feminist Literary Theory* (New York: Methuen, 1985) for a full discussion of the problems inherent in this approach. Her arguments with what she sees as various critics' demands for autobiographically based veracity inform the attack on Anglo-American criticism in the first section of her book (pp. 1–88).

55 Alpers, *Life of Katherine Mansfield,* p. 341.

56 Katherine Mansfield, "Prelude," *Short Stories of Katherine Mansfield,* pp. 232, 229–30, 245, 262.

57 "To Catherine Carswell," 7 November 1916, *The Letters of D. H. Lawrence,* ed. James T. Boulton and Andrew Robertson (Cambridge: Cambridge University Press, 1984), 3:25–26. All further references to this work, abbreviated LL, are incorporated in the text and accompanied by volume number.

58 Katherine Mansfield, "At the Bay," *Short Stories of Katherine Mansfield,* p. 272. All further references to this work, designated "Bay," appear in the text.

59 Susan Gubar, "The Birth of the Artist as Heroine: (Re)production, the *Künstlerroman* Tradition, and the Fiction of Katherine Mansfield," in *The Representation of Women in Fiction: Selected Papers from the English Institute, 1981,* n.s. 7, ed. Carolyn G. Heilbrun and Margaret Higonnet (Baltimore: Johns Hopkins University Press, 1983), p. 49.

60 Gilbert and Gubar do so in *No Man's Land* (1:39–39, 149–50), treating Lawrence's depiction of Gudrun as representative of male writers' hostility to female creativity.

61 D. H. Lawrence, *Fantasia of the Unconscious* (1923; rpt., London: Heinemann, 1933), p. 170; emphasis Lawrence's.

62 Janice S. Robinson, *H. D.: The Life and Work of an American Poet* (Boston: Houghton Mifflin, 1982), p. 92.

63 Bonnie Kime Scott, *James Joyce* (Atlantic Highlands: Humanities Press International, 1987), p. 81.

64 See Barbara Guest, *Herself Defined: The Poet and Her World,* for a good, concise analysis of their influence on each other's poetry ([Garden City: Doubleday, 1984], pp. 74–75).

65 Robinson, *H. D.,* p. 66.

66 Ibid., p. 96.

67 Guest, *Herself,* p. 204.

68 Ibid., p. 20; D. H. Lawrence, *Aaron's Rod* (1922; rpt., Harmondsworth: Penguin, 1950), p. 38. All further references to the latter work, abbreviated *AR,* are incorporated in the text.

69 H. D. (Hilda Doolittle), *Bid Me to Live* (*A Madrigal*) (New York: Dial, 1960), p. 7. All further references to this work, abbreviated *BML,* appear in the text.

70 Susan Stanford Friedman, "The Return of the Repressed in Women's Narrative," *The Journal of Narrative Technique* 19 (1989): 147.

71 Many critics have discussed the significance of H. D.'s identification with D. H. Lawrence, but Gilbert and Gubar seem right to emphasize the "mirror imagery" that marks him as different/opposite, a *"male* counterpart" rather than a simple double (*War of the Words,* p. 243). One may read the name H. D. gives Lawrence in *Bid Me to Live* as an implicit criticism of his sexual and artistic potential, since Rico is also the name of a character in *St. Mawr* who is a sexually inadequate dilettante. But H. D.'s lavish praise of Lawrence's art and her apparent fear of and respect for his virility make the reference to Lawrence's Rico seem coincidental or unconscious.

72 Sandra Gilbert and Susan Gubar, *Sexchanges,* vol. 2 of *No Man's Land* (New Haven: Yale University Press, 1989), pp. 307–8.

73 H. D. (Hilda Doolittle), *Tribute to Freud* (New York: McGraw-Hill, 1956), pp. 140–41.

74 Rachel Blau DuPlessis, *H. D.: The Career of That Struggle* (Bloomington: Indiana University Press, 1986), pp. 39–40, 76.

75 Harry T. Moore, Introduction to *D. H. Lawrence: An Unprofessional Study,* by Anaïs Nin (1932; rpt., Chicago: Swallow Press, 1964), p. 9.

76 Nin, *D. H. Lawrence,* p. 57.

77 Ibid., pp. 13–14, 36, 23, 58–59.

78 Luce Irigaray, "This Sex Which Is Not One," in *This Sex Which Is Not One,* trans. Catherine Porter and Carolyn Burke (Ithaca, N.Y.: Cornell University Press, 1985), pp. 23–33 passim.

79 Nin, *D. H. Lawrence,* p. 59.

80 Irigaray, "This Sex," p. 29. The second set of ellipses are hers.

81 Nin, *D. H. Lawrence,* pp. 34–35.

82 Margaret Homans, *Bearing the Word: Language and Female Experience in Nineteenth-Century Women's Writing* (Chicago: University of Chicago Press, 1986), p. 20.

83 Nin, *D. H. Lawrence,* pp. 64, 61.

84 Ibid., pp. 42, 49, 71, 50–51, 65, 37, 48.

85 Ann Rosalind Jones, "Writing the Body: L'Ecriture féminine," in *The New Feminist Criticism,* ed. Elaine Showalter, pp. 369, 371.

86 Marianne DeKoven, *A Different Language: Gertrude Stein's Experimental Writing* (Madison: University of Wisconsin Press, 1983), pp. 22–25.

87 Nin, *D. H. Lawrence,* pp. 84, 56, 20, 92.

88 Anaïs Nin, *The Novel of the Future* (1968; rpt., New York: Collier, 1970), p. 117.

Chapter Four: Lawrence's Female Successors

1 For a good example of this sort of study, see Carol Ohmann's "Emily Brontë in the Hands of Male Critics," *College English* 32 (1971): 906–13.

2 What seems to me still the best discussion of the problems implicit in the idea of anyone speaking as a woman is Shoshana Felman's "Women and Madness: The Critical Phallacy," *Diacritics* 5 (1975): 2–10 passim.

3 Julia Kristeva, "Women's Time," trans. Alice Jardine and Harry Blake, in *The Kristeva Reader,* ed. Toril Moi (New York: Columbia University Press, 1986), p. 207.

4 In the essay collection *New French Feminisms,* the editors Elaine Marks and Isabelle de Courtivron entitle a section that includes such texts "Utopias," but their "vision of the new world to which feminist thought and action are dedicated" seems to depend on a depressing vision of our literary past ([New York: Schocken, 1981], p. 231).

5 See Rita Felski's *Beyond Feminist Aesthetics: Feminist Literature and Social Change* for a concise discussion of the devastating effects of the theory of symbolic language as inescapably phallocentric on our valorization of women's literary texts ([Cambridge: Harvard University Press, 1989], pp. 40–44).

6 Patricia Yaeger, *Honey-Mad Women: Emancipatory Strategies in Women's Writing* (New York: Columbia University Press, 1988), pp. 177–78.

7 See Mark Spilka's Introduction to *D. H. Lawrence: A Collection of Critical Essays* (ed. Mark Spilka [Englewood Cliffs: Prentice Hall, 1963]) for a comprehensive discussion of Lawrence's critical history.

8 Hilary Simpson, *D. H. Lawrence and Feminism* (De Kalb: Northern Illinois University Press, 1982), pp. 13–14.

9 Kate Millett, *Sexual Politics* (New York: Avon, 1971), pp. 373, 317, 341.

10 D. H. Lawrence, letter to Mabel Dodge Luhan, 9 January 1924, in Luhan's *Lorenzo in Taos* (New York: Knopf, 1932), p. 134.

11 F. R. Leavis, *D. H. Lawrence: Novelist* (New York: Knopf, 1956), p. 332.

12 D. H. Lawrence, *The Fox,* in *Four Short Novels* (1923; rpt., New York: Viking, 1965), p. 179. All further references to these works, designated *Fox,* are incorporated in the text. Ancient Egyptians used the phrase "go west" as a euphemism for dying because the dead were entombed on the Nile's west bank. See Rose Marie Burwell's "Catalogue of D. H. Lawrence's Reading From Early Childhood" for a sense of the extent of his interest in Egyptian culture and religion (*D. H. Lawrence Review* 3 [1970]: 193–330; and 6 [1973]: 89–99).

13 Leavis, *D. H. Lawrence,* pp. 299, 317, 157–58. Later, Norman Mailer would claim, in *The Prisoner of Sex,* that because Lawrence had "the soul of a beautiful woman" he was better equipped to write about women than any normal man or *any* woman could be ([London: Sphere, 1972], p. 131).

14 Harry T. Moore, *The Life and Works of D. H. Lawrence* (New York: Twayne, 1951), p. 165.

15 Wayne C. Booth, *The Company We Keep: An Ethics of Fiction* (Berkeley and Los Angeles: University of California Press, 1988), pp. 4, 286.

16 Moore, *Life and Works,* pp. 295, 322–23.

17 Sandra Gilbert and Susan Gubar, *The War of the Words,* vol. 1 of *No Man's Land: The Place of the Woman Writer in the Twentieth Century* (New Haven: Yale University Press, 1988), pp. 168–70.

18 Tania Modleski, "Feminism and the Power of Interpretation: Some Critical Readings," in *Feminist Studies/Critical Studies,* ed. Teresa de Lauretis (Bloomington: Indiana University Press, 1986), p. 129.

19 Charles and Liebetraut Sarvan, "D. H. Lawrence and Doris Lessing's *The Grass Is Singing,*" *Modern Fiction Studies* 24 (1978): 535.

20 Doris Lessing, *The Grass Is Singing* (New York: Cowell, 1950), p. 139. All further references to this work, abbreviated *GS,* are incorporated in the text.

21 D. H. Lawrence, *The Rainbow* (1915; rpt., New York: Viking, 1961), pp. 2–5. All further references to this work, abbreviated *RB,* are incorporated in the text.

22 D. H. Lawrence, "The Princess," in *Complete Short Stories* (Harmondsworth: Penguin, 1976), 2:485–86; D. H. Lawrence, "None of That," in *Complete Short Stories* 3:706. All further references to this work, designated respectively "Princess" and "None," are incorporated in the text.

23 Sandra Gilbert and Susan Gubar, *The Madwoman in the Attic: The Woman Writer and the Nineteenth-Century Literary Imagination* (New Haven: Yale University Press, 1979), p. 83. They credit Ellen Moers's writings on "female Gothic" with inspiring their discussion of the tradition of "anxieties about space" in women's literature (p. 83).

24 Michele Wender Zak, "*The Grass Is Singing*: A Little Novel about the Emotions," in *Doris Lessing: Critical Studies,* ed. Annis Pratt and L. S. Dembo (Madison: University of Wisconsin Press, 1974), p. 71.

25 See Jane Gallop, *The Daughter's Seduction: Feminism and Psychoanalysis* ([Ithaca, N.Y.: Cornell University Press, 1982], p. 12), for a cogent discussion of the rhetorical and philosophical problems raised by Mitchell's gendering of language, in *Psychoanalysis and Feminism,* which seems, despite her disclaimers, to locate her own speaking position "outside the structure" of signification. Although I do not mean to imply that Mitchell is the only theorist about whose work this criticism can be made, the problem seems to me to continue in her *Women: The Longest Revolution* where her insistence that "one has to speak 'masculinely' in a phallocentric world" undermines her own authority to speak as a woman ([New York: Pantheon, 1982], p. 292).

26 Judith Kegan Gardiner, *Rhys, Stead, Lessing, and the Politics of Empathy* (Bloomington: Indiana University Press, 1989), pp. 91–92.

27 Roy Newquist, "Interview with Doris Lessing," in *Doris Lessing, A Small Personal Voice,* ed. Paul Schlueter (New York: Knopf, 1974), p. 52.

28 See Sarvan and Sarvan, "D. H. Lawrence" (p. 534), for a comparison of almost all identical passages of description in *Martha Quest* and *The Rainbow.*

29 Doris Lessing, *Martha Quest* (1952; rpt., New York: New American Library, 1970), p. 164. All further references to this work, abbreviated *MQ,* are incorporated in the text.

30 Dorothy Brewster, *Doris Lessing* (New York: Twayne, 1965), p. 159.

31 Sarvan and Sarvan, "D. H. Lawrence," p. 534.

32 Mark Spilka, "Lessing and Lawrence: The Battle of the Sexes," *Contemporary Literature* 6 (1976): 225, 232, 237.

33 Catherine R. Stimpson, "Doris Lessing and the Parables of Growth," in *The Voyage In: Fictions of Female Development,* ed. Elizabeth Abel, Marianne Hirsch, and Elizabeth Langland (Hanover, N.H.: University Press of New England, 1983), pp. 200–201.

34 Doris Lessing, *The Fifth Child* (New York: Knopf, 1988), pp. 10, 31, 20.

35 See Elizabeth Bowen's introduction to *Stories by Katherine Mansfield,* selected and ed. Elizabeth Bowen (New York: Vintage, 1956).

36 Victoria Glendinning, *Elizabeth Bowen: A Biography* (1977; rpt., New York: Avon, 1979), p. 86.

37 Elizabeth Bowen, "D. H. Lawrence," review of *The Portable D. H. Lawrence,* edited by Diana Trilling, reprinted in *Collected Impressions* (New York: Knopf, 1950), p. 157.

38 Elizabeth Bowen, "For Lawrence Life Was Not Peace But a Sword," review of *Portrait of a Genius . . . But,* by Richard Aldington, *New York Times Book Review* (21 May 1960): 3.

39 Elizabeth Bowen, *To the North* (1933; rpt., New York: Avon, 1979), p. 152. All further references to this work, abbreviated *TN,* are incorporated in the text.

40 D. H. Lawrence, *Women in Love* (1920; rpt., New York: Viking, 1960), p. 365. All further references to this work, abbreviated *WL,* are incorporated in the text.

41 Lawrence does betray a great deal of sympathy for Gudrun in both *Women in Love* and *The Rainbow,* where she appears as an idealized "*farouche*" young person too fine for the schoolgirl follies that trouble Ursula (p. 334). Farouche seems to be one of Bowen's favorite adjectives; it appears in at least half her works. Her valuation of human wildness and her depictions of it seem identical to Lawrence's.

42 Susan Gubar, " 'The Blank Page' and the Issues of Female Creativity," in *Writing and Sexual Difference,* ed. Elizabeth Abel (Chicago: University of Chicago Press, 1982), pp. 73–94 passim.

43 Edwin Kenney, *Elizabeth Bowen* (Lewisburg, Pa.: Bucknell University Press, 1975), pp. 42, 46.

44 Elizabeth Bowen, *The House in Paris* (1935; rpt., New York: Avon, 1979), p. 138.

45 D. H. Lawrence, *The Ladybird,* in *Four Short Novels,* p. 43.

46 Elizabeth Bowen, "The Disinherited," in *The Collected Stories of Elizabeth Bowen* (New York: Knopf, 1981), p. 379. All further references to this work, designated "Disinherited," are incorporated in the text.

47 Glendinning, *Elizabeth Bowen,* p. 105.

48 Elizabeth Bowen, *Eva Trout or Changing Scenes* (1968; rpt., New York: Avon, 1978), p. 17. All further references to this work, abbreviated *ET,* are incorporated in the text.

49 Virginia Woolf, *A Room of One's Own* (1929; rpt., New York: Harcourt Brace Jovanovich, 1957), p. 55.

50 Kenney, *Elizabeth Bowen,* p. 97.

51 Charlotte Brontë, *Jane Eyre,* ed. Richard J. Dunn (1847; rpt., New York: Norton, 1971), p. 55.

52 Mitchell, *Women,* p. 292.

53 D. H. Lawrence, "Sun-women," in *The Complete Poems of D. H. Lawrence,* ed. Vivian de Sola Pinto and Warren Roberts (Harmondsworth: Penguin, 1977), p. 526.

54 Virginia Woolf, "[Speech Before the London/National Society for Women's Service, January 21, 1931]," an early draft of the essay "Professions for Women" in *The Death of the Moth,* included in *The Pargiters,* ed. Mitchell A. Leaska (New York: Harvest–Harcourt Brace Jovanovich, 1977), pp. xxxviii–xxxix.

55 Joan Lidoff, "An Interview with Christina Stead, Surbiton, England, June, 1973," in *Christina Stead* (New York: Ungar, 1982), p. 204; Stead is not specific

about the date she began reading or the title of the book, but since she refers to it simply as Lawrence's poems, it was probably either *The Collected Poems of D. H. Lawrence* (1928) or Martin Secker's edition of *Selected Poems* (1934).

56 Diana Trilling, "Women in Love," *Nation* (28 October 1944): 535.

57 Lidoff, *Christina Stead,* p. 66.

58 Christina Stead, *For Love Alone* (1944; rpt., New York: Harcourt Brace Jovanovich, 1979), pp. 187, 256. All further references to this work, abbreviated *FLA,* are incorporated in the text.

59 Lidoff, *Christina Stead,* p. 84.

60 George Eliot, *Middlemarch* (1871–72; rpt., New York: New American Library, 1964), pp. vii, 811. All further references to this work, abbreviated *MM,* are incorporated in the text.

61 Jonathan frequently remarks, "I'm just an ordinary fellow," and although Stead shows he is worse, she makes plain the ordinariness of his flaws.

62 D. H. Lawrence, *Apocalypse* (1931; rpt., New York: Viking, 1966), pp. 137, 140.

63 D. H. Lawrence, *The Plumed Serpent* (1926; rpt., New York: Vintage, 1959), p. 436. All further references to this work, abbreviated *PS,* are incorporated in the text.

64 D. H. Lawrence, "Sun," in *Complete Short Stories* 2:534. All further references to this work are incorporated in the text.

65 Louise Yelin, "Overturning the Antipodes: Patriarchy, Colonialism, and Christina Stead's *For Love Alone*," paper presented at the MLA Convention, Washington, D.C., 29 December 1989.

66 Diana Brydon, *Christina Stead* (London: Macmillan Education, 1987), pp. 170–71.

67 Lidoff, *Christina Stead,* p. 93.

68 Christina Stead, *Cotter's England* (1966; rpt., London: Virago, 1980), p. 266. All further references to this work, abbreviated *CE,* are incorporated in the text.

69 Susan Sheridan, *Christina Stead* (Bloomington: Indiana University Press, 1988), pp. 131–33, 119–21.

70 Bowen, *Collected Impressions,* p. 158.

Conclusion

1 Elaine Showalter, "Towards a Feminist Poetics," in *Women Writing and Writing about Women,* ed. Mary Jacobus (London: Croom Helm, 1979), p. 28.

2 Adrienne Munich, "Notorious Signs, Feminist Criticism, and Literary Tradition," in *Making a Difference: Feminist Literary Criticism,* ed. Gayle Greene and Coppélia Kahn (New York: Methuen, 1985), p. 244.

3 In "The 'Mechanics' of Fluids," Luce Irigaray both examines this trend and

presents a meditation on woman-as-water. *This Sex Which Is Not One,* trans. Catherine Porter and Carolyn Burke (Ithaca, N.Y.: Cornell University Press, 1977), pp. 23–33.

4 Sandra Gilbert and Susan Gubar, *The Madwoman in the Attic* (New Haven: Yale University Press, 1979).

5 Eudora Welty, *Short Stories* (New York: Harcourt Brace Jovanovich, 1949), pp. 33–37. Eudora Welty, "Looking at Short Stories," in *The Eye of the Story: Selected Essays and Reviews* (New York: Vintage-Random, 1979), pp. 97–99.

6 D. H. Lawrence, *The Virgin and the Gipsy* (1930; rpt., New York: Vintage-Random, 1984), pp. 174–75. All further references to this work, abbreviated *VG,* are incorporated in the text.

7 Eudora Welty, "At the Landing," in *The Collected Stories of Eudora Welty* (New York: Harcourt Brace Jovanovich, 1980), p. 254. All further references to this work, designated "Landing," are incorporated in the text.

8 Marina Warner, *Monuments and Maidens: The Allegory of the Female Form* (New York: Atheneum, 1985), pp. 241–47.

9 Ibid., pp. 251, 266, 253–54.

10 Gail Kern Paster, "Leaky Vessels: The Incontinent Women of City Comedy." *Renaissance Drama,* n.s. 18 (1987): 51–54.

11 Stephen Heath, *The Sexual Fix* (New York: Schocken, 1982), pp. 116–117, 221–22.

12 Michel Foucault, *The Use of Pleasure,* vol. 2 of *The History of Sexuality,* trans. Robert Hurley (New York: Vintage-Random, 1986), pp. 84–85, 120, 129.

13 Warner, *Monuments,* p. 251.

14 Paster, "Leaky Vessels," pp. 50–51.

15 Michel Foucault, *Madness and Civilization: A History of Insanity in the Age of Reason,* trans. Richard Howard (1965; rpt., New York: Vintage-Random, 1973), pp. 86–89; Klaus Theweleit, *Women, Floods, Bodies, History,* vol. 1 of *Male Fantasies,* trans. Stephen Conway (Minneapolis: University of Minnesota Press, 1987), p. 272.

16 Theweleit, *Women,* pp. 249, 251, 380–82.

17 See Elaine Showalter, *A Literature of Their Own: British Women Novelists from Brontë to Lessing* ([Princeton: Princeton University Press, 1977], pp. 126–29), for a discussion of shared water images in the two texts.

18 Charlotte Brontë, *Jane Eyre,* ed. Richard J. Dunn (1847; rpt., New York: Norton, 1971), p. 261.

19 George Eliot, *The Mill on the Floss* (1860; rpt., Harmondsworth: Penguin, 1979), p. 649. All further references to this work, abbreviated *MF,* are incorporated in the text.

20 Mary Jacobus, *Reading Woman: Essays in Feminist Criticism* (New York: Columbia University Press, 1986), p. 78.

21 D. H. Lawrence, *The Trespasser,* ed. Elizabeth Mansfield (1912; rpt., London: Granada, 1982), p. 63.

22 D. H. Lawrence, *Kangaroo* (1923; rpt., New York: Viking, 1960), pp. 146–47, 348–49; D. H. Lawrence, *Sons and Lovers: Text, Background, and Criticism,* ed. Julian Moynahan (New York: Viking, 1968), p. 306.

23 D. H. Lawrence, *The Rainbow* (1915; rpt., New York: Viking, 1974), pp. 234–35.

24 Cornelia Nixon, *Lawrence's Leadership Politics and the Turn Against Women* (Berkeley and Los Angeles: University of California Press, 1986), pp. 63, 83–84.

25 D. H. Lawrence, *The Lost Girl* (1920; rpt., Harmondsworth: Penguin, 1950), p. 344.

26 D. H. Lawrence, *The Plumed Serpent* (1926; rpt., New York: Vintage, 1959), pp. 361, 386.

27 George Eliot, *Middlemarch* (1871–72; rpt., New York: Penguin, 1979), p. 811.

28 Welty, *Short Stories,* pp. 33–34.

29 William Jones, "Growth of a Symbol: The Sun in D. H. Lawrence and Eudora Welty," *University of Kansas City Review* 26, no. 1 (1959): 71.

30 Alfred Appel, Jr., *A Season of Dreams: The Fiction of Eudora Welty* (Baton Rouge: Louisiana State University Press, 1965), p. 118.

31 Jones, "Growth," p. 72.

32 Ibid., p. 72.

33 Ovid, *Metamorphoses,* trans. Rolfe Humphries (Bloomington: Indiana University Press, 1955), p. 89.

34 Eudora Welty, "Clytie," in *Collected Stories,* p. 83.

35 Eudora Welty, *Delta Wedding* (1945; rpt., New York: Harcourt Brace Jovanovich, 1979), pp. 158, 32–33. All further references to this work, abbreviated *DW,* are incorporated in the text.

36 John Edward Hardy, "*Delta Wedding* as Region and Symbol," in *Contemporary Women Novelists: A Collection of Critical Essays,* ed. Patricia Meyer Spacks (Englewood Cliffs, N.J.: Prentice Hall, 1977), p. 165.

37 Louise Westling, *Sacred Groves and Ravaged Gardens: The Fiction of Eudora Welty, Carson McCullers, and Flannery O'Connor* (Athens: University of Georgia Press, 1985), p. 91.

38 Noel Polk, "Water, Wanderings, and Weddings," in *Eudora Welty: A Form of Thanks,* ed. Louis Dollarhide and Ann J. Abadie (Jackson: University Press of Mississippi, 1979), pp. 97–100.

39 Michael Kreyling, *Eudora Welty's Achievement of Order* (Baton Rouge: Louisiana State University Press, 1980), p. 61.

40 John B. Vickery, "Myth and Ritual in the Shorter Fiction of D. H. Lawrence," *Modern Fiction Studies* 5 (1959): 77–78.

41 Bonnie Kime Scott, *James Joyce* (Atlantic Highlands: Humanities Press International, 1987), pp. 76–89, 97–98.

42 Keith Cushman, "The Virgin and the Gipsy and the Lady and the Game-keeper," in *D. H. Lawrence's Lady: A New Look at* Lady Chatterley's Lover, ed. Michael Squires and Dennis Jackson (Athens: University of Georgia Press, 1985), p. 165.

43 Theweleit, *Women,* pp. 422–24.

44 Cushman, "Virgin," pp. 62–63.

45 Sigmund Freud, *Civilization and Its Discontents,* trans. and ed. James Strachey (New York: Norton, 1961), pp. 13–19.

46 It seems necessary to note here that neither Freud nor Kristeva define the pre-Oedipal state as female, although, as Toril Moi says of Kristeva's work, "The fluid motility of the semiotic is indeed associated with the pre-Oedipal phase, and therefore with the pre-Oedipal mother" (*Sexual/Textual Politics: Feminist Literary Theory* [New York: Methuen, 1985], p. 165). That the pre-Oedipal mother is, in Freud's work and Kristeva's, "a figure that encompasses both masculinity and femininity" (Moi, p. 165) is important, but no more so than the less intentional statement made by Freud's re-use of *Civilization and Its Discontents'* archaeological analogy ("the discovery . . . of Minoan-Mycenaean civilization behind the civilization of Greece") in "Female Sexuality" to explain the primary attachment of daughter to mother, a relationship involving only female bodies, whatever masculine and feminine attributes they are assigned ("Female Sexuality," in *The Standard Edition of the Complete Psychological Works of Sigmund Freud,* trans. and ed. James Strachey [London: Hogarth, 1963], 21:226). In both cases, his analogy implicitly connects the pre-Oedipal/oceanic and the female.

47 Welty, "Looking," p. 98.

48 Luce Irigaray, "This Sex Which Is Not One," in *This Sex Which Is Not One,* trans. Catherine Porter and Carolyn Burke (Ithaca, N.Y.: Cornell University Press, 1977), p. 24.

49 Westling, *Sacred Groves,* p. 99.

50 Sandra Gilbert and Susan Gubar, *The War of the Words,* vol. 1 of *No Man's Land: The Place of the Woman Writer in the Twentieth Century* (New Haven: Yale University Press, 1988), p. 208.

51 Monique Wittig, *Les Guérillères,* trans. David Le Vay (New York: Bard-Avon, 1973), p. 9.

52 Teresa de Lauretis, "Eccentric Subjects: Feminist Theory and Historical Consciousness," *Feminist Studies* 16 (1990): 141–45.

53 Myra Jehlen, "Archimedes and the Paradox of Feminist Criticism," *Signs: Journal of Women in Culture and Society* 6 (1981): 585.

54 D. H. Lawrence, "We Need One Another," in *Phoenix: The Posthumous Papers of D. H. Lawrence,* ed. Edward D. McDonald (1936; rpt., Harmondsworth: Penguin, 1978), p. 194.

Bibliography

Alcoff, Linda. "Cultural Feminism Versus Poststructuralism: The Identity Crisis in Feminist Theory." *Signs* 13 (1988): 405–36.

Alpers, Antony. *The Life of Katherine Mansfield*. New York: Viking, 1980.

Appel, Alfred, Jr. *A Season of Dreams: The Fiction of Eudora Welty*. Baton Rouge: Louisiana State University Press, 1965.

Asquith, Cynthia. *Remember and Be Glad*. New York: Scribner's, 1952.

Bakhtin, M. M. "Discourse in the Novel." In *The Dialogic Imagination*, translated by Carl Emerson and Michael Holquist and edited by Michael Holquist, pp. 259–422. Austin: University of Texas Press, 1981.

Barr, Barbara Weekley. "Memoir of D. H. Lawrence." In *D. H. Lawrence: Novelist, Poet, Prophet*, edited by Stephen Spender, pp. 21–27. London: Weidenfield and Nicholson, 1973.

Basch, Françoise. *Relative Creatures: Victorian Women in Society and the Novel*. New York: Schocken, 1974.

Bauer, Dale. *Feminist Dialogics: A Theory of Failed Community*. Albany: State University of New York Press, 1988.

Baym, Nina. "The Madwoman and Her Languages: Why I Don't Do Feminist Literary Theory." In *Feminist Issues in Literary Scholarship*, edited by Shari Benstock, pp. 45–61. Bloomington: Indiana University Press, 1987.

Beauvoir, Simone de. *The Second Sex*. Trans. and ed. H. M. Parshley. 1953. Reprint. New York: Bantam, 1961.

Bedient, Calvin. *Architects of the Self: George Eliot, D. H. Lawrence, and E. M. Forster*. Berkeley and Los Angeles: University of California Press, 1972.

Bloom, Harold. *The Anxiety of Influence: A Theory of Poetry*. New York: Oxford University Press, 1973.

————. Introduction to *The Brontës*. Ed. Harold Bloom. Modern Critical Views. New York: Chelsea, 1987.

Booth, Wayne C. *The Company We Keep: An Ethics of Fiction*. Berkeley and Los Angeles: University of California Press, 1988.

Bowen, Elizabeth. *Collected Impressions*. New York: Knopf, 1950.

————. "The Disinherited." In *The Collected Stories of Elizabeth Bowen*, pp. 375–407. New York: Knopf, 1981.

————. *Eva Trout Or Changing Scenes*. 1968. Reprint. New York: Knopf, 1978.

————. "For Lawrence Life Was Not Peace But a Sword." Review of *Portrait of a Genius . . . But,* by Richard Aldington. *New York Times Book Review* 7 (21 May 1960): 3.

————. *The House in Paris*. 1935. Reprint. New York: Avon, 1979.

————. *To the North*. 1933. Reprint. New York: Avon, 1979.

Braidotti, Rosi. "The Politics of Ontological Difference." In *Between Feminism and Psychoanalysis,* edited by Teresa Brennan, pp. 98–105. New York: Routledge, 1989.

Brett, Dorothy. *Lawrence and Brett: A Friendship*. 1933. Reprint. Santa Fe, N. Mex.: Sunstone, 1974.

Brewster, Dorothy. *Doris Lessing*. New York: Twayne, 1965.

Brontë, Charlotte. *Jane Eyre*. Ed. Richard J. Dunn. 1847. Reprint. New York: Norton, 1971.

————. *Shirley*. Ed. Andrew and Judith Hook. Harmondsworth: Penguin, 1974.

Brontë, Emily. *Wuthering Heights*. Ed. William M. Sale, Jr. 1847. Reprint. New York: Norton, 1972.

Brydon, Diana. *Christina Stead*. London: Macmillan Education, 1987.

Burwell, Rose Marie. "A Catalogue of D. H. Lawrence's Reading from Early Childhood." *D. H. Lawrence Review* 3 (1970): 193–330.

————. "A Catalogue of D. H. Lawrence's Reading from Early Childhood: Addenda." *D. H. Lawrence Review* 6 (1973): 89–99.

Callow, Philip. *Son and Lover: The Young D. H. Lawrence*. New York: Stein and Day, 1975.

Carswell, Catherine. *The Savage Pilgrimage: A Narrative of D. H. Lawrence*. 1932. Reprint. Cambridge: Cambridge University Press, 1981.

Chambers, Jessie (E. T.). *D. H. Lawrence: A Personal Record*. Ed. and intro. A. J. Bramley. 1935. Reprint. New York: Barnes and Noble, 1965.

Connell, R. W. *Gender and Power: Society, the Person and Sexual Politics*. Stanford: Stanford University Press, 1987.

Corke, Helen. *D. H. Lawrence: The Croydon Years*. Austin: University of Texas Press, 1965.

————. "The Writing of *The Trespasser*." *D. H. Lawrence Review* 7 (1974): 227–39.

Culler, Jonathan. *The Pursuit of Signs: Semiotics, Literature, Deconstruction*. Ithaca, N.Y.: Cornell University Press, 1981.

Cushman, Keith. "D. H. Lawrence at Work: 'The Shadow in the Rose Garden.' " *The D. H. Lawrence Review* 8 (1973): 32–46.

———. "The Virgin and the Gipsy and the Lady and the Gamekeeper." In *D. H. Lawrence's Lady: A New Look at* Lady Chatterley's Lover, edited by Michael Squires and Dennis Jackson, pp. 154–69. Athens: University of Georgia Press, 1985.

Daleski, H. M. *The Forked Flame: A Study of D. H. Lawrence.* Evanston, Ill.: Northwestern University Press, 1965.

———. *Unities: Studies in the English Novel.* Athens: University of Georgia Press, 1985.

DeKoven, Marianne. *A Different Language: Gertrude Stein's Experimental Writing.* Madison: University of Wisconsin Press, 1983.

De Lauretis, Teresa. "Eccentric Subjects: Feminist Theory and Historical Consciousness." *Feminist Studies* 16 (1990): 115–50.

Delavenay, Emile. *D. H. Lawrence: The Man and His Work: The Formative Years, 1885–1919.* Trans. Katherine M. Delavenay. Carbondale: Southern Illinois University Press, 1972.

———. *D. H. Lawrence and Edward Carpenter: A Study in Edwardian Transition.* New York: Taplinger, 1971.

Devor, Holly. *Gender Blending: Confronting the Limits of Duality.* Bloomington: Indiana University Press, 1989.

Diehl, Joanne Feit. *Dickinson and the Romantic Imagination.* Princeton: Princeton University Press, 1981.

Dollimore, Jonathan. "Different Desires: Subjectivity and Transgression in Wilde and Gide." *Genders* 2 (1988): 24–41.

Doolittle, Hilda (H. D.). *Bid Me to Live: (A Madrigal).* New York: Dial, 1960.

———. *Tribute to Freud.* New York: McGraw-Hill, 1956.

DuPlessis, Rachel Blau. "For the Etruscans." In *The New Feminist Criticism: Essays on Women, Literature, and Theory,* edited by Elaine Showalter, pp. 271–91. New York: Pantheon, 1985.

———. *H. D., The Career of That Struggle.* Bloomington: Indiana University Press, 1986.

Eliot, George. *Adam Bede.* 1859. Reprint. New York: Signet Classics–New American Library, 1961.

———. *Daniel Deronda.* 1876. Reprint. Harmondsworth: Penguin, 1967.

———. *Middlemarch.* 1871–72. Reprint. New York: New American Library, 1964.

———. *The Mill on the Floss.* 1860. Reprint. Harmondsworth: Penguin, 1979.

———. *Scenes of Clerical Life.* 1858. Reprint. Harmondsworth: Penguin, 1973.

Felman, Shoshana. "Women and Madness: The Critical Phallacy." *Diacritics* 5 (1975): 2–10.

Felski, Rita. *Beyond Feminist Aesthetics: Feminist Literature and Social Change.* Cambridge: Harvard University Press, 1989.

Fetterley, Judith. *The Resisting Reader: A Feminist Approach to American Fiction.* Bloomington: Indiana University Press, 1978.

Forster, E. M. *Aspects of the Novel.* 1927. Reprint. New York: Harcourt, Brace, and Co., 1954.

Foucault, Michel. *Madness and Civilization: A History of Insanity in the Age of Reason.* Trans. Richard Howard. 1965. Reprint. New York: Vintage-Random, 1973.

———. *The Use of Pleasure.* Vol. 2 of *The History of Sexuality.* Trans. Robert Hurley. New York: Vintage-Random, 1986.

Freud, Sigmund. *Civilization and Its Discontents.* Trans. and ed. James Strachey. New York: Norton, 1961.

———. "Female Sexuality." In vol. 21 of *The Standard Edition of the Complete Psychological Works of Sigmund Freud,* translated and edited by James Strachey, 221–45. London: Hogarth, 1963.

Friedman, Susan Stanford. "The Return of the Repressed in Women's Narrative." *The Journal of Narrative Technique* 19 (1989): 141–56.

Fuss, Diana J. "'Essentially Speaking': Luce Irigaray's Language of Essence." *Hypatia* 3 (1989): 62–80.

Gallop, Jane. *The Daughter's Seduction: Feminism and Psychoanalysis.* Ithaca, N.Y.: Cornell University Press, 1982.

———. *Reading Lacan.* Ithaca, N.Y.: Cornell University Press, 1985.

Gardiner, Judith Kegan. *Rhys, Stead, Lessing, and the Politics of Empathy.* Bloomington: Indiana University Press, 1989.

Gaskell, Elizabeth. *The Life of Charlotte Brontë.* Ed. Alan Shelston. Harmondsworth: Penguin, 1975.

Genette, Gérard. *Palimpsestes: La Littérature au second degré.* Paris: Editions du Seuil, 1982.

Gilbert, Sandra M. "Life's Empty Pack: Notes toward a Literary Daughteronomy." *Critical Inquiry* 11 (1985): 355–85.

———. "Potent Griselda: 'The Ladybird' and the Great Mother." In *D. H. Lawrence: A Centenary Consideration,* edited by Peter Balbert and Philip L. Marcus, pp. 130–61. Ithaca, N.Y.: Cornell University Press, 1985.

Gilbert, Sandra M., and Susan Gubar. *The Madwoman in the Attic: The Woman Writer and the Nineteenth-Century Literary Imagination.* New Haven: Yale University Press, 1979.

———. *The War of the Words.* Vol. 1 of *No Man's Land: The Place of the Woman Writer in the Twentieth Century.* New Haven: Yale University Press, 1988.

———. *Sexchanges.* Vol. 2 of *No Man's Land: The Place of the Woman Writer in the Twentieth Century.* New Haven: Yale University Press, 1989.

Glendinning, Victoria. *Elizabeth Bowen: A Biography.* 1977. Reprint. New York: Avon, 1979.

Goreau, Angeline. "Aphra Behn: A Scandal to Modesty." In *Feminist Theorists: Three Centuries of Key Women Thinkers,* edited by Dale Spender, pp. 8–27. New York: Pantheon, 1983.

Grahn, Judy. *Another Mother Tongue: Gay Words, Gay Worlds.* Boston: Beacon, 1984.

Griffin, Susan. *Woman and Nature: The Roaring inside Her.* New York: Harper, 1978.

Gubar, Susan. "The Birth of the Artist as Heroine: (Re)production, the *Künstlerroman* Tradition, and the Fiction of Katherine Mansfield." In *The Representation of Women in Fiction: Selected Papers from the English Institute, 1981,* n.s. 7, edited by Carolyn G. Heilbrun and Margaret Higonnet, pp. 19–59. Baltimore: Johns Hopkins University Press, 1983.

———. "'The Blank Page' and the Issues of Female Creativity." In *Writing and Sexual Difference,* edited by Elizabeth Abel, pp. 73–94. Chicago: University of Chicago Press, 1982.

Guest, Barbara. *Herself Defined: The Poet and Her World.* Garden City: Doubleday, 1984.

Hahn, Emily. *Lorenzo: D. H. Lawrence and the Women Who Loved Him.* New York: Lippincott, 1975.

Hardy, John Edward. "*Delta Wedding* as Region and Symbol." In *Contemporary Women Novelists: A Collection of Critical Essays,* edited by Patricia Meyer Spacks, pp. 150–66. Englewood Cliffs: Prentice, 1977.

Heath, Stephen. *The Sexual Fix.* New York: Schocken, 1982.

Heilbrun, Carolyn. "Virginia Woolf in Her Fifties." In *Virginia Woolf: A Feminist Slant,* edited by Jane Marcus, pp. 236–53. Lincoln: University of Nebraska Press, 1983.

Henig, Suzanne. "D. H. Lawrence and Virginia Woolf." *D. H. Lawrence Review* 2 (1969): 265–71.

Heywood, Christopher. "Olive Schreiner's Influence on George Moore and D. H. Lawrence." In *Aspects of South African Literature,* edited by Christopher Heywood, pp. 42–53. London: Heinemann, 1976.

———. "Olive Schreiner's *The Story of an African Farm*: Prototype of Lawrence's Early Novels." *English Language Notes* 14 (1976): 44–50.

Higdon, David Leon. "Bertha Coutts and Bertha Mason: A Speculative Note." *D. H. Lawrence Review* 11 (1978): 294–96.

Homans, Margaret. *Bearing the Word: Language and Female Experience in Nineteenth-Century Women's Writing.* Chicago: University of Chicago Press, 1986.

Hough, Graham. *The Dark Sun: A Study of D. H. Lawrence.* 1956. Reprint. New York: Putnam's Sons, 1959.

Irigaray, Luce. *This Sex Which Is Not One.* Trans. Catherine Porter and Carolyn Burke. Ithaca, N.Y.: Cornell University Press, 1977.

Jacobus, Mary. *Reading Woman: Essays in Feminist Criticism.* New York: Columbia University Press, 1986.

Jardine, Alice A. *Gynesis: Configurations of Woman and Modernity.* Ithaca, N.Y.: Cornell University Press, 1985.

Jehlen, Myra. "Archimedes and the Paradox of Feminist Criticism." *Signs: Journal of Women in Culture and Society* 6 (1981): 575–601.

Johnson, Barbara. *A World of Difference.* Baltimore: Johns Hopkins University Press, 1987.

Jones, Ann Rosalind. "Writing the Body: L'Ecriture féminine." In *The New Feminist Criticism,* edited by Elaine Showalter, pp. 361–78. New York: Pantheon, 1985.

Jones, William M. "Growth of a Symbol: The Sun in D. H. Lawrence and Eudora Welty." *University of Kansas City Review* 26, no. 1 (1959): 68–73.

Keily, Robert. *Beyond Egotism: The Fiction of James Joyce, Virginia Woolf, and D. H. Lawrence.* Cambridge: Harvard University Press, 1980.

Kenney, Edwin. *Elizabeth Bowen.* Lewisburg, Pa.: Bucknell University Press, 1975.

Kermode, Frank. *D. H. Lawrence.* New York: Viking, 1973.

Knoepflmacher, U. C. "The Rival Ladies: Mrs. Ward's *Lady Connie* and Lawrence's *Lady Chatterley's Lover.*" *Victorian Studies* 4 (1960): 141–58.

Kreyling, Michael. *Eudora Welty's Achievement of Order.* Baton Rouge: Louisiana State University Press, 1980.

Kristeva, Julia. "Within the Microcosm of 'The Talking Cure.'" Trans. Thomas Gora and Margaret Walker. In *Interpreting Lacan,* pp. 33–48. Vol. 6 of Psychiatry and the Humanities, edited by Joseph H. Smith and William Kerrigan. New Haven: Yale University Press, 1983.

———. "Women's Time." Trans. Alice Jardine and Harry Blake. In *The Kristeva Reader,* edited by Toril Moi, pp. 187–213. New York: Columbia University Press, 1986.

Lawrence, D. H. *Aaron's Rod.* 1922. Reprint. Harmondsworth: Penguin, 1950.

———. *Apocalypse.* 1931. Reprint. New York: Viking, 1966.

———. *The Complete Poems of D. H. Lawrence.* Ed. Vivian de Sola Pinto and Warren Roberts. Harmondsworth: Penguin, 1977.

———. *The Complete Short Stories.* 3 vols. Harmondsworth: Penguin, 1976–77.

———. *Fantasia of the Unconscious.* 1923. Reprint. London: Heinemann, 1933.

———. *The First Lady Chatterley.* 1944. Reprint. Harmondsworth: Penguin, 1973.

———. *Four Short Novels.* 1923. Reprint. New York: Viking, 1965.

———. *John Thomas and Lady Jane.* 1954. Reprint. Harmondsworth: Penguin, 1973.

———. *Kangaroo,* 1923. Reprint. New York: Viking, 1960.

———. *Lady Chatterley's Lover.* 1928. Reprint. New York: Bantam, 1968.

———. *The Letters of D. H. Lawrence.* Ed. Aldous Huxley. London: Heinemann, 1932.

———. *The Letters of D. H. Lawrence.* 5 vols. Ed. James T. Boulton et al. Cambridge: Cambridge University Press, 1979–1989.

———. *The Lost Girl.* 1920. Reprint. Harmondsworth: Penguin, 1950.

———. *Mr. Noon.* Ed. Lindeth Vasey. Cambridge: Cambridge University Press, 1984.

———. *Phoenix: The Posthumous Papers of D. H. Lawrence.* Ed. Edward D. McDonald. 1936. Reprint. Harmondsworth: Penguin, 1978.

———. *Phoenix II: Uncollected, Unpublished, and Other Prose Works.* Ed. Warren Roberts and Harry T. Moore. Harmondsworth: Penguin, 1970.

———. *The Plumed Serpent.* 1926. Reprint. New York: Vintage, 1959.

———. *The Rainbow.* 1915. Reprint. New York: Viking, 1961.

———. *Reflections on the Death of a Porcupine and Other Essays.* 1925. Reprint. Bloomington: Indiana University Press, 1963.

———. *Sons and Lovers: Text, Background, and Criticism.* Ed. Julian Moynahan. New York: Viking, 1968.

———. *St. Mawr and The Man Who Died.* 1925 and 1929. Reprint in 1 vol. New York: Random, 1953.

———. *Studies in Classic American Literature.* 1923. Reprint. New York: Viking, 1964.

———. *The Symbolic Meaning: The Uncollected Versions of Studies in Classic American Literature.* Ed. Armin Arnold. New York: Viking, 1964.

———. *The Trespasser.* Ed. Elizabeth Mansfield. 1912. Reprint. New York: Granada, 1982.

———. *The Virgin and the Gipsy,* 1930. Reprint. New York: Vintage-Random, 1984.

———. *The White Peacock.* 1911. Reprint. Harmondsworth: Penguin, 1950.

———. *Women in Love.* 1920. Reprint. New York: Viking, 1960.

Lawrence, D. H., and Mollie Skinner. *The Boy in the Bush.* 1924. Reprint. Harmondsworth: Penguin, 1963.

Lawrence, Frieda. *Memoirs and Correspondence.* Ed. E. W. Tedlock, Jr. New York: Heinemann, 1965.

———. *Not I, But the Wind . . . .* New York: Viking, 1934.

Leavis, F. R. *D. H. Lawrence: Novelist.* New York: Knopf, 1956.

Lerner, Laurence. *The Truthtellers: Jane Austen, George Eliot, D. H. Lawrence.* New York: Schocken, 1967.

Lessing, Doris. *The Fifth Child.* New York: Knopf, 1988.

———. *The Golden Notebook.* 1962. Reprint. New York: Ballantine, 1968.

———. *The Grass Is Singing.* New York: Crowell, 1950.

———. *Martha Quest.* 1952. Reprint. New York: New American Library, 1970.

Lidoff, Joan. *Christina Stead*. New York: Ungar, 1982.

London, Bette. "*Wuthering Heights* and the Text Between the Lines." *Papers on Language and Literature* (Winter 1988): 34–52.

Luhan, Mabel Dodge. *Lorenzo in Taos*. New York: Knopf, 1932.

Mailer, Norman. *The Prisoner of Sex*. London: Sphere, 1972.

Mansfield, Katherine. *Journal of Katherine Mansfield*. Ed. John Middleton Murry. New York: Knopf, 1931.

―――. *Katherine Mansfield's Letters to John Middleton Murry 1913–1922*. Ed. John Middleton Murry. New York: Knopf, 1951.

―――. *The Letters of Katherine Mansfield*. 2 vols. Ed. John Middleton Murry. New York: Knopf, 1929.

―――. *The Scrapbook of Katherine Mansfield*. Ed. John Middleton Murry. London: Constable, 1939.

―――. *The Short Stories of Katherine Mansfield*. 1937. Reprint. New York: Knopf, 1950.

―――. *Stories by Katherine Mansfield*. Ed. Elizabeth Bowen. New York: Vintage, 1956.

Marcus, Jane. "The Niece of a Nun: Virginia Woolf, Caroline Stephens, and the Cloistered Imagination." In *Virginia Woolf: A Feminist Slant*, edited by Jane Marcus, pp. 7–36. Lincoln: University of Nebraska Press, 1983.

Marks, Elaine, and Isabelle de Courtivron, eds. *New French Feminisms*. New York: Schocken, 1981.

Meyers, Jeffrey. *Katherine Mansfield: A Biography*. 1978. Reprint. New York: New Directions, 1980.

Miller, Nancy K. "Arachnologies: The Woman, the Text, and the Critic." In *The Poetics of Gender*, edited by Nancy K. Miller, pp. 270–301. New York: Columbia University Press, 1986.

―――. "Changing the Subject: Authorship, Writing, and the Reader." In *Feminist Studies/Critical Studies*, edited by Teresa de Lauretis, pp. 102–20. Bloomington: Indiana University Press, 1986.

―――. "Emphasis Added: Plots and Plausibilities in Women's Fiction." In *The New Feminist Criticism*, edited by Elaine Showalter, pp. 339–60. New York: Pantheon, 1985.

Millett, Kate. *Sexual Politics*. New York: Avon, 1971.

Mitchell, Juliet. *Women: The Longest Revolution*. New York: Pantheon, 1982.

Modleski, Tania. "Feminism and the Power of Interpretation: Some Critical Readings." In *Feminist Studies/Critical Studies*, edited by Teresa de Lauretis, pp. 121–31. Bloomington: Indiana University Press, 1986.

Moers, Ellen. *Literary Women*. Garden City, N.J.: Doubleday, 1977.

Moi, Toril. *Sexual/Textual Politics: Feminist Literary Theory*. New York: Methuen, 1985.

Moore, Harry T. *The Life and Works of D. H. Lawrence*. New York: Twayne, 1951.

————. *The Priest of Love: A Life of D. H. Lawrence.* 1974. Reprint. Harmondsworth: Penguin, 1980.

Morgan, Thaïs E. "Is There an Intertext in This Text?" *American Journal of Semiotics* 3, no. 4 (1985): 1–40.

Moynahan, Julian. *The Deed of Life: The Novels and Tales of D. H. Lawrence.* Princeton: Princeton University Press, 1963.

Munich, Adrienne. "Notorious Signs, Feminist Criticism, and Literary Tradition." In *Making a Difference: Feminist Literary Criticism,* edited by Gayle Greene and Coppélia Kahn, pp. 238–59. New York: Methuen, 1985.

Nehls, Edward. *D. H. Lawrence: A Composite Biography.* 3 vols. Madison: University of Wisconsin Press, 1957–59.

Newquist, Roy. "Interview with Doris Lessing." In *Doris Lessing, A Small Personal Voice,* edited by Paul Shlueter, pp. 50–62. New York: Knopf, 1974.

Nin, Anaïs. *D. H. Lawrence: An Unprofessional Study.* 1932. Reprint. Chicago: Swallow, 1964.

————. *The Novel of the Future.* 1968. Reprint. New York: Collier, 1970.

Nixon, Cornelia. *Lawrence's Leadership Politics and the Turn against Women.* Berkeley and Los Angeles: University of California Press, 1986.

Ohmann, Carol. "Emily Brontë in the Hands of Male Critics." *College English* 32 (1971): 906–13.

Ostriker, Alicia. "The Thieves of Language: Women Poets and Revisionist Mythmaking." In *The New Feminist Criticism: Essays on Women, Literature, and Theory,* edited by Elaine Showalter, pp. 314–38. New York: Pantheon, 1985.

Ovid. *Metamorphoses.* Trans. Rolfe Humphries. Bloomington: Indiana University Press, 1955.

Paster, Gail Kern. "Leaky Vessels: The Incontinent Women of City Comedy." *Renaissance Drama* n.s. 18 (1987): 43–65.

Polk, Noel. "Water, Wanderings, and Weddings." In *Eudora Welty: A Form of Thanks,* edited by Louis Dollarhide and Ann J. Abadie, pp. 95–122. Jackson: University Press of Mississippi, 1979.

Pratt, Annis. "Woman and Nature in Modern Fiction." *Contemporary Literature* 13 (1972): 466–90.

Restuccia, Frances L. "'A Cave of My Own': E. M. Forster and Sexual Politics." *Raritan* 9, no. 2 (1989): 110–128.

Robinson, Janice S. *H. D.: The Life and Work of an American Poet.* Boston: Houghton Mifflin, 1982.

Robinson, Lillian S. *Sex, Class, and Culture.* New York: Methuen, 1986.

Sagar, Keith. *D. H. Lawrence: Life into Art.* New York: Viking, 1985.

————. "The Originality of *Wuthering Heights.*" In *The Art of Emily Brontë,* edited by Anne Smith, pp. 121–59. London: Vision, 1976.

Sarvan, Charles, and Liebetraut Sarvan. "D. H. Lawrence and Doris Lessing's *The Grass Is Singing.*" *Modern Fiction Studies* 24 (1978): 533–37.

Scheman, Naomi. "Missing Mothers/Desiring Daughters: Framing the Sight of Women." *Critical Inquiry* 15 (1988): 62–89.

Schneider, Daniel J. *D. H. Lawrence: The Artist as Psychologist*. Lawrence: University of Kansas Press, 1984.

Schor, Naomi. "Dreaming Dissymmetry: Barthes, Foucault, and Sexual Difference." In *Men in Feminism*, edited by Alice Jardine and Paul Smith, pp. 98–110. New York: Methuen, 1987.

Schorer, Mark. *D. H. Lawrence*. New York: Dell, 1968.

Schreiner, Olive. *The Story of an African Farm*. 1883. Reprint. Chicago: Academy, 1977.

Scott, Bonnie Kime. *James Joyce*. Atlantic Highlands: Humanities Press International, 1987.

———. *Joyce and Feminism*. Bloomington: Indiana University Press, 1984.

———. "The Strange Necessity of Rebecca West." In *Women Reading Women's Writing*, edited by Sue Roe, pp. 265–86. New York: St. Martin's, 1987.

———. " 'The World Split Its Husk': Woolf's Double Vision of Modernist Language." *Modern Fiction Studies* 34 (1988): 371–85.

Sedgwick, Eve Kosofsky. *Between Men: English Literature and Male Homosocial Desire*. New York: Columbia University Press, 1985.

———. "Epistemology of the Closet (I)." *Raritan* 7, no. 4 (1988): 36–69.

Sheridan, Susan. *Christina Stead*. Bloomington: Indiana University Press, 1988.

Showalter, Elaine. "Critical Cross-Dressing: Male Feminists and the Woman of the Year." *Raritan* 3 (1983): 130–49.

———. *A Literature of Their Own: British Women Novelists from Brontë to Lessing*. Princeton: Princeton University Press, 1977.

———. "Towards a Feminist Poetics." In *Women Writing and Writing about Women*, edited by Mary Jacobus, pp. 22–41. London: Croom Helm, 1979.

Simpson, Hilary. *D. H. Lawrence and Feminism*. De Kalb: Northern Illinois University Press, 1982.

Smith, Anne. "A New Adam and a New Eve: A Biographical Overview." In *Lawrence and Women*, edited by Anne Smith, pp. 12–48. New York: Barnes and Noble, 1978.

Smith-Rosenberg, Carroll. *Disorderly Conduct: Visions of Gender in Victorian America*. New York: Knopf, 1985.

Spacks, Patricia Meyer. *The Female Imagination*. New York: Knopf, 1975.

Spilka, Mark. Introduction to *D. H. Lawrence: A Collection of Critical Essays*. Ed. Mark Spilka. Englewood Cliffs: Prentice Hall, 1963.

———. "Lessing and Lawrence: The Battle of the Sexes." *Contemporary Literature* 6 (1976): 218–40.

Spivak, Gayatri Chakravorty. "Displacement and the Discourse of

Woman." In *Displacement: Derrida and After,* edited by Mark Krupnick, pp. 169–95. Bloomington: Indiana University Press, 1983.

Stead, Christina. *Cotter's England.* 1966. Reprint. London: Virago, 1980.

————. *For Love Alone.* 1944. Reprint. New York: Harcourt Brace Jovanovich, 1979.

Stimpson, Catherine R. "Doris Lessing and the Parables of Growth." In *The Voyage In: Fictions of Female Development,* edited by Elizabeth Abel, Marianne Hirsch, and Elizabeth Langland, pp. 186–205. Hanover, N.H.: University Press of New England, 1983.

Suleiman, Susan. "(Re)writing the Body: The Politics and Poetics of Female Eroticism." In *The Female Body in Western Culture: Contemporary Perspectives,* edited by Susan Suleiman, pp. 16–24. Cambridge: Harvard University Press, 1986.

Theweleit, Klaus. *Women, Floods, Bodies, History.* Vol. 1 of *Male Fantasies.* Trans. Stephen Conway. Minneapolis: University of Minnesota Press, 1987.

Trilling, Diana. "Women in Love." Review of *For Love Alone,* by Christina Stead. *Nation* (28 October 1944): 535–36.

Vickery, John B. "Myth and Ritual in the Shorter Fiction of D. H. Lawrence." *Modern Fiction Studies* 5 (1959): 62–82.

Warner, Marina. *Monuments and Maidens: The Allegory of the Female Form.* New York: Atheneum, 1985.

Welty, Eudora. *The Collected Stories of Eudora Welty.* New York: Harcourt Brace Jovanovich, 1980.

————. *Delta Wedding.* 1945. Reprint. New York: Harcourt Brace Jovanovich, 1979.

————. "Looking at Short Stories." In *The Eye of the Story: Selected Essays and Reviews.* New York: Vintage-Random, 1979.

————. *Short Stories.* New York: Harcourt Brace Jovanovich, 1949.

Westling, Louise. *Sacred Groves and Ravaged Gardens: The Fiction of Eudora Welty, Carson McCullers, and Flannery O'Connor.* Athens: University of Georgia Press, 1985.

Widmer, Kingsley. "Lawrence and the Fall of Modern Woman." *Modern Fiction Studies* 5 (1959): 44–56.

Wittig, Monique. *Les Guérillères.* Trans. David Le Vay. New York: Bard-Avon, 1973.

Woolf, Virginia. *The Diary of Virginia Woolf.* 5 vols. Ed. Anne Olivier Bell. London: Hogarth, 1977–84.

————. *Jacob's Room.* 1922. Reprint. London: Granada, 1977.

————. "*Jane Eyre* and *Wuthering Heights.*" In *The Common Reader,* pp. 159–65. 1st ser. 1925. Reprint. New York: Harcourt Brace Jovanovich, 1953.

————. "The Leaning Tower." In *Folios of New Writing,* edited by John Lehmann, pp. 11–33. London: Hogarth, Autumn 1940.

———. *The Letters of Virginia Woolf,* 6 vols. Ed. Nigel Nicolson. London: Hogarth, 1975–80.

———. Review of *The Lost Girl,* by D. H. Lawrence. *TLS,* 2 December 1920. In *D. H. Lawrence: The Critical Heritage,* edited by R. P. Draper, pp. 141–43. New York: Barnes and Noble, 1970.

———. "Notes on D. H. Lawrence." In *The Moment and Other Essays,* pp. 93–98. London: Hogarth, 1947.

———. *Orlando.* 1928. Reprint. New York: Harcourt Brace Jovanovich, 1956.

———. *The Pargitters.* Ed. Mitchell A. Leaska. New York: Harvest–Harcourt Brace Jovanovich, 1977.

———. *A Room of One's Own.* 1929. Reprint. New York: Harcourt Brace Jovanovich, 1957.

———. *Three Guineas.* 1938. Reprint. New York: Harcourt Brace Jovanovich, 1966.

———. *The Voyage Out.* 1915. Reprint. New York: Harcourt Brace Jovanovich, 1948.

Yaeger, Patricia. *Honey-Mad Women: Emancipatory Strategies in Women's Writing.* New York: Columbia University Press, 1988.

Yelin, Louise. "Overturning the Antipodes: Patriarchy, Colonialism, and Christina Stead's *For Love Alone.*" Paper presented at the MLA Convention, Washington, D.C., 29 December 1989.

Zak, Michele Wender. "*The Grass Is Singing*: A Little Novel about the Emotions." In *Doris Lessing: Critical Studies,* edited by Annis Pratt and L. S. Dembo, pp. 64–73. Madison: University of Wisconsin Press, 1974.

Zwerdling, Alex. *Virginia Woolf and the Real World.* Berkeley and Los Angeles: University of California Press, 1986.

Index